Migration, Development and Diplomacy

MIGRATION, DEVELOPMENT AND DIPLOMACY

Perspectives from the Southern Mediterranean

Edited by

Ivan Ureta & Derek Lutterbeck

The Red Sea Press, Inc.
Publishers & Distributors of Third World Books

P. O. Box 1892
Trenton, NJ 08607

RSP

P. O. Box 48
Asmara, ERITREA

The Red Sea Press, Inc.
Publishers & Distributors of Third World Books

| P. O. Box 1892 |  | P. O. Box 48 |
| Trenton, NJ 08607 | | Asmara, ERITREA |

Book and cover design: Saverance Publishing Services

Library of Congress Cataloging-in-Publication Data

Migration, development, and diplomacy : perspectives from the southern Mediterranean / edited by Ivan Ureta & Derek Lutterbeck.
   p. cm.
ISBN 1-56902-329-8 (cloth) -- ISBN 1-56902-330-1 (pbk.)
1. Mediterranean Region--Economic conditions. 2. Africa, North--Emigration and immigration--Europe. 3. Europe--Emigration and immigration--Africa, North. 4. Emigration and immigration--Government policy. 5. International cooperation. I. Ureta, Ivan. II. Lutterbeck, Derek.
   HC244.5.M54 2010
   338.9182'2--dc22

                                        2010028879

Table of Contents

Abbreviations

—◆◆—

AMERM	Association des Association Marocaine pour les Études et les Recherches en Migration (Morocco)
AMU	Arab Maghreb Union
API	Agency for the Promotion of Industry (Tunisia)
APIA	Agency for the Promotion of Agricultural Investments (Tunisia)
ATIME	Travailleurs Marocains en Espagne (Morocco)
BCT	National Bank of Tunisia
BMENA	Broader Middle East and North Africa
CARIM	Consortium for Applied Research on International Migration
CCDH	Consultant Council on Human Rights (Morocco)
CCME	Council of the Moroccan Community Abroad (Morocco)
CEMM	Centre d'Etudes sur les Mouvements Migratoires Maghrébins (Morocco)
CEMP	Comprehensive European Migration Policy
CENAP	National Centre for Planning and Development Studies (CENAP)

CERIST	Research Centre on Scientific and Technical Information (Algeria)
CISP	International Committee for Solidarity between the Peoples (Algeria)
CNE	Commission for New Energies (Algeria)
CNEPRU	National Commission of Planning and Evaluation of Academic Research (Algeria)
CNERMN	National Research Centre on the National Movement and the Revolution of 1st November 1954 (Algeria)
CNES	National Economic and Social Council (Algeria)
CNR	National Council of Research (Algeria)
CNRPAH	National Centre for Prehistoric, Anthropologic and Historic Research (Algeria)
CNRST	National Centre for Scientific and Technical Research (Morocco)
CRASC	Centre for Social Anthropology and Cultural Research (Algeria)
CRATE	Central Record of Available Technical Equipment
CREAD	Centre of Research in Applied Economics for Development (Algeria)
EFTA	European Free Trade Association
EMP	Euro-Mediterranean Partnership
ENP	European Neighbourhood Policy
EU	European Union
FDI	Foreign Direct Investment
FINCOME	Global Forum of Moroccan Competences Abroad (Morocco)
FLN	Front de Libération National (Algeria)
FNA	Front National Algérien (Algeria)

FRONTEX	European Agency for the Management of Operational Cooperation at the External Borders
FTA	Free Trade Agreement
GCIM	Global Commission on International Migration
GNI	Gross National Income
GRES	Groupe de Recherches et d'Etudes sociologiques (Morocco)
HCR	High Council for Research (Algeria)
ICMPD	International Centre for Migration Policy Development
IER	Equity and Reconciliation Commission (Morocco)
ILO	International Labour Organization
IMO	International Maritime Organization
INESG	National Institute of Global Strategy Studies (Algeria)
IOM	International Organization for Migration
ISM	Institute for Mediterranean Studies
JHA	Justice and Home Affairs
LADDH	Algerian League for the Defence of Human Rights (Algeria)
LD	Libyan Dinars
LOSC	United Nations Law of the Sea Convention
LSC	Laboratory for Social Change (Algeria)
MAD	Moroccan Dinar
MDG	Millenium Development Goals
MEDAC	Mediterranean Academy for Diplomatic Studies
MESRS	Ministry of Higher Education and Scientific Research (Algeria)
MRE/CME	Moroccans Residing Abroad (Morocco)

NATO	North Atlantic Treaty Organization
OCME	Observatoire de la Communauté Marocaine à l'Etranger (Morocco)
ODA	Overseas Development Aid
OECD	Organization for Economic Co-Operation and Development
ONRS	National Organization of Scientific Research (Algeria)
OSIM	Organisation de Solidarité Internationale de Migrants (Morocco)
RABIT	Rapid Border Intervention Teams
RCC	Rescue Coordination Centre
RND	Rassemblement National Démocratique (Algeria)
RS	Research Secretariat (Algeria)
SAR	International Convention on Maritime Search and Rescue
SARP	Algerian Society of Psychological Research (Algeria)
SOLAS	International Convention on the Safety of Life at Sea
UNDP	United Nations Development Program
UNESCO	United Nations Educational, Scientific and Cultural Organization
UNHCR	United Nations High Commissioner for Refugees
UNHDR	United Nations Human Development Report
UNHLD	United Nations High Level Dialogue
UNITWIN	University Twinning and Networking
UfM	Union for the Mediterranean
VIS	Visa Information System

Acknowledgements

———

This book is a result of a project on migration, development and diplomacy launched jointly by the Institute for Mediterranean Studies at the University of Lugano and the Mediterranean Academy of Diplomatic Studies in Malta. Numerous people have been involved since the beginning. We firstly thank Dr. Annick Tonti, former head of the Middle East and North Africa section at the Swiss Agency for Development and Cooperation and senior academic advisor at the University of Lugano. The entire team of the Institute for Mediterranean Studies in Lugano, composed at the moment by Mr. Claudio Naiaretti, Dr. Federica Frediani, Dr. Anna Omodei Zorini and Dr. Mauro Martinoni, have been very supportive throughout the project.

We are also indebted to Professor Guido De Marco, Professor Stephen Calleya and Dr. Omar Grech from the Mediterranean Academy of Diplomatic Studies for their hospitality and contribution to the Forum on Migration, Development and Diplomacy which was held in Malta in July 2008, and where first drafts of most of the papers contained in this volume were presented.

For their contribution to this workshop we would also like to thank Professor Mohammed Maougal from Algeria; Mr. Mohammed Bernoussi, Professor Khadija Elmadmad, Professor Moha Ennaji and Ms. Naima Baba from Morocco; Dr Ali Errishi, Professor Bashir Al-Kut, Prof. Amal Obeidi, Mr. Abdulhadi Giuma and Mr. Ibrahim Gaet from Libya, and Mr. Tarak Ben Salem, Mr. Ali Jawani and Professor Abderrazak Bel Hadj

Zekri from Tunisia. Ms. Paola Constantino and Mr. Rafe di Domenico were very helpful during the editorial process. Finally, thanks go to Ms. Angela Ajayi and to Mr. Kassahun Checole, chief publisher of Africa World Press/Red Sea Press Inc., who has shown great dedication to this project from beginning to end. This book has been funded entirely by the Institute for Mediterranean Studies at the University of Lugano.

Introduction

In recent years, migration across the Mediterranean has become an issue of growing concern to the countries of the region and beyond. It has also become a rather divisive issue between the two shores of the Mediterranean, as the interests of countries to the North and those of the South have often conflicted in questions related to migration in the region. The countries to the North have increasingly come to perceive irregular migration from the African continent as being "out of control" and as a threat to their national welfare systems and domestic peace and stability. Consequently, they have attempted to find ways to curb the flow of undocumented migrants across the Mediterranean. This has involved not only measures on their own territories to prevent irregular immigration such as enhanced border and maritime patrols, but they have also demanded stricter controls from their southern neighboring countries.

For the countries along the southern rim of the Mediterranean, the situation has in many ways been more complex. As far as they themselves have become destination or transit countries for would-be migrants coming from further south, they too have come to view irregular migration as a growing burden, and have been espousing an increasingly restrictive immigration control agenda. On the other hand, as migrant-sending countries, southern Mediterranean countries have also been interested in opening channels for legal migration into the EU for their citizens in order to relieve pressure on their saturated labour markets. As a consequence of these diverging interests, collaboration between the countries north and south of the Mediterranean in the area of migration policy has generally been rather difficult to achieve, and at times the migration issue has led to considerable tensions between north and south Mediterranean countries.

Finally, clandestine boat migration across the Mediterranean has also become a growing humanitarian challenge. According to (conservative) estimates, at least 10,000 would-be immigrants have died over the last ten years seeking to cross the Mediterranean from the south, and the numbers seem to be rising rapidly.

More recently, the political debate on migration across the Mediterranean towards Europe has increasingly focused on the nexus between migration and development. Development cooperation has been advocated by European countries as a means to achieve a long-term solution to the 'migration crisis' in the region. In recent years, the European Commission, for instance, has issued a number of communications on how development assistance could be used as a policy instrument to address the 'root causes' of migration. Moreover, in July 2006, a first Ministerial Euro-African Conference on Migration and Development was held in Rabat, which brought together some 60 African and European countries, to discuss migration and development, and to find ways out of the seemingly persistent crisis of irregular migration from the African continent towards Europe. In the context of the Euro-Mediterranean partnership, as well, the migration-development nexus has become an increasingly prominent focus. In November 2007, a first Euro-Mediterranean Ministerial conference on migration was held in Algarve, where migration and development were key items on the agenda.

However, while some have hailed the Rabat and subsequent conferences as important milestones in EU-African relations, or in relations between migrant-sending and migrant-receiving countries, there have also been numerous critical voices. Many critics have in particular pointed out that the process has been driven largely by the EU's restrictive immigration control agenda and its very narrow understanding of the relationship between migration and development. Within the framework of the Rabat process, the nexus seems to have been largely reduced to using the carrot of increased development aid in return for enhanced cooperation from southern Mediterranean and African countries in preventing migration from and through their territories. By contrast, other relevant aspects of the linkage between migration and development, including the potentially positive impact of migration on the development of both sending and receiving countries, do not seem to have received much attention.

Against this background, the aim of this volume is twofold: to offer a broader perspective on the migration-development nexus, and to give a stronger voice to the often-overheard voices of southern Mediterranean countries on migration and development issues. The majority of the contributions contained in this volume explore various facets of the relationship between migration and development from the perspective of the countries along the southern rim of the Mediterranean, although some of them also provide critical analyses of EU policies in this area. First drafts of the papers were presented at a workshop on migration and development organized jointly by the Institute for Mediterranean Studies at the University of Lugano (ISM) and the Mediterranean Academy of Diplomatic Studies (MEDAC) in Malta in June 2008.

The first chapter by Abderrazak Zekri focuses on migration and development issues in Tunisia. He explores the social and economic impact of emigration in Tunisia in the post-WWII period. He argues that emigration had the important effect of reducing the manpower surplus and thus unemployment in Tunisia. Moreover, by sending back remittances, Tunisian émigrés have significantly contributed to improving the financial and social situation of their families back in Tunisia. However, Zekri also highlights the thus far only relatively limited effectiveness of funds sent back on the development of the home countries; according to him, only around 10 percent of remittances are actually used for productive purposes. As a consequence, Zekri calls for the establishment of more effective financial mechanisms which would lead both to an increase in remittances as well as to their more effective and productive use in the country of origin.

The second chapter by Hocine Labdelaoui takes stock of research carried out in Algeria on migration and development-related issues. Labedelaoui argues that, as in many other countries affected by international migration, the topic of "migration and development" has become increasingly fashionable in Algeria. He distinguishes between five different areas of research under this broad theme: Algerian emigration, return migration, transit migration, migration and development and immigration into Algeria. However, Labdelaoui points out that scientific interest in these areas has not yet translated into a satisfactory understanding of how migration has impacted on development in Algeria. While the official state discourse has been largely limited to declarations of principle on the need to 'manage migration,' scientific research in Algeria has faced a number of institutional and other constraints.

Fethi Boulares, also from Algeria, discusses the phenomenon of irregular migration from Algeria, or what are often referred to in Algeria as the so-called 'harragas.' He underlines that migration in Algeria has increasingly evolved from being an exceptional event to being a real national tragedy. In reflecting on the reasons which lead young Algerians to risk their lives trying to reach Europe on rickety boats, Boulares ultimately points to the still authoritarian nature of the Algerian regime, which has hampered the social and economic development of the country. While the hydrocarbon sector in Algeria has generated considerable wealth for the elite, this has not translated into more economic opportunities for the majority of the population. Moreover, Boulares also highlights how the EU's securitiarian approach towards migration has increasingly been replicated by the Algerian regime.

This is followed by a contribution by Moha Ennaji on emigration from Morocco. Morocco has traditionally been a very important source country of migration which, in the words of Ennaji, has developed a strong 'culture of emigration.' With the help of survey data, Ennaji explores the migratory intentions of Moroccan youth. The surveys show that Moroccan youth generally have a favorable attitude toward migration, which they consider a strategy to improve their living conditions and to contribute to their development. According to Ennaji, Morocco's socio-economic situation is the main factor driving emigration from the country; its main causes include the lack of future prospects, economic instability, unemployment and poverty.

The chapter by Naima Baba focuses specifically on how to optimize the benefits of emigration in Morocco. Baba highlights the need for more effective internal and international cooperation mechanisms in areas such as labour migration, remittances, social issues and return migration in order to maximize the benefits of international migration to sending countries such as Morocco. So far however, according to Baba, the development of effective policies in this area has been hampered by an often negative perception of migration in Morocco which tends to be associated with phenomena such as brain drain, illegal migration, as well as trafficking and smuggling in human beings. Moreover, there is still no real science of emigration in Morocco which would look at the phenomenon in a holistic manner.

The last case study on Morocco, by Khadija Elmadmad, provides an overview of Morocco's legislation on issues related to migration, including the legal situation of migrants in Morocco. Elmadmad argues that, overall, Morocco has adopted increasingly comprehensive and unified legislation in this area, regulating issues such as entrance and stay of foreigners and irregular migration. However she also points out that legal protection of migrants in Morocco remains limited. In particular, when it comes to expulsion of irregular immigrants, legal guarantees are practically absent. In this area, Morocco's legislation and practice, she argues, are contrary to international agreements which Morocco has signed.

The following contribution by Bashir al-Kut focuses on irregular migration in Libya. He points out that, in recent years, Libya has emerged both as an important destination country for migrants from sub-Saharan Africa as well as a transit country for irregular migrants seeking to reach the EU. Al-Kut also highlights the inconsistencies of Libya's policies in this area: on the one hand, it has adopted an open door policy towards Africa, on other it has sought to implement increasingly restrictive immigration control policies. From Libya's perspective, the role of the EU is key in addressing the challenge of irregular from the African continent. Given both its colonial past and high levels of development, Europe is seen as having a historic responsibility both to alleviate the root causes of migration in African countries and to assist transit countries such as Libya in addressing the migration issue.

Subsequent chapters adopt a more regional perspective on migration in the Mediterranean region. Derek Lutterbeck focuses on the evolution of irregular migration across the Mediterranean as well as the EU's main policy responses in this area. He argues that despite the EU's official discourse on the need to adopt a 'global' or 'comprehensive' approach to the migration issue, its policies have thus far focused largely on more security-oriented measures, and in particular the strengthening of border and immigration controls. He also highlights some of the negative consequences of these measures, in particular the diversion of the migratory flows towards longer and more dangerous routes across the Mediterranean.

The chapter by Patricia Mallia looks at the legal regime governing state's actions with regard to irregular migration by sea. She highlights the tension that exists between states' rights and duties when it comes to dealing with seaborne migration: on the one hand, states have security interests and are are entitled to take any action in accordance with international law which will minimise the risks posed by irregular immigration. On the other hand, at the core of states' activities lie *persons* on the move, therefore requiring consideration of issues of human welfare and dignity. Mallia also looks at the specific situation of Malta, which has been confronted by a rapid growth in irregular migration by sea in recent years.

The following chapter has been written by Ivan Ureta, who provides a critical analysis of the current economic and political underpinnings of migration and development policies in Europe. Ureta looks at three interlinked issue areas: migratory trends, development policies and policy coherence in the Euro-Mediterranean area. He argues that while OECD countries have experienced a general growth in migratory movements in recent years, it is in particular migration from developing countries which has attracted public attention. Immigration from the third world is closely bound up with images of poverty, illegality and exploitation, which has made this type of migration much more visible than immigration from other parts of the world.

Moreover, after 9/11 and the global recession, migration policies of developing countries have generally become more restrictive.

The final chapter by Mark Furness and Alina Khasabova examines the role of the European Union in managing illegal migration in the Mediterranean. While member states concerned about border sovereignty have been reluctant to allow greater EU involvement in this sensitive policy area, awareness that the scale of illegal immigration is beyond the capabilities of individual countries has grown amid concerns about terrorism and transnational organized crime. An increased EU dimension in managing illegal immigration and protecting external borders has the potential to generate a more efficient and legitimate response, and yet given current political realities the EU's main role will remain complementary to existing member states' efforts. According to Furness and Khasabova, bilateral cooperation with origin and transit states has long been a policy priority for EU member states, but these relationships lack a coherent institutional framework. Moreover, their general lack of transparency raises issues of consistency with the European Convention on Human Rights.

Overall, we hope that the contributions to this volume will add to the current debate on migration and development as well as to the adoption of more effective policies in this area on both sides of the Mediterranean.

Chapter 1

— ❧ —

MIGRATION AND DEVELOPMENT: SOCIO-ECONOMIC IMPACT OF EMIGRATION IN TUNISIA
— Abderrazak Zekri —

INTRODUCTION

Tunisia has long been a country of emigration. Since the 1960s, it has sent several waves of emigration to European countries, especially France. Due to a slowdown in this emigration to Europe and difficulties for the Tunisian workforce, even the highly skilled, to access the European labour market, other destinations for Tunisian emigration emerged, particularly the Gulf States. Since the 1970s, Tunisia, through cooperating organizations, placed around 28,000 officials, experts and technical experts. 10,000 currently work in the framework of technical cooperation. Essentially, this consists of temporary emigration that lasted between 5 and 10 years according to the length of the work contract.

Since 1973, migratory flows towards Europe experienced a shift because of decisions by European countries to quell immigration. With the end of organized emigration, family emigration started to substitute workforce emigration, which subsequently increased permanent settlement in host countries.

The impact of these migratory flows on employment translated to an erosion of manpower surplus and, consequently, to the reduction of unemployment. The economic impact is evident in funds transferred to the country of origin. Even when permanently settled in various host countries, Tunisian emigrants are determined to preserve a link with their home country. They save or transfer part of their incomes to help maintain and improve the financial and social situations of their families remaining in the home country and to development of the region.

The contribution the macro-economic character of Tunisian emigration brings emerges from an analysis of the evolution and practice of migratory movements and evaluation of the quantitative and qualitative importance of the investments generated by the immigrants.

This must be balanced with an analysis of the impact skilled emigration has on development in Tunisia—an aspect important to studies on the links between migration and development—through its contributions to knowledge transfer and university training, technological research and health. In this context, it is necessary to point out that Tunisia provides a perfect example of this category of migrants who are ever-increasing in many European and American countries.

TUNISIAN EMIGRATION: A GENERAL OUTLOOK

Tunisian emigration to France increased after Tunisian independence. It became greater than that of other North African countries. Between 1954 and 1962, the average rate of annual growth was 15.2 percent for Moroccans and 23.9 percent for Tunisians. The period from 1962 to 1974 was marked by a drastic change in migratory flows originating from the Maghreb. The number of departures became larger year after year while also seeing an improvement of the migrants' profiles (e.g., education level and professional qualifications). In addition, North

African emigration became characterized by better organization. The departures of North African workers were governed by bilateral agreements between each state of the Maghreb and the different European workforce importers (France, Germany, Belgium, and Holland). North African countries, confronted with critical economic difficulties, encouraged the expatriation of the active population in the hope of an economic recovery which would eventually put an end to this 'temporary' exodus and allow the emigrants to reintegrate back into Algerian society. Tunisian administrators conceived of emigration as a solution that would reduce the problems caused by unemployment and underemployment. However, if emigration was an objective set by these internal factors, it was equally encouraged by a request from European countries experiencing strong economic growth and needing continuously growing manpower. This was utilized by European entrepreneurs who wanted to attract compliant, mobile and cheap workers to the European labor market.

Evolution and Geographic Distribution of Tunisian Emigration

The number of Tunisians overseas continued to increase since the explosion of international migration in Tunisia, particularly after the 1960s; the number is, according to statistics from the Ministry of Foreign Affairs (end of December 2007), 1,018,173 people, which represents one-tenth of the total population.

European countries host 83.1 percent of Tunisian residents abroad. The majority, 54.5 percent, lives in France. In Arab countries, the Tunisian Community is estimated at 142,655 (14.1percent), of which 98,109 (9.6 percent) live in North African countries. As for Tunisian emigration in the American continent, it only appeared later when compared to the migratory movements to Europe; Tunisian residents in the United States of America and Canada represent 26,133 people, i.e., 2.6 percent of all Tunisian emigrants abroad.

The size of the Tunisian community abroad shows a continuing progression. It grew from 436,806 in 1987 to 1,018,173 in 2007. This represents an average annual growth rate of 4.3 percent.

European countries such as Italy, Germany and Switzerland experienced a pattern of continuous extraordinary increases in general registrations, with average annual growth rates of 14.9 percent, 5.9 percent and 6.7 percent respectively. Libya distinguished itself with constant gains between 1989–2007, recording an average annual growth rate of 4.6 percent, slightly above average. On the other hand, the number of Tunisians living in Algeria experienced a continuous decrease from 1987–2007 at a rate of 6.6 percent. Available statistics show a growth in the number of Tunisians settled in Canada and The United States of America between 1994 and 2007 with average annual growth rates of 4.8 percent and 9.2 percent respectively.

Main Characteristics and Transformations of Tunisian Emigration

Since the beginning of the 1980s, various factors of the community's *demographic structure* have also gone through important transformations, particularly family groupings, marriages and births that took place out of the country. By way of example, 51,471 Tunisian families, made up of 89,215 family members, had 'family reunions' in France between 1976 and 2006. The consular estimations show that 78 percent of emigrated Tunisian families in Europe live in France.

This demographic structure, which was characterized by masculine first-generation emigrants, changed composition since women and children reached 46 percent of the whole community.

In addition, sociological changes were observed in the behaviour of Tunisians abroad, such as regard for their future and the objectives for their migration. These changes brought about a new attitude within the emigrants, which is evident by the extension of their stays abroad, a tendency for permanent settlement and their integrations into host countries.

In the same way, *the level of education and training* of emigrants improved, particularly with new generations of emigrants joining the ranks of the scientific and technological elite. This consolidated the economic successes already achieved by the first

4

generations in several domains such as the sciences, technology and culture.

The *economic structure and the population distribution by socio-professional category* were also marked by significant progress. Statistics collected by the Ministry of Foreign Affairs emphasise that the number of workers constantly increases and includes more and more women who are accessing the labour market in the host countries. In addition, Tunisian executives, businessmen and merchants reached 108,026 people in 2007, representing 10.6 percent of the entire Tunisian community abroad.

One has to note that Tunisian emigrants in Arab countries, particularly those of the Gulf, are predominantly aid workers. In 2007, 8,093 of the 9,949 Tunisian aid workers worked in Persian Gulf countries. This represents 81 percent of Tunisian aid workers settled overseas.

The Characteristics of Emigrants as Determining Factors in Migratory Movements and Investment

The increase of Tunisian migrants, the evolution of their professional characteristics and the emergence of new categories of businessmen and entrepreneurs were factors that explained a continuous progression of migratory movements. In addition, the birth of new migrant categories composed of entrepreneurs who came because of encouragements from the state and investment incentives also contributed to the creation of economic establishments that promoted local, regional and national development of Tunisia.

MIGRATION AND DEVELOPMENT: CONTRIBUTIONS OF TUNISIAN MIGRATION

Revenue Transfers: Importance of Fund Transfers and Their Evolution

Two methods are used for fund transfers by Tunisian residents abroad: cash and in-kind transfers. Cash transfers represent bank transfers, money orders and post office transfers, direct transactions through cash dispensers and, finally, salaries and social benefits transferred by employers and social security institutions. In-kind transfers include cars and personal property imported in the context of their temporary or definite return in the country and the equipment acquired for the accomplishment of economic projects in Tunisia. This equipment mainly consists of transportation materials and supplies imported for transportation projects or for small construction businesses.

One should note that in-kind transfers exploded from 1983 to 2007; they represented 2 percent of total transfers in 1983 and grew to 28.2 percent in 1999 and 23.6 percent in 2007. In actual value, they represent an important amount of money, equivalent to 518 million dinars injected in the Tunisian market in the form of merchandise of all sort (cars, appliances, textiles, various equipments...).

In 2007, fund transfers rose to 2,199 million Tunisian dinars, of which 1,681 million were cash (76.4 percent on the total). Their distribution, by country and continent, shows that most of these transfers originate from Europe. 48.7 percent come from France alone. Transfers originating from Arab countries represent only 8.9 percent of the total, with 3.3 percent coming from Saudi Arabia.

The evolution of financial transfers between 1982 and 2007 by Tunisian residents abroad (see table below) shows the following elements: the annual growth rate is 8.7 percent; cash transfers increased from 407 million dinars in 1992 to 1681 million dinars in 2007, an annual growth rate of 10 percent; in-kind transfers experienced an increase from 101 million dinars in 1992 to 518 million dinars in 2007, an annual growth rate of 11.7 percent. According to figures from the Central Bank, financial transfers by Tunisian emigrants during the first 8 months of 2008 amounted to 1882 million dinars, which represent an increase of 9 percent compared to the same period in 2007. Furthermore, one can note the fact that informal transfers are not counted as part of these figures, which can also add to the overall transfers if one can correctly estimates their value.

TABLE 1. EVOLUTION OF REVENUE TRANSFERS OF TUNISIANS LIVING ABROAD (1982-2007)

YEAR	CASH TRANSFERS		IN-KIND TRANSFERS		TOTAL IN MILLION DINARS (M.D.)
	M.D.	% OF TOTAL	M.D.	% OF TOTAL	
1982	210	95.5	10	4.5	220
1983	239	98.0	5	2.0	244
1984	211	85.5	35	14.2	246
1985	180	79.6	46	20.4	226
1986	245	85.4	42	14.6	287
1987	357	88.6	46	11.4	403
1988	393	84.2	74	15.8	467
1989	359	77.5	104	22.5	463
1990	442	84.0	84	16.0	526
1991	472	89.6	55	10.4	527
1992	407	80.1	101	19.9	508
1993	450	75.0	150	25.0	600
1994	499	71.7	197	28.3	696
1995	546	7607	166	23.3	712
1996	592	74.2	206	25.8	798
1997	616	72.8	230	27.2	846
1998	676	74.9	226	25.1	902
1999	732	71.8	288	28.2	1020
2000	810	74.2	281	25.8	1091
2001	1014	76.0	320	24.0	1334
2002	1124	73.9	398	26.1	1522
2003	1316	75.5	395	24.5	1611
2004	1346	75.5	437	24.5	1783
2005	1391	77.0	416	23.0	1807
2006	1537	76.5	473	23.5	2010
2007	1681	76.4	518	23.6	2199

Source: Tunisian Central Bank (BCT).

Money Orders

Money transfers of Tunisians living abroad are essentially composed of bank transfers and money orders. Money orders represent fund transfers carried out by expatriate Tunisians through the postal office. Money orders amounted to 477 million dinars in 2007, representing 21.7 percent of the total revenue transfers of expatriate Tunisians (i.e. 2199 million Dinars) and 28.3 percent of cash transfers (i.e. 1681 million Dinars). With regard to the regional distribution of money order transfers in 2007, Tunis held the first position with 87 million dinars (18.2 percent of the total). Sousse and Nabeul tie for third place with 32 million dinars (6.7 percent of the total).

The North monopolizes the distribution of money orders by region with 53.8 percent (more than half of money order transfers are sent to the northern region), the centre receives 28.7 percent of money order transfers (more than one-fourth of the money orders). In 2007, the number of postal orders sent by Tunisians settled abroad amounted to 905,822, with an average value of 527 dinars per money order. Finally, money orders increased from 291 million dinars in 2003 to 477 million of dinars in 2007, with an annual growth rate of 13.2 percent. Fund transfers of Tunisians abroad sent through the post network have also increased by 24 percent, swelling from 489 million dinars in 2005 to 606 million dinars in 2006.

Main Usage of Money Transfers by Tunisian Emigrants

Money transfers by Tunisian emigrants have contributed to the improvement of household social and economic situations, an objective generally set by emigrants when they migrate. In fact, the conclusions of different investigations conducted in Tunisia and a number of North African countries show that these transfers helped achieve this. The emigrants also made an effort in qualitatively changing the life conditions of families, which is clearly illustrated by real estate investments. In addition, one notes that migration also contributed to achieving the millennium objectives to make education and health the predominant household expenditures.

TABLE 2. PRINCIPAL EXPENDITURE OF FUNDS: COMPARATIVE DATA

NATURE OF EXPENDITURE	TUNISIA	MOROCCO	ALGERIA	EGYPT
Consumption expenses	32	46	45	43
Education expenses	23	31	13	12
Lodging expenses	19	16	34	18
Investment	18	5	8	15
Others	8	2	-	12
Total	100	100	100	100

Source: Data of National studies cited by Khachani Med

Investments Made by Emigrants

Tunisia counted on internal capacities as well as on expatriated resources for its economic development. In this context, economic competences abroad constitute a privileged medium. Emigrated Tunisians' contributions in creating businesses and technology transfer are undeniable.

Overview on the Participation of Emigrants in the Investment to Their Countries of Origin

Official statistics on the projects promoted by Tunisian residents abroad exclusively cover structured economy. However, in order to improve the analysis, it is important not to ignore the dynamic informal economic contribution of migrants: the trade sector, transportation and services.

In evaluating the contribution of Tunisian emigrants in business creation, the following agencies provided national statistics for reference: The Agency for the Promotion of Investments (API), which was renamed, in the mid 1990s, 'The Agency for the Promotion of Industry' and The Agency for the Promotion of Agricultural Investments (APIA), which offers specialized assistance to the emigrant 'investors.'

Examination of the statistics shows that between 1988 and 2007, the emigrants' accepted projects numbered 10,304 and theoretically mobilized an investment of 385,171 million dinars that could create 43,914 jobs.

The service sector comprises most of the projects carried out by emigrants (64 percent), while industry and business creation attracts only 26 percent of investments. Finally, farming remains the least attractive activity for emigrant investors.

In regards to actual investment, one has to remark that the projects in the service sector do not mobilize most of the capital invested by emigrants. While this sector makes up 64.2 percent of the total projects, it only invests 43.5 percent of all the projects. This could be explained by the fact that these projects mainly consist of transportation, commercial and repair activities, which require little financial means. On the other hand, businesses in the manufacturing sector make up 40 percent of the investments made between 1987 and 2007, despite the fact that they represent only 26.2 percent of the projects.

For the period in question, 43,912 jobs were created by Tunisian migrants' investments. More than half of those were in the 'industry sector,' which is double the amount of businesses created in the same sector. This is followed by the service sector, which created 45 percent of the total jobs. Finally, it is notable that the agricultural sector, while creating 9.6 percent of the projects and mobilizing 16.6 percent of the capital invested, only generated 4.1 percent of the total jobs. This shows that agricultural projects are relatively capital-intensive, but not big job creators.

Investments by the Emigrants: What Impacts the Economy?

The investments and businesses created by the emigrants indicate the importance Tunisian migrants give to developing their country of origin. Certainly, at the beginning they remained relatively modest.

In fact, a study carried out by the agencies in charge of investments (API, APIA) highlighted that the projects by Tunisian emigrants mobilized only 3 percent of currency transfers for the period 1995–2001. These investments appear even more modest when one compares them to the investments made by the private sector during the 9th economic plan (1997–2001) since they represented only 1 percent of the total investment of the private sector.

As for employment, the contribution of these projects does not exceed 2 percent of the jobs created during the period in question.

Attitudes eventually changed, since, according to recent data (see table on funds expenditure), one can observe that investments now represent 18 percent of the transfers. This tendency was confirmed by analysis from the European Investment Bank in a recent conference dedicated to the transfer of migrant funds in the Mediterranean region.

Nevertheless, it is useful to remember that fund transfers of migrants to Tunisia remain a visible element of their participation in developing their country of origin. The economic role of these transfers, their impact on the balance of payments and on the exterior economic and financial stability in general were affirmed in the course of the economic development plans.

Giving the importance of these transfers, Tunisia and other countries face the following challenges:

- how to stimulate these transfers despite certain constraints and transformations that affect migrations, particularly the tendency of migrants to permanently settle in Europe and the restrictions of migration policies in Arab and Western countries;
- how to direct informal transfers towards formal means, considering the importance of informal channels that most often supply parallel markets;
- how to negotiate the host countries' financial systems with the issue of transfer costs, which are sometimes excessive;
- how to develop a strategy of financial systems in view of this resource;

- how to diversify the financial products proposed to consume these funds and face the competition of the banks of the host countries;
- how to increase the awareness of senders and beneficiaries to use bank networks;
- how to provide benefits for emigrant households, the holders of financial transfers, while consolidating their use in the form of investment.

Migration and Development: Impacts of 'Intangible' Transfers

The impact of brain-drain migration, although it is a recent element in the debate on migration in Tunisia, seems to attract the attention of decision-makers due to the role that these emigrants can play in the development of the country. In fact, the interest in this issue was particularly stressed at the end of the 1990s when considering the role that it could play in the field of technology transfer and the development of several training sectors and scientific research.

The work started with an attempt to measure the degree of Tunisian competences abroad and one can see this in consular statistics under the section professionals and businessmen (reference to economic competences). The inventory of professionals in 2007 is important. It led to actions that maintain a direct relationship with these professionals in order to increase their awareness and to associate them with national programs of scientific and technological research. In addition, the private sector is reinforcing collaboration with these professionals to develop innovation, quality and competitiveness in its products.

Conclusions on the Links between Migration and Development

Emigration remains a crucial issue in the relations between Tunisia and other North African countries in general and the European Union since the latter has traditionally been the destination for North African emigrants. It still remains so in the present and the trend appears like it will continue into the future. It is especially pertinent since European countries are determined to manage immigration as a security issue. It is necessary to keep in mind that foreign manpower in general, and North Africans in particular, was in strong demand during the periods of economic growth (the euphoria during the reconstruction of the old continent, from 1945-1975) and rejected as soon as the 'economic crises' started.

Today, despite improvements, the social and economic situations in North African countries remain sources of migration pressure. In fact, the *differences of development levels* with European countries are still accentuated and the gap between the income of European and North Africans continues to grow, maintaining favourable conditions for the continuity of migratory flows. The GNP per person in the countries of the European Union is 17 times higher than the Maghreb).

In addition, the classic logic for rejecting manpower surplus (internal factor) and economic call (external factor), which is full of consequences for a migratory phenomenon that favours the expansion of what one could call the 'migratory dream,' is changing. The economic call is becoming informal and is being encouraged by businesses from the tertiary sector. It is also creating a new organization of movements with different forms. This migratory dream is a phenomenon that takes dramatic dimensions. Structured networks were formed on either side of the Mediterranean to send illegal migrants to Europe.

Migration constitutes a durable phenomenon that needs to be understood in a way that it represents an opportunity for countries of origin as well as host countries. In fact, today, migrations are in a way an extension of the national labour market: the migrant leaves his country for a labour market that can offer him better opportunities and more advantageous salary conditions; scientists leave to look for an appropriate work structure or to open new qualification perspectives.

These exchanges in human resources generate a substantial advantage on a global scale. The figures are eloquent. The World Bank estimates that the contribution of migrants to worldwide revenue will reach 772 billion dollars in 2025. It is therefore important that this global contribution is equally distributed between the North and the South. This objective, which needs to be achieved, remains dependent on the perception of migration as a development factor.

The many policies based on the close connection between migration and development, particularly those of the UN, must rely on principles of solidarity and shared interests. This orientation is extremely urgent and it should be included in the framework of a global, multilateral partnership that strives against poverty as has been put in the objectives of the millennium and for the promotion of sustainable development.

Of course, such policies are not ambitious enough to gain control of the migratory flows but look for domains of common interest and for incentives that are prone to formulate migration as a contribution to development.

Countries sending and receiving fund transfers, as well as international organizations, give special attention to these funds, their evolution and their spending. This interest is shown by a concern in the optimization of their usage as financial supports to development. The encouragement of the emigrant initiative leading to productive investments in sectors of high added value and in regions of the origin country is an expression of such a move.

When it comes to revenue transfers, one should note that they totalled 232 billion dollars in 2006, of which 167 billion went to developing countries. The Mediterranean region, particularly North Africa, is affected by these significant financial flows.

Next to these money transfers, other forms of 'transfers' are also important especially technology and knowledge transfers and their implication in the development of the emigrant and immigrant countries. Migration could contribute through expatriate elites.

Nevertheless, the judicious use of this global contribution, through consumption of savings and population contributions, implies the implementation of a real partnership between all countries (immigration and emigration countries). Host countries must commit to set up actions and *encourage migrants settled in the Northern countries to developing the economies of the South.* This is what we call 'co-development.'

In this spirit, co-development policies could focus on two major objectives. First, it is a matter of *concentrating the revenues of migrants towards productive investment in their countries of origin.* This constitutes a major stake. One estimate is that there are some seven billion Euros transferred solely through formal channels every year from European to Mediterranean countries, neighbors and partners of the European Union. In a general manner, these savings constitute an essential source of finance for the countries concerned, which is more important than development assistance. However, this presents two problems. Not all countries benefit according to their needs, and one estimates says that only 10 percent of the total is used for productive investments. These are the reasons why recommended policies in this field must have a two-fold objective: to increase the expenditure of these savings where most needed, and to improve the effectiveness of these transfers.

To achieve these two goals, a narrow link must exist between financial systems in the countries that receive the migrants' savings. Thus, along with North/South actions associating migrants, transfer operations can be an occasion to reinforce loan capacities of bank or micro-finance institutions of emigration countries.

The second objective of this co-development policy consists of *mobilizing the qualified community.* The elite community, be they teachers, doctors, researchers, engineers or computer scientists, represent several thousands of highly skilled people, initially trained in their countries of origin and who equally took advantage of supplementary training in the universities and high schools of host countries. Generally, they kept a bond with their countries of origin, but do not envisage resettling there. Through co-development, they are therefore encouraged to work more directly to develop their countries (or regions) of origin. This skilled workforce carries out monetary transfers of this fashion in domains and on matters defined by the authorities and institutions of their origin countries in order to ensure a good connection with national strategies for development.

Chapter 2

—◆—◆—

MIGRATION AND DEVELOPMENT: HOW MUCH DO WE KNOW ABOUT IT IN ALGERIA?
– Hocine Labdelaoui –

INTRODUCTION

In Algeria, the theme of 'migration and development' is one of the main bases of reflection on migration issues. The political discourse between different ministerial and state departments shows an interest in the topic. The elaborate reports and studies on these issues by university researchers and theses and dissertations of university students tackle, directly or indirectly, its different aspects.

However, this revived interest for reflection on the 'migration and development' issue has not yet produced a collection of satisfactory knowledge to understand the different problems of Algerian emigration in the economic and social development of Algeria. The political discourse of the state simply reaffirms positions of principle in matters of emigration management. The state departments responsible for 'Algerian community settled abroad' excel at experimenting with movement formulas and the majority are limited to declarations of intentions. In regards to research, they cannot overcome the difficulties of setting up scientific research on migrations.

Recently, the difficulties in producing quality knowledge on this subject have begun to disappear. It seems that by its very nature, the demand emerging in this field could reinvigorate the objective conditions for instituting a research tradition on the migration issue.

The aim of this work is to analyse the scientific knowledge generated from the research and work carried out on Algerian migration.

We will start by making an inventory of the works on migration at universities and research centres to identify the importance put on the theme of 'migration and development.'

We will try to explain the deficit of scientific knowledge on 'migration and development' with an analysis of the difficulties in setting up scientific research on migration as part of the general obstacles to scientific research in Algeria.

Finally, by highlighting the right research tracks in ongoing projects, we will conclude with a reflection on the perspectives to developing scientific research on 'migration and development.'

THE STATE OF RESEARCH ON MIGRATIONS AND ON THE THEME, 'MIGRATION AND DEVELOPMENT'

Algeria, though mainly a country of emigration, but also becoming a country of immigration, produces surprisingly little scientific work on migratory questions. Produced by isolated individual project initiatives or in response to sporadic demands by the public service, these works did not produce a significant collection of knowledge on the matter. In fact, the studies' inventories of research centres and university research (dissertations/ theses) show a deficit in knowledge on migration issues. This deficit is found again in the topic of 'migration and development.'

An Account of the Work Produced
by Research Centres

The six socio-economic and socio-historic Algerian research centres show disparate interest in migration studies. The exception is the CREAD (Centre for Research in Applied Economics for Development) which, during the last 30 years, produced about ten studies on:

- the situation of Algerian emigrants in Europe (Benattig & al. 1978; Musette & al. 1994);
- the impact of the transfers of migrants' savings on rural society in Algeria. (Benattig, 1981);
- training of students abroad (El Kenz, Benguerna & Khelfaoui, 1999);
- Algerian emigration and the country of origin (Khendriche, 1999);
- migration and the labour market (Musette 2002; Musette & al. 2004; 2006);
- the rights of migrants (Musette, Labdelaoui, Kherdoun & Souaber, 2002; Musette, 2006);
- return Migration (Musette, Hammouda, Belhaouari— Musette & Labdelaoui, 2006; Musette, Labdelaoui, Kherdoun & Belhaouari—Musette, 2007);
- the movement of Algerian Migrants (Musette, Hammouda, Khaldoun, 2008).

The CENAP (National Centre for Planning and Development Studies) gives particular interest to the study of Algeria within the topic of international migration. After producing a study on the evolution of Algerian emigration in the context of the construction of the European Union (CENEAP, 1992), it is presently preparing a vast survey on international migration of Algerians.

This research direction corresponds with the studies conducted by this centre—even under its former designation—on the situation of Algerian emigration to France, which was the subject of a vast national survey at that time (AARDES, 1980) and to a second, expanded report in 1981 (INEAP, 1981).

As a research institution specializing in historical studies, the CNERMN (National Research Centre on the National Movement and the Revolution of 1st November 1954) has completed two studies on the history of Algerian emigration: One on emigration towards Western Europe (Sari, Ali-Mazighi & Labdelaoui, 2004); and the other on emigration to Arab countries of the Middle East (Tarchoune, Yahiaoui & Khaldi, 2003).

The work of the INESG (National Institute of Global Strategy Studies) is on the situation of Algerian emigration to France (INESG, 1989) and the strategies of Arabic emigration (Labdelaoui, 1999).

The Centre for Social Anthropology and Cultural Research (CRASC) attributes a particular interest to the analysis of the migration problem. After publishing, through a research department, various texts on Algerian emigration (Kouidri, 1989; Carlier, 1983), it is presently carrying out two studies of its own. The first concerns contemporary international migration in Algeria (Moulay Hadj & al, 2007). The second deals with youth emigration, based on a survey in Kabylie (Hadibi & al, 2007). Presently, it participates in the framework of the FSP (Fonds de Solidarité Prioritaire - Priority Assistance Funds) in a Franco-Maghreb research and training programme called 'Foreign Students in the Maghreb and in the Euro-Mediterranean Area: Towards Which Kind of Globalisation for Higher Education and Skills Circulation?'

The CNRPAH (National Centre for Prehistoric, Anthropologic and Historic Research) has taken the initiative to relaunch the study on Algerian emigration (CNRPAH, 2007) from a sociological approach entitled "Emigration—Immigration." This was announced in June 2007 at an international seminar in honour of Abdelmalek Sayad.

In its consulting mission with the Algerian political authorities, the National Economic and Social Council (CNES) produced four reports on Algerian emigration: two studies on the situation of Algerian emigration in France (CNES, 1989 &

1998), a third one on the contribution of the national community in France for the economic and social development of its country of origin (CNES, 2002), and a forth report on European policy on migration (CNES, 2004).

An Account of University Research Groups and Laboratories

Parallel to its principle mission of providing training, the University of Algeria, undertakes research activities with groups recognised by the National Commission of Planning and Evaluation of Academic Research (CNEPRU) and, in recent years, with research laboratories established under laws on scientific research orientation.

The first studies completed at the Algerian University go back to the 1990s, to the launch of the second phase of the university groups. In fact, the University of Algiers produced the majority of the work.

Applying its research to a sociological method focusing on migratory issues in terms tightly linked to the country of origin, the first group, composed once again of the members of this university, chose the following theme: The integration of returning Algerian migrants' children into Algeria's education system.

The study, made through a questionnaire prepared in two colleges of Algiers placed these students in specialized classes. It led to the evaluation of teaching the Arabic language as a pedagogical way to integrate students into Algerian schools (Ali-Mazighi, Djabri, Labdelaoui & Sahraoui, 1992).

A second group, through the CNEPRU system, pursued the study on migration issues by moving the centre of interest towards training Algerian students abroad. The completed research demonstrated the way the management of this training has generated a phenomenon of non return and, thus, of loss.

To expand the field of their studies, the members of this second group have also examined the migration of Southern Mediterranean students to European universities (Streiff-Feinart, 1994).

With the creation of the Laboratory for Social Change (LCS) in 2000, migration research's approach evolved. It shifted from the analyses of emigration to the study of the mobility of academic and technical competencies. It is through this evolution that members of the laboratory group participated in the research and training programme "The New Migration Movements: Young Graduates, Scientists, Intellectuals and Intelligentsia in Western Mediterranean: Circuits, Networks, Social Logics and Representations." This was done through the Franco-Maghreb project FSP (Fonds de solidarité prioritaire - Priority Assistance Funds) and with the participation of different universities (Paris 8, Meknès, Tunis, Florence and Bari).

The first part of the project accredited by the CNEPRU and based at the LCS, covers all Algerian institutions of higher education and a sample of 1200 teachers of different grades (Labdelaoui, Amira & Akkeb, 2005). Initial results of the research show that the organization and the administrative management of the training systems abroad, short internships and scientific conventions trigger teacher mobility to function as an auxiliary means to a situation of professional precariousness (Labdelaoui, 2006).

Due to a lack of financial means, the surveys planned by the three projects mentioned above were limited solely to the region of Algiers. This makes generalising the results of the three studies necessary.

The University of Constantine followed the steps of the University of Algiers. Researching the image of Algerian emigration in the Spanish media (Dellio Fodhil, 2001) was followed by the establishment of a specialized laboratory in migration research. Founded as the "Laboratory of Socio-historic Research and Studies on Migratory Movements" it is presently leading ten studies on the themes of local and international migration (LERMM, 2008).

Through this overview on migration research by the University of Algiers, it is clear that the amount of research is insufficient to envisage an approach to evaluating the actual state of forming research traditions on the matter.

EVALUATION OF DISSERTATIONS AND THESES ON MIGRATION

One can imagine that by its accumulated research traditions as the first Algerian university, the University of Algiers is naturally the one with the most post-graduate dissertations and theses on the theme of migration.

Examining files from the central library of the university and the registers of theses permitted the gathering of information on post-graduate research work carried out between 1970 and 2007. The documents that were consulted give only short and incomplete indications on works carried out prior to 1970.

The table provided hereunder shows that while the number of dissertations and theses carried out at the University of Algiers on the theme of migration during that period only amounts to 35, that is not important. It is the range of topics that is in fact important.

TABLE 1. EVALUATION OF DISSERTATIONS AND THESES ON MIGRATION AT THE UNIVERSITY OF ALGIERS FROM 1970 TO 2007

FIELD	DISSERTATIONS		THESES	TOTAL
	DEA OR DES	MASTER		
Sociology	04	08	01	**13**
Arts	03	05	01	**09**
Political Science	02	04	-	**06**
Economics	01	02	-	**03**
Islamic Sciences	-	01	-	**01**
Law	03	–	-	**03**
Total	**13**	**20**	**02**	**35**

Source: Register of Theses of the University of Algiers, University Research Network of CERIST.

Students of sociology and the arts show more interest for migration studies. In sociology, theses and dissertations on the subject represent more than half of the titles listed (13). In the arts, though they only represent about a fourth of the total (9), they still clearly remain superior compared to the number of academic papers on immigration produced in other fields of study.

The distribution of dissertations and theses by degree type shows that the researchers stand mainly at masters and DEA or DES level (Diplôme d'études approfondies: a post-graduate qualification which is a prerequisite for PhD candidates; Diplôme d'études supérieures spécialisées: a university degree awarded after a five-year course of study). The 31 dissertations at this level represent nearly 94 percent of the total titles listed. This fact makes us think that students who have worked on migration experience some difficulties in following their research beyond their first post-graduate diploma, either because they are not prepared enough to conduct this type of research, or due to a lack of support or means.

Reading the undertaken themes reveals a slow, but regular, evolution of the research objective: they go from objectives centred on emigration issues to objectives built around a wider range of what makes up migrations. At the beginning of this evolution, students focused on the causes of emigration and the situations of emigrants in host countries.

In most of the sociological and political science research works, the causes of emigration analysis are examined starting from the case of the exodus of students and academic competencies. This is what we find in a dissertation analysing emigration plans among postgraduate students (Mabrouk, 2007) and in a work exploring the causes that push Algerian intellectuals to flee their countries while proposing recommendations for solution (Laadjel, 1990). The same topic of 'brain drain' emigration is tackled using the training of Algerian managers abroad in research on business enterprise.

The works of those students reading economy or law examines the causes of emigration from the point of view of capital growth (Djebbara, 1980), in terms of the relation between emigration and agricultural development (Larbi, 1977) and from an approach relating to the impact of emigration on rural society (Benyounes, 1977).

Emigration analysis as a means to understand the situation of emigrants was handled in two ways: by its occurrence in French or Arabic fictional masterpieces and through the conditions of the life of emigrants.

The work of students reading French literature tackled the situation of Algerian emigrants in the host country as it was romanticised in French language literature and which was often linked to the causes of emigration (Mokadem, 1977; Hadj Naceur, 1976; Azouz, 1982; Aït Hamou, 1978). The issue was also studied through the image of emigration in fictional master-pieces by French and Arabic authors (Chekroun, 1992; Bayhou, 2002). The research works of students reading Arabic literature analyses the novel: *The Season of Emigration to the North.* This was done by looking at the causes of migration (Ouali, 2003), the composition of time and space (Achour, 2003) or, uniquely, by looking at the significance of space (Medkem, 2001).

The students also deal with the living conditions of emi-grants in the host countries. Their socio-economic and socio-political aspects are analysed by the students of Sociology and Political Science. The studies carried out in this context involve: the adaptation of emigrant families in France (Taftaf, 2002), the everyday living conditions of North Africans at the mines of Frei-berg (Maarouf, 1970), the political management experience of Algerian emigration in France in the 1920s (Carlier, 1976), the problems of mixed marriages (Kacimi, 2008), and the incidents of the Franco-Algerian crisis on Algerian emigration following fuel nationalisation (Duteil, 1972). The living conditions in the host countries are, in addition, analysed from the point of view of law and Islamic studies with a dissertation on the judicial status of Algerian workers in France (Akacha, 1973) and another on an analytical evaluation of the Koran and religious texts related to stays in non-Islamic countries (Ibn Ameur, 2002).

The evolution of research exclusively focusing on emigration issues as they affect migratory issues has taken new dimensions following the disappearance of emigration policy and also an intellectual reorientation of issues related to the reintegration of emigrated Algerians. These issues are naturally subscribed to the context of the time, which was that of 'rotating emigration' that concerned the return plans of Algerian workers (Le Masne, 1974) and the reintegration of emigrants in Algerian industry (Hanachi, 1985).

Schematically, the framework of this evolution of the research objectives reveals that students' interest in migration is shown by four themes:

- the return of Algerian emigrants in the context of the new state of migration, especially 'migration for settlement purposes';
- the settlement of immigrants on Algerian territory;
- the situations of migrants in other countries;
- the scientific stakes of migrations within State relations.

Today, repatriation problems come along with the renewed approaches on migration by countries of emigration somewhat familiar with an altogether different situation of emigration and immigration. Nevertheless, sociology students analysing return migration highlight the difficulties of reintegration into the country of origin. This is done by studying the difficult socio-cultural adaptations of emigrant girls who returned to the country (Begtache, 1992) and also through retired emigrants going back to their place of origin (Daabouze, 2002).

Sociological analysis of foreign nationals' presence in Algerian territory began in the 1980s with works on Protestant missionaries in Algeria (Bockerman, 1980) and the 1930s Spanish emigration in Algeria (Menjel, 1983). This continued with a study on the conditions of Palestinians in Algeria (Eddeks, 1981) and the presence of a Jewish minority in Algeria during the colonial period (Doudah, 2003). These studies somewhat precede ongoing works on the question of transit migration and illegal immigration. New categories of immigration in Algeria (e.g., illegal, transit, etc.) promote the renewal of regulations governing foreigners' rights of entry and their stays in countries. A legal analysis on the status of foreigners in Algeria (Kabache, 1980) focused on these regulations.

The analysis of foreign migrants' conditions in other countries attracted University of Algiers students. This theme is found in three works: a sociological study on the creation of a Palestinian business in Jordan (Hassan Sari, 1992), an economic study of Jewish immigration's consequences on the economy of occupied Palestinian territories (Ayad Teisser, 1994) and a sociological study on images of foreigners from a collective Israeli perspective (Sedki, 2004).

The evolution of migration fluxes, which turned into important issues in international and regional policy, pushed political science students to analyse the importance of emigration in Euro-Maghreb relations (Menad, 2004), its consequences on their relations (Bougara, 2002) and the rise of the extreme right in Western Europe as a result of migration issues (Sahel, 2002).

The choice of these themes clearly shows that the authors of the mentioned studies are conscious that migration problems are no longer caused by the relations between two countries united by a common colonial history, but by these relations' evolution in the context of international migration and relations between states. The dissertations and theses done by research teams of other Algerian universities reveal a failure to consider the migration problem. Excluding the studies carried out by the University of Algiers, the only registered dissertation (a master's thesis) on Algerian emigration is by the University of Constantine (Taftaff, 1989).

The Status of the Theme 'Migration and Development' in Migration Research

Through this outline on the works carried out at universities and at the different research centres dealing with migration, one may observe that 'migration and development' is studied as a component of four different fields.

The issue of Algerian emigrants returning to their countries of origin was the subject of several university dissertations and theses during the '70s and '80s. These works analyse this issue through the disposition of individual projects (Lemasne, 1974), socio-professional integration (Hanachi, 1985, Daabouze, 2002) and, finally, through socio-cultural adaptation (Bagtache, 1999). They also studied aspects of return migration concerning executives who were trained abroad (Harbi, 1982) and the 'brain drain' phenomenon (Laadjel, 2004). The CREAD's participation in investigations on return migration turns up in three projects: the first looks into the question of emigrants' relations with their countries of origin (Khendriche, 1999); the second tackles the problem of students who do not return back to their countries (El Kenz et al, 1999); and, finally, the third project examines the re-emergence of problems related to Algerian emigrants returning to their country in the last ten years (Musette & all, 2007).

University research groups' works on return migration deal with different questions than the ones tackled by the studies mentioned above. Sociologists from the University of Algiers studied the integration of returning emigrants' children into the educational system (Mazighi & all, 1992). The return of students educated abroad is also studied (Labdelaoui & all, 2001) and the problems involving skilled mobility was the subject of a third project (Labdelaoui & all, 2006).

On a whole, the studies carried out in the 1970s and 1980s were completed in a context marked by a classification of return migration as a venture of the emigrants themselves and as an application of policies from the Algerian State and the countries hosting these immigrants. The current works are in line with another approach that views repatriation as a mobility that emigrants undertake within the framework of developing European policies to manage global migratory movements.

The mobilization of highly skilled Algerians trained abroad was the subject of investigations on the theme 'migration and development.' University studies mentioned above analyse the different aspects related to the reintegration and the adaptation of students in their home countries and to skilled mobility. They give special attention to explaining the causes of non-return and the difficulties of social and professional reintegration. Further explaining the causes and effects, the works of research centres attempt to analyse the methods to use for an adapted mobilization of the skilled force settled abroad (INESG, 2002). They also attempt to analyse emigration's contributions to developing Algeria (CNES, 2002).

The theme of resettlement did not stimulate interest deserving of its importance. Researchers and university students did not deal with this theme and the CREAD is the only research centre offering two studies on the issue (Benattig, 1988, accordian Music, 2008).

The impact emigration has on the development of regions exporting manpower is a theme sometimes tackled by university economy students (Djebbabra, 1980, Larbi, 1977, Benyounes, 1977).

To conclude this first part, the studies on 'migration and development' confirm the general research on migration. They demonstrate a deficit in the collection of scientific knowledge on the migration phenomena, which requires explanation.

Research Difficulties on Migrations and on the Theme of 'Migration and Development'

After reviewing the current state of migration research, it is obvious that the little interest given to the theme of 'migration and development' is due to the difficulties in setting up general scientific research on migration. We can explain the deficit of scientific knowledge on migrations in Algeria as a twofold problem: the difficult conditions for scientific research in general and the difficulties inherent to research on migration in this context.

The Difficulties of Setting Up the Conditions for Scientific Research

Algerian scientific research on migrations bears the negative effects of a public policy that substitutes fundamental research by applied research imposed as an obligatory exercise of successful activities. If, at the level of political texts, the will to create scientific and technological research was constantly expressed, the conversion of this will into strategies and clear political actions remained just wishful thinking.

Before the application of Law 98.11, the scientific research sector experienced institutional instability. It also suffered from a shortage of clear policy and immediate and long-term strategies for developing scientific research.

Not having produced precise and detailed evaluations of their reports, the national Organization of Scientific Research (ONRS) and the National Council of Research (CNR), both institutions created in the spirit of the 1972 higher education reform, were dissolved in 1982. This brought about the functional reorientation and the dissolution of the majority of the research centres and the teams that they managed.

The Commission for New Energies (CEN), created to replace these two institutions, met its end in 1986 and was replaced by the High Council for Research (HCR), which succumbed to the Research Secretariat (SR) that was then replaced by the current Ministry (Ministère délégué) in charge of scientific research. These transformations led to restructuring the research administrative organization at the level of the Ministry of Higher Education and Scientific Research (MESRS). Theoretically, this would provide better coordination of the two categories of scientific research (training and development research) and harmony between the activities of the two authorities (Ministry and Ministère délégué) and the institutions under their respective supervision.

Lacking clear policies and subject to institutional instability, the scientific research sector became a place for proliferating scientific activities (sometimes even scientistic) and not a place for the establishment of effective scientific research and real coordination of research activities. The different establishments were satisfied by orientation operations and the project evaluation without specifications or the obligation to provide real scientific results (the only obligation was the targeted time-frame). This 'freedom' in choosing research themes paradoxically became an obstacle to scientific research development. Apart from not being followed by fixed devices that can amalgamate several interesting initiatives, it also failed to produce the financial and logistic resources to invest in strategic fields.

Under the burden of these constraints, the research projects carried out by the centres or the CNEPRU and the works of universities or publishers respond more to career strategies and the legitimization of the weakened social status of teachers and researchers. In such a context, the reason themes on migrations are infrequently undertaken is obvious since they are rarely requested or an ordered by authorities or sponsors.

Inherent Difficulties to Research on Migrations

The non-institutionalization of research on migrations

Occupying a secondary place in the system governing scientific activities, migration research suffers from an institutional organization deficit. In contrast to Morocco and Tunisia which enjoy research centres, associations and think tanks on the matter, this research suffers in Algeria due to an absence of permanent specialized institutions. Employees within 'research groups' in charge of completing tasks within their time-frame complete the few activities the country does produce.

From the time the first scientific research organization started in 1972 until today, even while awaiting the launch of a new five-year research plan, the number of teams that worked on migration can be counted on the fingers of one hand. Of the 514 recognised research laboratories, since the application of law 98.11, we count only a single laboratory that deals with migration issues (LERMM, University of Constantine, 2007). Located at the University of Constantine, this laboratory has not published its results as of this writing.

The deficit in migration research in Algeria compared with its Tunisian and Moroccan neighbors can be partially explained by differences in the application of the emigration issue by the three states. In Tunisia and Morocco, emigration is both an essential financial resource to the economy and a political force of control. This explains state requests for economical and social knowledge. On the other hand, emigration is more an issue of internal politics and a strategic factor in foreign relations, particularly with France.

Non-institutionalization of migration research in the scientific research sector, be it at universities or otherwise, is not exclusively explained by the organizational outline of the sector but somewhat by the prevailing contextual management of emigration. It does not require establishing permanent research institutions. This explains the instability of the ministerial organization's policy management and on Algerian emigration research and the resignation of the ministry in charge of the national community abroad (Labdelaoui, 2005).

The failure to set up a research and documentation centre on migratory questions also demonstrates the predominance of this sporadic research logic (according to the political and economic concerns of the moment).

The shortage of specialized researchers in migratory studies

Algeria's higher education program does not include any training programmes or areas of studies that train specialized researchers in migration studies. The 1972 reform of higher education was devised and structured to facilitate the implementation of socialist development programs. It privileged the training of graduates in specialities that had direct associations with those goals. As for the other reforms that followed, they brought new structure to the configuration of subjects created by the 1972 reform. Theoretically, this was to allow universities to adapt themselves to the socio-economic evolution of the country, namely, politically provoked economic liberalism.

Since it was not being directly considered by these internal economic priorities, the migration question was not given particular attention in the different programs of research or training. If we focus on the different bachelor's degree programs in humanities and social sciences, we cannot fail to notice that sociology is the only subject that offers a study unit entitled "North African migrations" through its 'demography' specialization. The aspects relating to international or local migrations and to the history of emigration are not intended to be studied as specialisations at either graduate and post-graduate levels (University of Algiers, 2006).

The absence of demand for migration research

As well as not being institutionalized and not able to mobilize qualified researchers, the scientific knowledge on migration is not subject to a social request for research. Like other types of scientific research, it is subject to the negative effects of knowledge and science statuses in society, particularly those involving decision-making and the use of power. Its place and importance are especially weakened by the fact that its issues are an external 'solution' to an internal problem which the society is not able to solve itself. In regards to making policy, the emigrant does not cause any problem by his departure and absence and constitutes a social figure that does not require scientific consideration but administrative management.

This account explains why the Algerian state, while constantly reaffirming the interest granted to the expatriated community abroad, did not set up a system for the collection of scientific information on the migration phenomena. The few reports available on these questions are produced by the CNES or other research institutions. So far, the officially created bodies at the ministerial level, as well as other institutions (CN, APN, UGTA, etc.), did not generate any scientific research or solicit any scientific institutions, university or other, to perform it.

RESEARCH DIFFICULTIES ON THE THEME OF 'MIGRATION AND DEVELOPMENT'

Confronted by these different problems, the scientific research on migration has been unable to produce a discourse on migratory questions. The creation of knowledge on these issues takes place in an institutional and academic framework which is adverse to the development of research traditions in the migration field. It also occurs in a social context marked by difficulties declaring principle positions favouring the institutionalization of scientific knowledge production on migration issues. The effects of this last difficulty clearly appear in the 'migration and development' issue's scientific knowledge deficit.

The Position of the 'Migration and Development' Issue in the Management of Migration by the State

The issue of 'migration and development' occupies a central place in Algerian political discourse. With the exception of the 1970s and the beginning of the 1980s, this interest has led to the creation of policies that were never fully developed or implemented.

Reintegration Policy of the '70s and '80s

Following the cessation of sending of workers abroad in 1973, the Algerian state implemented an aggressive policy for the reintegration of emigrants living abroad to achieve a triple objective: to allow those Algerians forced into exile during the colonial period to benefit from the independence of their country and to enjoy the freedom to choose the place where they wanted to live and work, to mobilize emigrated manpower to complete development plans and assume official positions of the newly transformed Algerian government, and to face the potential French menace of massively discharging Algerian emigrants after political relations deteriorated between the two countries over the nationalization of French fuel companies.

To implement this policy, Algeria supported reintegration of emigrants by granting them fiscal exemptions to complete their repatriation and to transfer their means of production and funds. The government also provided extensive resources to carry out projects, settle in the regions of their choice, find jobs and send their children to school (Labdelaoui, 2005). It deliberately chose a collective management involving the majority of the ministerial departments to apply the decisions made during the 'one party' and 'the assemblies for emigration' meetings.

This policy brought positive results to the migrant reintegration plan (Benattig, 1988) and answered the socio-cultural problems caused by reintegration. Mainly, this involved the providing education for students who benefited from the experience of progressive integration and preparation for reintegration in the country of residence (Alimazighi, Labdelaoui, Sahraoui, Djabri, 1992).

Policy on Skilled Emigration and Fund Spending

Since the late 1980s, with the consequences of the collapse in petrol profits and the faded return plans of emigrants, 'development migration' became an issue for mobilizing the highly skilled settled abroad and their investments. In this regard, we have three remarks:

- At a symbolic level, the Algerian political discourse marks a sensitive evolution towards recognizing the self-organized Algerians settled abroad as a means of mobilizing the scientific and financial capacities of the community. (Labdelaoui, 2006)
- On an organizational level, the process of this mobilization necessitated setting up a governmental structure that would coordinate participation with other state institutions.
- Finally, on a statutory level, the mobilization of the competences and capacities of emigrants renewed the judiciary. New enactments on investment support to support the development of Algeria (Labdelaoui, 2007) emerged.

This policy's implementation tested several organization configurations of government participation in the management of mobilizing emigrants. After trying to work through a secretary of state, management of the Algerian community settled abroad was handed over to a ministry attached to the government leader. In 2008, after this department disappeared for more than two years, the community's administrative matters were amalgamated and handed over to the Ministry of National Solidarity. We note a renewed interest on the matter in Parliament (which organized an international symposium in June 2008) at that time. This interest is also demonstrated by the national agency responsible for developing investment, which is initiating a project on the consumption of capital investment established abroad, a project that was implemented in France and in certain countries of the Mediterranean. The skilled workforce settled abroad wants to provide ideas while founding its own organizations, such as the Algerian Competences Association that has just organized its second conference for Algerian executives settled abroad participating in the development of their country in December 2008.

Lack of Scientific Knowledge Request son the Theme: Mobilization of the Skilled Workforce Settled Abroad

From this quick overview of the interest given to the discourse and governmental activities on the issue of mobilizing the competences and capacities of the Algerian community settled abroad, one notes that the 'migration and development' topic occupies a central place in Algeria's management of migration. However, examining this established perspective shows that it tends to only produce research of political and symbolic visibility. The decisions made are only rarely applied and there is no apparent motivation to elaborate, apply and evaluate projects. This reflects negatively on the development of 'migration and development' research traditions at universities and at the level of research for training and development.

Outlook on the Foundation of Scientific Research on Migrations and 'Migration and Development'

Even though research on Algerian migration is carried out in an unfavourable institutional and organizational context, it seems that it finds factors of its revival and development in emigration's evolution as well as in the appearance of transit migration and the materialization of immigration in Algeria. In this evolution, the research on 'migration and development' constitutes one of the tracks for migration research redeployment on.

For the first time since independence, national research programs, in particular the "Population and Society" or "History, Prehistory and Archaeology" programs, adopted emigration themes as recommended targets or selected research (MESRS, 1998).

The factors favoring the foundation of migration scientific research

Evaluating current research perspectives confirms that factors which drive the desire to establish migration research traditions exist.

The contextual factors

Pressured by other states dealing with immigration, Algeria is committed to updating knowledge on migratory fluxes to and from its territory. Algeria should not only study the migration phenomenon but should also provide useful knowledge for its migration policies.

- Necessity for knowledge about the new state of migration: This knowledge became a condition to making effective migration management policies. The Algerian State cannot do without a study on its emigration's relationships with the hosting countries and the international migration flow between these countries and Algeria. In the same way, it cannot minimize the importance knowledge has on the evolution of migrants' profiles, emigration's causes and the variety of destinations. Finally, it cannot fight illegal immigration on its territory without relying on scientific knowledge.
- Importance of regional and international cooperation: Algeria's participation in projects initiated by the European Union (E.U.), the UNDP, the ILO and the OMI shows this perspective. Creating an office to fight illegal migration demonstrates its cooperation with the

European Union and, at the same time, shows Algerian authorities' will not to find themselves isolated in matters concerning migration management (Labdelaoui, 2005).

At a scientific level, Algerian universities and research centres have expanded cooperative relationships, where reflection on migratory issues will have an important place. However, to take full advantage of these opportunities, it is important to benefit from the experiences of other universities and research institutions to consolidate the efforts of developing research on Algerian migration.

The grounds for the creation of research careers in migration

Even if well prepared, or not prepared at all, to take up research on migratory issues, students at under-graduate and post-graduate levels embark on research projects in the field. Even if the number of students preparing dissertations and theses on emigration and immigration does not increase, it at least remains stable. This indicates that, in the future, areas of study such as sociology, the arts, history and political sciences will become fields of development in research traditions on migration.

The signs of fracture with the European models of sociological analysis on migrations

The research themes prepared at universities and at the CERIST (Research Centre on scientific and technical information) reveal a tendency to develop methodology on migration studies in Algeria. Whether the themes relate to the situation in the hosting countries, to the causes of emigration, or to the immigration phenomenon in Algeria, the dominating process seeks to put the relationship between emigration and immigration into perspective.

The thematic fields of future university research

This tendency to break with the sociological immigration adopted in Europe is not limited to research carried out for the achievement of university degrees. It conspicuously appears in ongoing research projects at the university level as well as at research centres (mainly: CREAD, CENEAP, CNRPAH and CNERMN).

Starting with the ongoing research themes, we offer the hypothesis that migration research in Algeria is composed of five thematic fields.

Algerian emigration

Besides simply continuing to persist, the exodus of Algerians overseas has also changed deeply. The new causes of emigration created new migrant profiles, destination extensions and diversification of the types of migration. A number of ongoing research studies at the University of Algiers and at several research centres such as the CREAD and the CRASC attempt to understand this evolution. The researchers analyse current phenomena, such as new causes of emigration, skill mobility and illegal Algerian emigration by sea known as 'harragas' or harga.'

Return migration

The works currently carried out by the CREAD mark a separation from current models on immigration research. They show that the repatriation of Algerian emigrants became a changeable component on migratory circulations. Their return no longer includes only the retired and repressed as it did in the past, but different categories, including the skilled workforce (Musette, Kheldoun, Labdelaoui, 2007).

Transit migration

Transit migration, in its illegal forms, constitutes the third field of migration research in Algeria. Three projects are in progress: The Department of Sociology at the University of Algiers, which accepted work on the situation of sub-Saharan migrants in the cities of Southern Algeria, carries out the first. The second project, undertaken by the Algerian Society of Psychological Research (SARP), in collaboration with the International Committee for Solidarity between the Peoples (CISP), is completing an investigation on the profile of sub-Saharan migrants in Algeria (CISP, SARL, 2007). Finally, a team of researchers from the University of Annaba investigates the interactions between transit migration and the urban environment (Spiga, 2007).

Migration and development

The problems related to the 'migration and development' issue will be an important track for migration research. In this context, the CREAD has just accepted a new research project on the theme of 'migration and development in Algeria.' This project maintains a triple objective: to understand the economical and social impact of migration flows (internal and international) on the development of Algeria, to carry out a comparative impact study on migration at two localities (Algiers and Tlemcen) and to propose mechanisms that will accompany these dispersions' contributions to development. Hence, this project helps fill the knowledge deficit on the contributions of migration to decreasing social inequalities and also in stimulating the local labour market.

'Migration and development' is currently the subject of PhD students who are carrying out research on two topics: the return of Algerian emigrants and the relationships between migration, work and development.

Foreign immigration in Algeria

Finally, the fifth research area on migration involves the phenomenon of foreign immigration in Algeria. The LCS team from the Department of Sociology at the University of Algiers, within the framework of the CNEPRU, deals with the connection between the new context of international migration and the general tendency for Algeria to evolve as a country of immigration and emigration (Labdelaoui, and other, 2008).

CONCLUSION

Due to the complexity of migration data, and while focusing on migration through these five fields, Algerian research cannot do without the integration of the 'migration and development' theme in its future projects. This requires establishing an organization to consolidate ongoing projects and to coordinate future projects that will most likely emerge as the new national research programs make calls for studies.

The initiative to create an associated research laboratory on population and migration in Algiers stays within this perspective. This laboratory would be open to national and international researchers, both domestic and abroad, who investigate the Algerian migration issue. The founding of this laboratory will rely on the future association of migration research.

Chapter 3

— ◆ ◆ —

CLANDESTINE IMMIGRATION IN ALGERIA: THE FAILURE OF THE SECURITY APPROACH
– Fethi Boulares –

"It is better to be devoured by fishes than by soil worms."
– Harragas' Motto

INTRODUCTION

During the past few years, the status of illegal immigration in Algeria has evolved from exceptional to one of real national tragedy. Not a week passes without the press reporting on corpses washed up by the sea or boats carrying young people making desperate SOSs to ships, coast guards or even, as a last resort, calling their families on land to alert the Algerian rescue authorities.

Despite the legal arsenal adopted by the Algerian Parliament, categorising illegal immigration as criminal conduct, dozens of young people, every day, leave their families, villages and country to risk their lives finding ferry men, paying them significant sums and still end up in European prisons.

The question that researchers and experts, as well as journalists, do not cease to raise is: why are these young Algerians so desperate to flee their country?

This paper tries to answer this question and highlight the illegal immigration phenomenon commonly called '*the harragas*' and the reasons driving these young people to sail away. We further try to analyse Algeria's approach to this matter, European politics aside.

DELIMITATION OF THE 'HARRAGA' CONCEPT

The word '*harraga*' refers to a category of Algerian society that has chosen to migrate illegally. The action of the '*harga*' (in English 'to burn') refers to the illegal migrants' destruction of their identification documents once they have reached their destinations (Hammouche & Labdelaoui, 2005). The word 'harragas' also derives from 'sneak in' and 'burn the steps.'

These young people are determined to flee from Algeria, whatever the price, because they understand the seriousness of the multi-dimensional crisis which has gripped the entire country for the last few decades. This situation pressed itself on the entire society, especially on the youngest. They have lost all hope. They find no comfort when Algerian officials insist the currency reserves deposited in American banks exceed140 billion dollars (*El Watan,* 4 October 2008).

Assuming that the illegal immigrants are victims of a Western mirage spread by the Internet and satellite television networks is an insult to the memory of the young victims of the Algerian crisis. The 'harraga' are aware of the situation prevailing in their poor country. By deciding to run the risk, they have only one desire, to start a new life in the host country, even if it is far from their families (Zerrouki, 2004).

The various reports published on this phenomenon in Algeria clearly demonstrate that illegal immigration has attained alarming proportions during recent years, especially since President Bouteflika is in power. Every day we note coast guard interventions to save or hinder migrants to leave their home waters.

STATISTICS OF A NATIONAL TRAGEDY

While Algeria's neighbors, Morocco and Tunisia, for example, have lower illegal immigration levels, this does not suggest the situation in Algeria will change for the better.

In summer 2009, for instance, the phenomenon has risen again and with even more strength. From East to West, young Algerians leave from everywhere. Young, middle aged, men, women, children, entire families. On the night of August 7, 2009, off the shore of the Annaba province, the Coast Guard pursued a boat with 46 young, prospective illegal immigrants on board. Refusing to surrender, the makeshift boat turned against the Coast Guards ship. The following day, another group of 28 people were also intercepted off the Annaba coast.

The number of *harraga* corpses retrieved by the National Marine Coast Guard has tripled in four years, from 29 in 2005 to 98 in 2008. The interception of 1,327 young Algerians, mostly between 21 and 29, means that the majority of these illegal migrants come from the eastern coast of the country with 636 migrants, out of which 442 come from the province of Annaba alone.

2008 has been the bloodiest year for the *harraga*. Officials fished 98 corpses from the sea, i.e., an increase of 37 percent compared to 2007, during which the Coast Guard had recorded 61 deceased people. In the same period, the Navy made 88 interventions. In 2008, the authorities of various European countries turned away 639 intercepted illegal migrants. This is another increased figure compared to those recorded in 2007 and 2006, which saw 189 and 532 cases. During the past three years, 1,350 illegal migrants were intercepted and later repatriated.

In 2008, over 67,000 people have crossed the Mediterranean Sea seeking asylum in Europe, out of which, according to the United Nations High Commissioner for Refugees (UNHCR), more than half of them reached Italy and Malta. The attempts of illegal migration significantly increase in respect to the last four years. 246 people were intercepted in August 2008. In 2007, the Navy intercepted 1,259 illegal migrants and retrieved 61 corpses. 2006 saw 1,016 people intercepted and 73 bodies recovered. In

2005, the numbers were only 335 and 29. So, from 2005 to 2008 there were 261 deceased and 3,937 people intercepted by the Navy (Zerrouki, 2004).

Seventy-five percent of Algerian immigrants are illegal, of which 63 percent are students and workers. Most of them dream of leaving the country for Europe. Contrary to Tunisia and Morocco, the majority of migration candidates have a high level of education. We note that 38 percent of them are university students and 40 percent have an average level. In regards to their financial situations, we can affirm that this is not so bad. The 'harraga' phenomenon mostly concerns the insecure middle classes (Afroun, 2009).

Most *harraga* are between the ages of 18 and 40. They include students, public servants and free-lance professionals. They move illegally on-board makeshift boats. Most of the immigration candidates choose Sardinia, Italy or Almerìa, Spain, aided by people called 'ferry-men' with compasses and life preservers (*Le Jour d'Algerie*, 29 September 2007).

Along these lines, an investigation carried out by an activist with the LADDH (Algerian League for the Defence of Human Rights), Dr. Kamel Daoud, reveals that the *harraga* phenomenon has attained alarming proportions since 2007. The Coast Guard has succeeded in impeding approximately one thousand young illegal migrants about to reach the Spanish and Italian coasts. Moreover, more than 400 migrants went missing, while the Navy recovered another 100 bodies. In addition, hundreds of illegal Algerian migrants remain in Tunisian and Libyan prisons after they were arrested in the home waters of these two countries.

As it regards the social categories concerned with this phenomenon, Dr. Kamel Daoud's investigation reveals that, expect for the elderly people, all social classes in Algeria are tempted by illegal immigration. The same investigation reveals that the majority of Eastern Algerian families deal with illegal immigration. In the eyes of the desperate young people, Algeria has become a big, open-air prison. In this framework, criminalizing this conduct and arresting immigration candidates does not mean anything to these young people since they feel trapped. This situation can have fatal repercussions on their mental and moral stabilities.

Official statistics show that, between 2005 and 2007, an aggregate number of 2,340 candidates to illegal immigration were intercepted offshore, out of which 1,301 were rescued while in danger of death. Some 400 prospective illegal immigrants travelling by boat have been intercepted since January 2008, according to a recent figure from the Coast Guard. However, 12,753 migrants have reached Sicily during the first nine months of 2007, besides the 1,396 who made it to Sardinia. Furthermore, 53,842 immigrants were arrested and deported to Libya in 2006, which imprisoned 60,000 migrants and refugees in May 2007. 200,000 migrants were expelled (NGO Fortress Europe—according to a confidential report from the European agency Frontex for EU borders security).

On the other side of the phenomenon, the French speaking newspaper *Liberté* carried out a survey from November 3–14, 2008 throughout five Provinces of the centre, five of the East and four of West Algeria. Fifteen interviewers asked fourteen questions of 1,364 males between the ages of 15 and 34. The questionnaire was drawn up in Arabic and French and structured in two parts: socio-demographic identification and the questions themselves. It revealed that 43.8 percent of those interviewed knew several close associates (family, friends, and neighbors) who had left their country through illegal networks.

Through this survey, we can infer that the phenomenon is entrenched in Algerian society. Nearly all, or 98 percent, of the polled people admitted to knowing about this phenomenon. This figure definitively demonstrates the reach of the plague within the milieu of the Algerian youth. Moreover, a large number of the interviewed consider the *harga* as an adventure. The survey found that 43 percent of the interviewed youngsters hold that opinion. Conversely, 26.3 percent think it is a suicidal act.

Those viewing the ordeal as an adventure are aware of the dangers of such a trip across the sea and of the major risk to losing their lives. In addition, 25.8 percent of those interviewed believe that the *harga* is the only solution to escape their misery. Hope for a decent and stable life is the strongest motivation for these youth to brave the dangers of leaving their country. In addition to the 43.8 percent who say they know of several people who have left their country via illegal networks, 39.3 percent admit to currently knowing at least one person who has illegally reached Europe that way.

However, 16.8 percent of the interviewed people deny knowing any similar case in their immediate acquaintances. On a different note, the survey carried out by *Liberté* reveals that 28.5 percent of the polled say they know several examples of harragas who succeeded in life abroad and who are more or less integrated into their host countries. 56.6 percent of them state they have at least one example of a person who illegally went abroad, succeeded in life and has even attained a good situation, compared to 14.9 percent who state they have never heard of such a person. Still, 43.1 percent of the people polled said that, among their acquaintances, there are several persons still wishing to illegally leave Algeria and live somewhere else.

It seems these people often talk about these wishes. In this survey, 37.9 percent of this population confessing hearing at least one person mention wanting to become a *harraga* and leave Algeria illegally, even risking his/her life against, while only 19 percent of the people polled alleged knowing no one in their immediate circles who would plan to reach Europe.

Nonetheless, a number of elements determine the success of such a venture: favourable weather conditions, the command of the trip route, the navigation means and materials it is equipped with, the taken food and rescue equipment are extremely important for the success of maritime trips. However, to many poor *harragas*, the ferrymen offer only inflatable dinghies or old, obsolete boats. By the time many young people see their accommodations, with the money already paid, it is too late.

Even if they continue, in most cases, the Coast Guard intercepts the *harragas* before even leaving the domestic territorial waters. Lately, the Navy has multiplied their patrols along the Algerian coast with the purpose of stopping this phenomenon. The 3,937 interceptions made in the last four years are proof of this. Those who escape these blockades do not necessarily succeed on account of other circumstances, like weather or boat conditions. Many *harragas* are declared missing at sea before their bodies wash up onto various beaches. In 2008, at least 1,502 people died trying to reach the European coasts of the Gibraltar

Strait, offshore the Canary Islands, in the Aegean Sea and even on land, in the African deserts. For those escaping this awful fate, the difficulties are not over yet. They have just begun. They must figure out how to live without personal documents, resources or work in countries which employ increasing means to fight against illegal migration (Daoud, 2008).

WHY DO PEOPLE FLEE ALGERIA?

In years past, Algeria was a transit country and today has become a country supplying illegal migrants. The question of why *'the harragas'* risk their lives to escape Algeria is a core question researchers and experts have tried for years to sufficiently answer.

At a conference on youth expelled from Europe and *'the harraga'* held in September 2007 by the Ministry of National Solidarity and the Family, which representatives of the ministries, the public and diplomats of thirteen African and European countries attended, Minister Djamel Ould Abbas declared this phenomenon is new and unique. So, it was established that illegal immigration does not only concern the young and unemployed seeking jobs their idealized countries, but also executives, students, traders, women, handicapped and children as young as 12. The category involved with the *'harraga'* phenomenon draws from the entire middle-class.

To the expert observers there are many factors behind this phenomenon: hard lives, poverty, feelings of exclusion, lack of development, shortage of welfare, the discovery of other horizons. These are some of the many triggers pushing Algerians to confront the sea and take excessive risks to reach Spain, Italy, Great Britain, France or even Switzerland. In the past, France was the most popular destination for the *harraga*; that, like the place of embarkation, has changed. Now, 65 percent of the persons who try to sail away illegally come from Western Algeria, 34 percent from Central Algeria, 1.5 percent from Eastern Algeria and 1 percent from Southern Algeria (Safta, 2008). Similarly, Algerian experts agree that this phenomenon is the result of the legitimacy crises, meaning that those who rule are not necessarily the ones chosen by the masses. The power in Algeria is based upon co-optation, clientelism, bribery and, of course, the exclusion and marginalisation which have become methods of governance in this country.

The phenomenon of '*the harraga*' shows that the relationship of trust between government and the young has crumbled. Many may think, "These official servants have marginalised and forgotten us." This sentence, directed at the Ministry for Solidarity by the candidates to illegal emigration whose attempts to reach the northern side of the Mediterranean shore have failed, demonstrates the Algerian youths' exasperation. The relationship of trust between government and the youngsters seems to be non-existent. Neither job-promising politics nor pompous speeches can deter young Algerians from risking their lives at sea, pursuing a dream. Prospective illegal emigrants increase daily and the Algerian coast witnesses a crowd of hopefuls for the 'great crossing' the likes of which it had never seen before.

At a social level, we notice an increasingly sharp antagonism within the population. It is forming between a wealthy minority and a penniless majority, growing due to the dwindling of the middle class. At an economic level, the country holds great yet underexploited potential despite the significant financial resources obtained by the exportation of hydrocarbons. At a political level, the country is governed by a very authoritarian regime that has a propensity to suffocate all opposing institutions, parties or political leaders. This is also explained by the lack of democracy in Algeria, as far as the principle of self-determination for the populations is concerned, since the Algerian population lacks that right. The political system in Algeria does not allow power rotation. The President has concentrated all powers in his hands.

At the level of legislative power, no laws enact the parliamentarians' proposals. Everything comes from above. For judicial power, the executive branch manages that too; judges are designated and dismissed at will. With 200 cases to be decided every day, justice is decided by statistics, not by quality decisions. A worldwide ranking showing that democracy is still non-existent in Algeria substantiates this argument.

The proof is in a report drawn up by The Economist Intelligence Unit on the democracy index worldwide where Algeria's rank is 133rd out of 167 countries. This report was drawn up with very specific criteria such as pluralism, free voting and citizens' right to bring legal actions against government executives or members of the intelligence service. The report split the countries into four lists: countries with full democracy, which number 30; countries whose democratic systems have some flaws (50); countries whose regimes qualify as 'hybrids' (36) and, finally, the authoritarian regimes (51). Thirty countries have perfect democracies, 50 run defective democracies, 36 are hybrid regimes and 51 are authoritarian regimes. The authors of this document placed Algeria in the category of 'authoritarian regimes.' This ranking of Algeria actually confirms recent reports drawn up by international organizations, pointing at carelessness in justice, restrictions of expression, bribery and not being able to incorporate associations.

Ali Bensâad believes that this upsetting reality has been hidden for a long time by authorities who have used rhetoric to reduce the migration issue to a one belonging to Sub-Saharans. He observes that while no attempts were made from the Algerian coasts as Algeria applied itself to holding back African migrants, of those crossing through Morocco, the majority were Algerian (Mkedchi, 2008).

The authorities in Algeria behave keep themselves in denial. They bury their heads in the sand, refuting the reality of the social order and refusing to calmly analyse the origins of illegal immigration. In order to understand it, we must examine this phenomenon in the context of state failure. 'The *harraga* phenomenon' is an indicator of severe crises of territorial integrity. There is no doubt that when the political field, like the media, offers no opportunities to the population, they look for an outlet to express themselves. If they have no legal means of expression, naturally, their alternatives are illegal.

According to the sociologist Addi Lahouari, there is a political void in Algeria and the state institutions do not represent the power they are vested with. The State Chief lacks the power he is vested with by constitution. The ministries have no power at all. This situation has spread to all levels of government administration. Some public servants try to profit from their functions. Bribery has become commonplace and the citizens has lost faith in their government executives. The country has become a jungle where the strongest take the greatest portions and it is impossible to govern a population with a securely. Addi concludes that if Algeria does not make drastic changes, in ten years the country will be like Somalia (*El-Khabar*, 27 August 2008).

ALGERIA SURRENDERS TO EUROPEAN PRESSURES: SUB-CONTRACTING AND CRIMINALIZATION OF IMMIGRATION

The phenomenon of the *harraga* shows the state is powerlessness to find a solution for young people tempted by illegal immigration. So, instead of using oil to boost the Algerian economy and create thousands of employment posts, the state preferred to use the security approach to attempt to put an end to this plague, showing where Algeria's priorities lie. This is not surprising since a state of emergency has been in effect since military force ended the electoral process in 1992.

Before the phenomenon of illegal emigration and proliferation of migrant-smuggling networks reached the proportions of today, the state decided to take a hard line. Thus, the Algerian government adopted a bill amending the criminal code, dated June 8, 1966, which considers human and organ trafficking 'illegal immigration' crimes. Simply leaving the national territory without authorisation may be construed as a crime by virtue of the bill. On the basis of these new amendments, courts can render hard detention sanctions against the *harraga* and especially against the illegal immigration networks.

Among the amendments to the criminal code we note that the penalty for illegal exit from Algerian may be up to six months of incarceration. Smuggling migrants may bring as many as ten years of incarceration, namely in cases involving minors or migrants subjected to inhuman or degrading treatment. This punishment is worsened if the crime is committed by a person or organisation dedicated to moving migrants or involving weapons. Incapable of finding any actual solutions to this phenomenon concerning thousands of young Algerians longing for a better future, the government intends to use repression--a practice in conflict with universal human rights principles.

These measures have been criticised by the United Nations Commission for Human Rights, which has shown genuine concern over the incarceration of illegal emigrants in Europe and Northern Africa (*El-Khabar,* 27 August 2008).

Moreover, the criminalisation of illegal immigration is far from a unanimous opinion in political and legal environments. Thus, the FLN (*Front de Libération National*), the biggest political party in Algeria, believes that incriminating the illegal immigration will not stop the haemorrhaging of people. According to this party, it is better to approach the issue from its roots, trying to understand the reasons pushing university students, the unemployed, women and even elderly people risk trying to reach the Southern European shore (*El Watan*, 8 April 2008).

Contrary to the FLN, the RND (*Rassemblement National Démocratique*), part of the presidential alliance, has applauded this measure, believing that this is going to efficiently contribute to the fight against illegal immigration. The FNA (*Front National Algérien*) has expressed its opposition to this law though the voice of its parliament deputy Mohamed Benhamou. In his opinion, criminalising the *harragas* will change nothing. He added that the government must attack the roots of the reasons pushing university graduates, the unemployed, women and even old people to run such risks to reach Europe instead of opting for the easy solution. According to the FNA deputy, the solution consists of establishing a real social peace, creating employment and regulating the housing problem. This new code, he concludes, means that Algeria surrenders to European pressure to slow down this issue (*Magharebia*, 4 September 2008).

The legal scholar Mohand Issad believes that the term 'harraga' is inappropriate, since he does not see any reason to condemn the young people who try to reach Europe illegally. He instead proposes taking responsibility of this phenomenon. This eminent legal scholar declared that the law criminalizing the *harragas* is called a villain law.

In the same theme, Saïd Musette, researcher with the CREAD of Algiers, believes that embarking on commercial ships with foreign destinations is a crime under Algerian law, but it is not punished like '*the harraga*' who leave in makeshift boats. In his opinion, the *harraga* phenomenon has always existed. Illegal migrants used to travel to prized destinations via Morocco and Tunisia. However, while these two nearby countries strengthened control at their borders, the Algerian *harraga* have turned back to the Algerian coasts. Some other scholars think that, by criminalising illegal immigration, the Algerian authorities confuse the maritime code and the criminal code, arbitrarily using them against these youth through the application of articles 23 and 24 of order no. 166/211 related to foreigners' stays in Algeria. The courts apply the maritime code, which has no links with this phenomenon. Similarly, experts note that all persons arrested in Algerian territorial waters with Algerian identification documents and on-board Algerian boats are put in jail. This constitutes a violation of personal freedom.

According to observers, Algeria has complied with the requests of Northern countries, which never cease demanding that Southern countries do more to control illegal migration. Europe, which has shut its doors to migrants, seeks increasingly determined actions from Maghreb countries against the ferrymen to fight illegal immigration. Europe seems to have won. After having convinced Tunisia and Morocco to implement reception centres for illegal immigrants in their respective territories, the North wins another battle, that of seeing Algeria sharpen its legal system against illegal immigration, making the Maghreb a shield against illegal immigration.

Within the scope of international commitments, Algeria has launched a project to create a Mediterranean observatory. It shall be implemented next January. The purpose of this structure is to implement some awareness mechanisms, communication programmes and a database on illegal immigration in the Mediterranean. This structure aims at drawing up a plan of action to take care of the youth in cases of illegal emigration. Several ministers of Parliament and representatives of the Northern shore, such as France and Italy, will prepare the first steps of the project (Habib, 2005).

On the other hand, this action has raised interrogations of the observers as to the role played by the states of the Maghreb, whose territories have become a transit spot for the African exodus towards Europe. This makes it seem natural that they should be the guardians of the European borders.

This is definitely what the EU would like to get in exchange for some commercial or economic concessions. Observers believe that the European states desire to integrate Maghrebi countries into their system of protection against illegal immigration is stronger than they show in negotiations with them and other African countries. They wish to stamp out this immigration by progressive drying up of the causes at its origin (Kateb, 2006).

While the issue of illegal immigration continues to antagonise the European Union, it is still unsuccessful to stop it. Before this situation, the European Commissioner for Cooperation and Development, M. Louis Michel suggested creating 'migration agencies' in African countries. The European commissionaire preaches 'assisted migration,' which regulates supply and demand through these agencies. They might, for instance, manage seasonal issues; the permanent food supply for the diasporas; and exchanges between universities, hospitals, companies, etc. Experts in this matter have been sceptical as to its effectiveness in eradicating the phenomenon of the illegal immigration. They assert that migration agencies, which are supposed to regulate the supply of African manpower and the demand of European countries, would only intensify the seriousness of the plague (Makedchi, 2009).

Another point to consider is that Europe has made no effort to help the poorer countries develop their economies and provide more attractive living conditions for the potential emigrants. This is, however, something the Southern countries need. In the beginning of June, Abdelkader Messahel, the state minister in charge of the Maghrebi and African Affairs announced, "Our priority is now that the development issue be at the core of the regulation and solution of the migration problems" upon William Lacy Swing's visit to Algeria, as director general of the International Organisation for Migration (IOM). European contributions for the development of the Southern countries are still lacking, while repression against illegal immigration continues (Fattani, 2008).

Under the pretext of fighting against terrorism, the EU has strengthened its external borders. Surveillance on the external EU borders is the task of the European agency Frontex (the European Agency for the Management of Operational Cooperation at the External Borders, established in 2004). In 2006, the EU established a 'European patrol against illegal immigration' with a budget of 3.2 million euros. The Europe 'pact,' decided in July 2008, provides regularisation for people present in Europe. Irregular administrative statuses shall be made on a 'case-by-case' basis. It further toughens the conditions for family reunion. This document was considered the 'shame directive.' Almost all European countries have enacted measures limiting immigration.

Committing themselves to a better regulation of illegal immigration, the European countries try to export their plans to the African continent. A three-year cooperative programme (2009–2011) was adopted in Paris at the Euro-African conference.

This conference, the 2nd of its kind (after one in Rabat in 2006), saw the participation of the 27 EU countries and only the same number of African countries. The issue of the false documents plagued this conference. It is in this sense that counter documentary fraud became part of this adopted plan of action. The proposal to "strengthen the border control," helping the "creation of joint border posts" was a contentious one. However, this 'unanimous' agreement on the plan does not hide the divergences existing between the representatives of the two continents.

The European pact on immigration and asylum, proposed by France upon its EU presidency and adopted by all member states, constitutes the bone of contention at this conference. A great number of African countries refuse this document. African representatives believe that the restrictive European migration policy may increase the irregular migration flows. The African ministries have requested softening the entry conditions in Europe or risk continuing the same problems (Talbi, 2009).

Besides strengthening the conditions to obtain visas and reinforcing expulsion procedures, the EU expends a vast amount of effort and resources trying to quell illegal immigration. For this reason, on January 15, 2009, four countries of the European Union (Italy, Greece, Cyprus and Malta) requested tangible and cooperative action against illegal immigration from their partners at a meeting held in Prague.

The Italian minister of internal affairs has suggested reinforcing Frontex (European agency for the management of operational cooperation at the EU external borders) by entering into bilateral agreements with the countries from which illegal migrants come. Without those agreements, it is very difficult for each member state to proceed with expulsions. In his opinion, it is the beginning of a process.

The composition of this four-member group is relevant since they represent the countries suffering the greatest pressure from illegal immigration in the Eastern Mediterranean. In fact, in 2008, over 67,000 people crossed the Mediterranean Sea seeking asylum in Europe. According to the United Nations High Commissioner for Refugees (UNHCR), more than half of them reached Italy and Malta. Italy alone has seen 36,900 immigrants unloaded on its coasts during the past year, a figure increased by 75 percent compared to 2007. In the same period, 2,770 migrants, out of whom 1,400 were Somalis, reached Malta. Greece and Cyprus function as transit spots for illegal migrants to reach the countries of Western Europe. Along the same line, in a law submitted for its approval, the European Parliament provides criminal sanctions to the employers of people with no documents in order to make companies and individuals more aware of the fight against immigration. The European Parliament has approved language at its January 19, 2009 plenary session. The Parliament report notes that between 4 and 8 million illegal immigrants work legitimate jobs in European construction, farming and hotel sectors (Le Cour Grandmaison, 2008).

In addition, on June 18, 2008, the Strasbourg Parliament voted in favour of the 'return' directive, bringing the maximum period of custody of irregular foreigners to eighteen months. This text provides the possibility of expelling persons from the EU states for five years. Despite the recommendation, issued by the UN Human Rights Council working group on arbitrary detention, to the states "to make use of the detention towards the asylum seekers and illegal immigrants only as last attempt," we notice that the prevailing European practice makes a rule of the exception. Custody camps (224) are multiplying on the Old Continent. Identical phenomena exist in countries both near and far, such as Libya, well known for its violations to fundamental human rights. This state has not even signed the Geneva Convention on refugees. It is not at all surprising that geopolitical, economic and financial interests prevail over any other consideration in the pursuit of illegal migrants now organized on the two coasts of the Mediterranean Sea (Blidi, 2009).

All the measures taken by the European Union haven't changed anything. Increasing numbers of people departure on the adventure. On March 29, 2009, 200 migrants have drowned offshore Libya (Bensaad, 2008).

In this humanitarian tragedy, the Maghrebi states must play a bad hand. They must demonstrate that they are ready to take the commitments arising from their candidacy for economic integration into the European block.

Along the same lines, Ali Bensâad, an Algerian expert in the matter, does not hesitate to ascribe the situation to the failure of various policies, namely the 'Barcelona Process.' In fact, he mentions that cooperation between the two shores has failed on the account of the Mediterranean policies on migration. In his opinion, the problem is much more complex than the picture disclosed by the *harraga* issue. The issue is a tool for geopolitical leverage. For five years, the migration issue has been confined to Sub-Saharans. Bensâad declares that the Maghrebi countries have become sub-contractors on behalf of Europe, which has explicitly exercised pressure from 2000–2004, abandoning all decencies. The Maghrebi countries have submitted to the aid conditions dictated by the European Union, including "those showing nationalist shade, such as Libya and Algeria which have easily put on the cloth of the auxiliary repressor". The outcome is that, for five years, Sub-Saharans have been abandoned in the middle of Sahara by Moroccan services, as wells as by the Algerians. During this time, all countries have enacted new repressive laws governing the access of foreigners into their territories to meet the European mandates (Bensaad, 2005).

This makes apparent that the illegal immigration phenomenon is related to European security. The European Union has conditioned its aid to the states of Maghreb to their willingness to sub-contract for the Old Continent, patrolling their southern borders and stopping the migratory flows from the South.

The Algerian approach to the issue reveals several truths unknown by the general public. Algeria's battle against illegal immigration stems from its desire for European aid. The European Union exploits this to make Algeria submit to its will, as it was at the time of the negotiations between the states of Maghreb and the EU in 2004. Then, the two parties agreed that the issue of illegal immigration will be incorporated in all current or future negotiations. The EU has demanded that the states of Maghreb be fully involved in the control of their borders and in the fight against immigration. Those states that comply get full political and financial support (Benyoub, 2009).

It should be noted that the European Union has replaced its policy to deny all aids to the states of Maghreb with one to fight illegal immigration. This fact not only shows that Europe has turned its back on its universal commitments, but also that it has made its borders more vulnerable than they used to be.

CRIMINALIZING IMMIGRATION: A PROCESS DESTINED TO FAIL

There is no doubt that the law criminalising illegal immigration has not produced the expected impact. Article 75, punishing persons attempting to leave the country illegally with detention and fines, has not discouraged prospective migrants. Experts on the matter believe that the security approach adopted by the Algerian government is destined to fail for the simple reason that the young candidates to illegal emigration run much higher risks than the sanctions provided by the law. In other words, the *harragas,* defying the sea and its dangers, will not fear serving the current six-month jail sentence. The judicial repression measures recently put into place by the authorities to end the *harraga* phenomenon seem to have no effect on the uncompromising will of the young people to reach the other side of the Mediterranean Sea. Most *harragas by leaving the court* declare they will try the adventure again until they succeed or perish. Since the government has no vision or imagination to find a final solution to the phenomenon, it is satisfied by mere superficial reports and analysis. Some political executives have even treated the *harragas* as anti-nationalists, amplifying the disdain of the desperate youth. This attitude is at the origin of the rift between governors and governed and their mutual mistrust (Malika, 2009).

For more than two years, the phenomenon has not ceased spreading. Despite the risk they run, every day, young Algerians try the dangerous adventure of crossing the Mediterranean Sea in makeshift boats. In 2008, the Coast Guard brigades of the western maritime side intercepted 418 boats attempts, i.e., more than one boat per day headed for Europe from the Oran coasts.

Besides the interceptions, the Coast Guard also disclosed they had recovered 48 bodies from the sea, to which a dozen missing persons must be added. At the beginning of 2009, 17 persons had already been rescued by Coast Guard brigades. Moreover, 6 persons have drowned and 4 others are missing at sea, besides the number of *harraga* corpses recovered offshore by the Marine Coast Guards, which has tripled in five years. Thus, 2008 has been the bloodiest year for the *harragas*. The Coast Guard have fished out 98 corpses, an increase of 37 percent compared to 2007, during which time the Coast Guards recorded 61 deceased. In the same period, the Navy have made 88 interventions in the fight against this plague. These operations have intercepted 1,327 young Algerians between 21 and 29 years old. The majority of these illegal emigrants, notes the same source, came from the Eastern coast of the country with 636 people, out of whom 442 came exclusively from the province of Annaba (*El Watan*, 16 May 2009).

It has also been established that the *harragas* generally make their trip during the summer because of favourable weather conditions that time of the year. A significant increase in the number of deceased and of the attempts to cross the sea is noticeable over the last four years. In the month of August 2009, 246 people were intercepted. In 2007, the navy forces intercepted 1,259 illegal migrants and 61 corpses were recovered. The 2006 amounts were 1,016 people intercepted and 73 dead by drowning. In 2005, the numbers only amounted to 335 and 29 bodies. All in all, from 2005 to 2008, there were 261 dead at sea and 3,937 people intercepted by the naval forces.

Each day records new numbers of illegal immigration and this year is already appearing busy for the Coast Guard. In the first ten days of January, they intercepted 17 *harragas* offshore Mostaganem (West of Algeria). However, these figures do not reflect the actual extent and scale of the phenomenon since they do not mention the number of missing persons at sea and the bodies recovered by foreigner coast guards, besides those who actually made it to shore.

CONCLUSION

To conclude, it is clear that only democracy and equal opportunities can put an end to this plague. That does not mean that a complete example of democracy needs to be introduced into Algeria. Democracy, to which the Algerians aspire, partially derives from a respect for the popular will, majority decisions, freedom and justice for all and development and prosperity.

In the present form, the path to democracy undeniably passes two steps. First, a transition, consisting of creating a separation of powers between the military and the presidency, allowing elections to be freely held, is needed. It must also provide a democratic parliament and government with an economic and social programme. This would make democracy in Algeria real, progressive, peaceful, smooth and without bloodshed. The regime must assign the main portion of the power to the Algerian population. It should be vested with, and granted, the right to choose and manage its fate in a democratic manner.

These two solutions are the only ones that guarantee shelter from threats to national security and the plague of the *harraga* phenomenon.

Some people believe '*the harraga*' is proof that the youth feels confused, while others think that it shows the young people must be heard and that it requires conferences and seminars be held in order to understand the concerns of the youth and, at last, control it through concrete measures. Lawyers, psychiatrists and sociologists may help find the solutions to restore confidence in the young and demonstrate that they have a future at home in Algeria. The only way to achieve this would be by establishing an economic and social policy for research of the deep causes behind the phenomenon.

Chapter 4

Intentions of Migration Among the Moroccan Youth
– Moha Ennaji –

Intention is a force in the universe,
and everything and everyone is
connected to this invisible force.

– Wayne W. Dyer

Introduction

Migration is a crucial social phenomenon that draws the attention of government and non-government organizations all over the world. Migration triggers change in both the receiving and the sending countries involving the movement of people across political, cultural and administrative borders. Similarly, migration is closely linked to the search for better job opportunities. Migration is perceived by most migrants as a means to realize a goal to improve their socio-economic statuses.

Morocco is an emerging country with an economy based on agriculture. Regular droughts, inflation, overpopulation and weak economic growth have increased unemployment and poverty over the last two decades. The high unemployment rate is also caused by the government's decreases in public administration job (Ennaji 2006). Staggering poverty is the root cause of most Moroccans intentions' to migrate.

Migration can only alleviate part of the pressure on Morocco's labour markets and it plays a small role in solving the country's employment puzzle. More importantly, migration cannot be the only solution to the country's unemployment problem. Migration has not only helped decrease the unemployment rate of the country, it has supplied needed workers for Europe. In this regard, migrants significantly contribute to development in both Morocco and the host countries, hence the importance of establishing joint policies and strategies of co-development.

This chapter explores the intentions of migration among Moroccan youth. Given the growing number of Moroccan migrants abroad, especially in Europe, and the economic impact of migration on Morocco, it is interesting to examine the real intentions of young Moroccans so far as migration is concerned.

MIGRATION INTENTIONS

The desire to migrate among young Moroccans is very strong, as the survey by Ennaji and Sadiqi (2008: Chapter 7) reveals. The survey concerned the migration intentions of young students and employees.

According to this research, almost one-fifth of actively employed Moroccans would like to emigrate to Europe. This readiness to migrate is especially high in rural and semi-urban zones where people live in precarious conditions because of the lack of resources and investments. The above survey reveals that in these regions, 63.82 percent of Moroccans wish to emigrate to better their living conditions and 16 percent of them thought of emigrating illegally despite the risks; however, only 29 percent of those wishing to migrate mentioned that they would like to migrate on a legal basis (Hamdouch and Khachani 2005).

To the question whether they were interested in migration to further their studies or to develop job prospects, 57 percent of students at Fès University answered that they would like to migrate mainly to pursue their postgraduate studies abroad. 32 percent mentioned that they wanted to work in Europe where wages are much higher than those in Morocco; the minimum wage in Morocco being approximately $200 a month, whereas in Europe it is at least triple that amount. Only 2 percent of the students stated that they wanted to migrate for family reunification or for marriage.

It is well known that many students do not return to Morocco after finishing their studies because of the high unemployment rate in their country of origin. The majority of respondents thought that migration might be a positive move, especially if the aim was to pursue one's studies or to improve one's living conditions through work. This may be due to the fact that the situations and infrastructures at their universities are deficient. Indeed, most students are not satisfied with the Moroccan educational system, which they believe is disconnected from the job market. They complain mainly about the traditional methods of teaching, mismanagement and lack of resources.

The vast majority of respondents revealed that they would prefer to migrate to Europe or North America. At the top of the list of European countries, France is first with 17.7 percent, followed by Germany (13.1 percent), Belgium (12.0 percent), Holland (11.5 percent), Spain (10.6 percent) and England (8.0 percent).

Given these statistics, it is clear that most students look to Europe as an interesting place to be. When asked why, they said because one could get a good job in the European Union where salaries are attractive. This attitude may be attributed to the fact that most informants long for an easy, comfortable and happy life. They also stated that, in Europe, there is respect for human dignity and workers' rights are guaranteed by law.

Concerning the question of whether Moroccan mass media encouraged migration or not, most respondents (55.5 percent) answered that they did, especially television talk shows with Moroccan emigrants who have succeeded in their migration projects. By contrast, 43.3 percent thought that media reports on migration did not have an impact on young people and their families.

Most respondents (55.5 percent) think that mass media, especially the national television channels, indirectly encourage migration because they often give the public an idealistic view of Europe. For example, *Noujoum Al Hjra* (*The Stars of Migration*) is a television program that shows how Moroccan migrants have succeeded in the host country; *Canal Atlas* is another television program that advises migrants who have amassed significant savings to invest in Morocco. Another television program called *Biladi* (*My Homeland*) shows the major reforms and changes that have taken place in Morocco in order to persuade migrants to invest in the country. Moroccan television rarely shows the difficult daily lives of migrants in the European 'paradise' or the living conditions of their families left behind.

In contrast with students' favourable attitudes to migration, the data Rob Van der Erf and Liesbeth Heering (2002) compiled reveals that the majority of Moroccans do not want to migrate. This is due to the fact that most young Moroccan students, particularly males, are interested in migrating only because they want to pursue their studies abroad in order to obtain good degrees from prestigious European universities.

The majority of those who do not wish to migrate state that they are either satisfied with their economic situations and, therefore, do not need to migrate or that they wish to migrate but do not have the financial means.

According to Van der Erf and Heering (2002:48), the highest percentage of people (23 percent) favouring migration can be found in Nador (15 percent), a city in northern Morocco that is well known for its high rate of migration, and in Khenifra (15 percent), one of the provinces of the Middle Atlas where the phenomenon of migration is recent.

With regard to gender, men are often more inclined to migrate than women. For men, the main reason for their intention to migrate is overwhelmingly economic. As heads of households, men have the responsibility of securing an income for their families. Thus, the vast majority of males (90 percent) and return migrants (80 percent) state that the decision to migrate is motivated by unemployment, low wages or poverty (see Van der Erf and Heering 2002: 49).

Similarly, women indicate that the major cause of migration is economic, followed by non-economic motives like family reunification and family creation. Thus, most men and women who intend to migrate state that they wish to do so mainly for economic reasons.

Nevertheless, intentions just partly reflect wishes and dreams and are not sufficient to solely predict future behaviour. In order to weigh the intentions, those who said they intended to migrate abroad were also asked when they intended to do so. If this was within two years, they were also asked whether they had actually taken any steps to realize their intentions. While intentions to migrate vary from 4 percent for women to 29 percent for men, the percentage of those with intentions to migrate within the next two years is actually much lower: 1 percent for women and 6 percent for men. These significant differences are due to a large percentage of people who say they do not know when they will migrate (see Van der Erf and Heering 2002: 53).

CAUSES OF MIGRATION

Concerning the reasons for migration, students were unanimous in stating economic and social factor as the main motivation for migration (65.3 percent), followed by educational (16 percent), political (10.6 percent) and historical reasons (5.8 percent).

The reasons for migration are so interwoven that it is difficult to determine the real causes; different individuals may have different motives. Nonetheless, social and economic motives are the most important reasons for migration since, more than any other social category, university graduates are hit by unemployment and poverty. Those who are lucky enough to find jobs are often underpaid. Educational issues may themselves be migrational motivators since the Moroccan educational system suffers from many deficiencies, especially from a shortage of technological equipment and resources and a divorce between academia and the job market. As for the political reasons that some respondents stated, it is interesting to note that these emanate from personal ideologies. As a case in point, some students think that the political system is so centralized and restrictive that it does not offer opportunities to the new generation of Moroccans. Likewise, many mentioned social injustice, unequal opportunities, and corruption as examples of problems that make students think of migration.

According to Hamdouch and Khachani (2005), there are various internal and external causes of migration in Morocco, the most important of which is the huge economic gap between Morocco and European countries. The income per capita in Morocco is much weaker than in Europe (see Ennaji and Sadiqi 2008: Chapter 7).

By comparison, Morocco has only 5.6 percent of Europe's average per capita income. This gap is widened by the discrepancy between different social categories of people and the different regions of the country. For example, it is a fact that the northern region is much poorer than its central region, which accounts for the very high rate of international migration in the former. Because of these difficult economic conditions, migratory flows are expected to increase in the future.

Another internal cause of migration is the instability of the economy, which is essentially based on agriculture. This instability is caused by the numerous droughts that the country has suffered and the sky-rocketing oil prices which have combined to reduce economic growth, as outlined above.

Despite measures taken by the government, since the 1970s, to reduce the demographic growth (for instance, through family planning), the population of Morocco has continued to steadily increase since independence. This factor has directly impacted employment since the job market is inundated each year by a greater labour force than either the public or private sectors can absorb. As a result, unemployment has increased, especially among university graduates.

Parallel with the population growth, the number of jobless people has also increased. Thus, from 1994 to 2004, the rate of unemployment has increased from 12.1 percent to 13.7 percent. This is partly due to the fact that the state has cut public administration jobs and drastically reduced recruiting for the public sector. Due to the liberalization of the economy, the state has decreased public investments and employment.

The state, which had, since 1976, created an average of 400,000 jobs annually, decided, in 1983 (following the World Bank scheme of structural adjustment), to reduce the creation of public administration jobs to about 14,000 annually. The structural adjustment programs have had very negative effects on the job market, although they helped redress the economic balance.

In addition, privatization and liberalization led to restructuring public and private enterprises which suffered as a result of severe competition with European firms. As a consequence, many businesses were obliged to reduce their work forces.

All these reasons are 'push' factors for migratory flows, inferring that unemployment has social ramifications for migration. The high rate of unemployment and the poverty that such factors engender push many young Moroccans to emigrate legally or illegally.

Poverty is another important reason for migration. According to the Moroccan Department of Statistics (1999), more than 5.3 million Moroccans (i.e., 19 percent of the overall population) live under the poverty line. This figure fell to 4 million in 2004 (14 percent of the population), according to government statistics (cf. the Moroccan Daily *Le Matin,* January 2006). This reveals that poverty in Morocco, especially in urban areas, has considerably regressed, according to the general report on fifty years of development and perspectives for 2005. However, it is clear that the number of people economically vulnerable is higher in reality. For instance, although the minimum salary is 2,000 MAD (approximately 190 Euros) per month, many businesses in the private sector pay their employees less. Trade unions have, on several occasions, criticized this precarious situation since it applies to the majority of workers. The bulk of potential migrants are from this vulnerable category of the population (Achoual 1983).

In addition to economic causes, there are other important factors that determine migration. For instance, psychological and sociological factors can incite people to migrate. The positive image of successful migrants returning to their home country during summer vacation is remarkable, especially for those young

Moroccans living under the constraints of unemployment and poverty. They begin to envisage migration as a solution. Many of these 'successful' migrants drive luxurious cars, own nice apartments, and sometimes have important investments in Morocco. They become models for potential migrants whom they generally help to realize their migration ambitions.

This positive image of the migrant is magnified by the power of television. With satellite dishes, millions of Moroccans in urban and rural areas can watch European channels that generally portray a liberal and wealthy Europe. This makes many of them think of migration as a solution to their misery and frustration. Migration is also fostered by the geographical proximity of Morocco to Europe. Tangiers is only forty minutes by boat from Algeciras, Spain, which makes many young illegal migrants think of crossing the Mediterranean Sea by means of *pateras* to reach Spanish shores.

Migration is equally encouraged by networks of traffickers on both sides of the Mediterranean. These traffickers charge high fees and often make false promises to potential illegal migrants. Spanish traffickers, who are very active in Ceuta and Melilla, have made fortunes out of this 'business,' which generates between five billion and seven billion dollars a year, according to a recent Moroccan 2M television program (see also Hamdouch and Khachani 2005).

Similarly, networks have an impact on the intentions of future migration at the household and individual levels. At the individual level, perceptions and attitudes (or social norms) form the basis of intentions for future moves, but household and individual circumstances cause changes of intentions; socioeconomic conditions determine whether intentions will be implemented.

These factors push many young Moroccans to migrate. Nonetheless, the causes of migration have evolved over the decades. In addition to economic reasons, migration can also be motivated by family reunification, studies abroad and other social reasons. Social causes involve the influence of family members or of other migrants and the desire to 'do like' friends or relatives who have migrated.

CONCLUSION

Migration intentions among the young in Morocco are strong in students and underpaid employees, but less than 30 percent of the respondents actually intend to migrate. Most are discouraged by the visa restrictions and by the high cost of migration.

The lack of future prospects, economic instability, unemployment and poverty are the major causes of migration. The socio-economic situation of Morocco is conducive for migration, which is considered a strategic answer to the woes of the youth. The Moroccan youth generally have a favourable attitude toward migration, which they consider a strategy to improve their living conditions and to contribute to their development.

The search for a job is ranked first among the economic motivations for migration in both rural and urban zones. The second cause is the desire to find a better paying job to ensure a decent income in order to satisfy the needs of the family and to face the high costs of living. The third cause is family reunification, which has become a common reason in rural zones. The fourth cause of migration concerns the desire to pursue higher education in Europe, a tendency relevant mainly in young urban migrants.

Under such circumstances, it is vital that Morocco and its European partners adopt an approach of co-development. They ought to collaborate and coordinate their efforts and migration policies in order to solidify the Euro-Mediterranean partnership with respect to migration.

Chapter 5

Emigration and Development in Morocco: The Challenge to Optimize Positive Outcomes

– Naima Baba –

Introduction

Morocco is constantly searching for formulas enabling it to expand its development. Considering the significant presence of its citizens abroad, at issue is whether or not this country will acquire the appropriate means to overcome the migration-development challenge. This country has increasingly become an emigration and immigration crossroad because of domestic emigration, transit space and also certain migrants choosing it as final destination. As such, Morocco requires domestic and international cohesion in directing the aid programs given to migrants, agreements with other countries, managing work, funds remittances, social affairs and migrant returns. Often perceived only under its negative aspect, Moroccans' migration towards European countries is stigmatised by such bias as brain drain, illegal migration, trafficking and smuggling in human beings, negatively exposing the migration phenomena under the sight of the field's activists.

However, in Morocco, positive outcomes conflict with the difficulty and hesitation to define a real emigration policy built upon an institutional frame which is harmonised and established by regulation capable of governing all the components of the migration phenomenon. This can only be achieved through an inner force of will, together with suitable elements and external forces.

Moreover, making the migratory outcome profitable requires simultaneous implementation of two operations. The first requires immediate action, but the second involves creating a long-term building site, despite the fact that this concerns the socio-economic fields or the scientific research contribution. Although this approach is limited to Moroccan migration, especially towards European countries, the migratory phenomenon cannot be analysed by isolated aspects; it is therefore necessary to observe the immigration debate in any analysis generally concerning migration.

ENDOGENOUS OPTIMIZATION FACTORS

Morocco emphasises implementing a real, strategic emigration policy. The entities directly involved are the various ministries, governmental bodies and agencies dealing with issues concerning international migrations. This also presumes the adoption of an appropriate legal structure. Since it regards scientific capital in matters of migration, it considers any progresses in this field.

IMPLEMENTATION OF AN EMIGRATION POLICY

Launch of an Emigration Policy in Morocco

Moroccan history shows that the emigration policy has been an 'intrinsically' domestic public policy. In the '80s, the emigration policy was in line with a domestic politics logic tightly linked to the political situation of that time (Lacroix, 2005).

And it further organized the state concerns through associations to optimise the economic contributions of its citizens.

The '80s initiated Morocco's desire to involve its migrants in developing their country. Presently, the state is still arranging, through certain programs, migrants activities and creating an elite Moroccan lobby abroad in cooperation with foreign Moroccan community organisations; this lobby seeks to be systematically involved in the protection of national causes before the European states.

Within this context, two governmental strategies are being established.

- The 2008-2012 five-year plan was submitted by the ministry in charge of the Moroccan community residing abroad, in coordination with the Ministry of Foreign Affairs and cooperation from the Foundation Hassan II and the MRE (Moroccans Residing Abroad). It is a preliminary plan for the promotion of Moroccan citizens residing abroad. On February 5, 2008, the Mixed Governmental Commission in charge of the MRE issues, presided over by the Prime Minister validated the proposal. This 2008-2012 five-year plan, the guidelines of which are structured around a number of practical proposals, aims to draw up a new strategic view as it concerns the public politics addressed to the MRE. On a social level, this plan launches action programs for the benefit of Moroccan competences abroad. It also supports the associations' actions to encourage cooperation between the state and other associations active in this field. From an economic and financial standpoint, this plan provides for the reduction of custom duties. In addition, it proposes measures for promoting MRE investment projects and emphasises upgrading the public financial mechanisms in charge of funding the investment and seeking new incentive tools.
- The Global Forum of Moroccan Competences Abroad (FINCOME) program is a national strategy imple-

mented by the Moroccan Government in partnership and cooperation with involved public and private establishments. This program constitutes an interme-diation tool, set up to facilitate the participation and involvement of Moroccans living abroad by revealing the various work-sites and development initiatives of their native country. This brings alternatives to the various abilities of Moroccan diaspora so as to accomplish mis-sions locally, and/or from a distance, based on voluntary action and ethical commitment.

Towards the Clear Redefinition of Moroccan Emigration Policy

The migration phenomenon is composed of two equally complex components, both placing migrants at the core of the relationships between his/her native country and the host country. Migration, within the scope of public politics, depends upon all other domains. This is why implementing a domestic emigration policy requires the control of politics from several branches, e.g., economy, social, health, labour, culture and security.

Drawing up a clear Moroccan emigration policy first goes through a global diagnostic of the migration element with respect to all these domains in order to detect the failures of politics already in force and try to engender the means of overcoming these failures. It further presumes the introduction of programs fulfilling, on one hand, Morocco's duties to maintain strong, rich relationships with its emigrants and, on the other hand, its obliga-tion to positively meet the multi-dimensional expectations which nourish this community with respect for its native country. This is because an effective emigration policy must seek to maintain balance between the measures which deal with the different migra-tion issues without hiding any aspect or harming another. A clear emigration policy has the merit of being defined by a governmental strategy. This enables it to carefully manage or even substantially avoid the complex issues which often characterises emigration.

INSTITUTIONS AND LEGAL SCOPE

Legal Scope

In Morocco, the legal framework comprising the migration issue remains embryonic and fragmented despite the effort deployed in the process of the reforms implemented in the last ten years.

There is still a lot to do in respect to the adoption and application of legal provisions capable of simplifying the administrative and procedural measures related to the Moroccan community. As it regards personal status, consolidating reform of the Family Code creates standardization through simplifying the marriage and divorce procedures applicable to the MRE. It is also necessary to introduce specific provisions to the contractual frame of mixed marriages and to keep orienting family law towards the preservation of childrens' rights. This includes family code provisions for the status of expatriate children and children born within mixed marriages, lining them up with the international conventions ratified by Morocco.

In order to optimise the actions of emigrants to develop their country, additional legislative reforms might be undertaken with respect to the commercial code and investment bill, adopting measures aimed at promoting investments in Morocco through the reduction of investment costs, relief of the tax burden related to acquiring materials and equipment and cadastral charges, as well as reducing return taxes. An additional requisite is implementing a preferred tax regulation favouring regional development and export companies.

For illegal emigration, it should conduct a critical analysis of legislation arranging and structuring the terms of control and the management of the mobilised populations.

There are three key mechanisms at the core of the migration national scheme.

- The MRE Ministry was established in 1990. The MRE ministry is vested with the role of consolidating the rights and benefits of the Moroccan community residing abroad.

It also strives to mobilise the community to defend national causes; in this same direction, it further aims to create favourable conditions so the community may participate in public life. Among its goals, the ministry tries to provide some elements to help the community integrate into the hosting societies without affecting their Moroccan identity. It is also vested with the role of mobilising the Moroccan community abroad to defend national causes. As an influential lobby, it also plays a conclusive role in the choice of both national and international strategy options. One of its crucial goals is cooperating with host countries to adopt reasonable immigration policies.

- The Overseas Moroccan Community Council (CCME) is born from the recommendations made by the Equity and Reconciliation Commission (IER) in 2005. Three royal speeches followed thereafter. In November 2005, the King explained the need for MRE representation in the Parliament. On November 6, 2006, he ordered the CCDH (Conseil Consultatif des Droits de l'Homme) to submit proposals for creating a representative council. The CSCME was established in November 2007, although since the beginning was very criticised (Daoud, 2008). Its major function is to represent the Moroccan government in all matters concerning the Moroccan community abroad. We should remember how it delivered a number of recommendations to the Moroccan State for bills regarding Moroccan citizens living abroad or in relation to their interests in the residence countries. The council can also bring its perspective on all bilateral negotiations and agreements between residence countries and Morocco and arrange cyclic reports on the social, economic and political environment where the MRE evolve. Therefore, it is also necessary for this body to promote the dialogue between cultures and religions and to take part in all debates regarding this matter.

- The Foundation Hassan II was established by royal decree in July 1990. It is entirely addressed to the MRE. Its fields of action are culture, social matters and economy. However, the foundation is not subject to government control and it has no representative powers. It is a non-profit organisation which aims to maintain and strengthen the fundamental ties that the MRE retains with their country, helping them to overcome the difficulties they encounter in emigrating. The Foundation Hassan II for Moroccans Residing Abroad has become an observer in the International Organisation for Migration. The MRE Foundation Hassan II's main missions are: ensuring the teaching of the Arabic language and Moroccan culture; organising culture camps for the benefit of the MRE children; provide humanitarian, social and legal assistance to those who are facing difficulties; and advise Moroccans living abroad who wish to invest in Morocco. It also observes and analyses the conditions of the Moroccan community settled abroad through the *Observatoire de la Communauté Marocaine à l'Etranger* (OCME), set up in 2003.

Additional bodies should be added to these three, namely, the Foundation Mohamed V with a return tool for the MRE and other mechanisms within the Ministry of the Interior.[1] Since migration constitutes their main concern, it is essential to raise the question of separating the functions and prerogatives of these different bodies. If the presence of different institutions in the Moroccan institutional system demonstrates the migration issue's priority in the government agenda, we ask, how well do they cooperate and coordinate both actions and rhetoric.

THE PROMOTION OF RESEARCH ON MIGRATIONS

Global Outline of the Research System in Morocco

Since its independence, Morocco has experienced a long reform process in the research promotion field. In these reforms, the government targeted the higher education institutions. The research institution has therefore gone through several steps to make scientific research one of the vital keys of national Moroccan politics. Since the '90s, in fact, Morocco has become conscious of the need for national policies on scientific research to make it a tool for economic and social development. This resulted in action on matters of research administration, management, structuring, orientation and planning.

Therefore, the implementation of numerous mechanisms confirms this tendency: the Academy of the Sciences Hassan II, [2] the governmental authority in charge of the scientific research with the Ministry of National Education, higher education, training of executives and scientific research, [3] the permanent, interdepartmental committee in charge of scientific research, [4] the National Centre for Scientific and Technical Research (CNRST)[5] and the National Commission for the Coordination of Higher Education. [6]

These, and a number of additional mechanisms, aim to upgrade the approach of scientific research in the country, and integrate Moroccan researchers abroad who conduct important scientific and technical research and who, so far, have been marginalised by the lack of coordination and integration authorities. As for scientific and technical national policy, its various mechanisms focus, through research, on the means to realise the priorities and national goals.

Scientific Research at the Migration Service

Some research centres and laboratories in Morocco attempt to understand and analyse population movements. They try to fix the lack of migratory information. Below are some of these organizations.

Centre d'Etudes sur les Mouvements Migratoires Maghrébins (C.E.M.M.M) was established in 1990 following the first international meeting on the Maghrebi migration movements. It is a multi-disciplinary centre of research on the Maghrebi migration phenomenon in Europe. Affiliated with the board of the *Université Mohammed Ier d'Oujda*, it groups together researchers of several complementary competences to study migration matters:

sociologists, economists, geographers, political scientists and legal experts. Among these goals, is inciting and encouraging multi-disciplinary scientific research of population movement and collecting vast, quality data relating to Maghrebi migration movements in order to create a migration databank.

The *Centre Jacques Berque pour le Développement des Sciences Humaines et Sociales au Maroc* was established in 1991. It coordinates, enlivens and leads the research programs for the doctorates of the centre as well as other Moroccan, Maghrebi and European partners (centres of research, universities, etc.). Among its programs, there is one called Migration Flows Africa-Maghreb-Europe. The multi-disciplinary study of cross-border mobilizations newly created in Tangier constitutes one of this program's components.

The *Centre MigCom* is the result of a close cooperation between COOPI and Afvic. [7] The centre's mission has expanded to become a reference for communication of the migration issue in Morocco. The Migcom centre is active in numerous media and migration topics. The aim is to communicate the dangers of illegal emigration to young people and orient public opinion to being more friendly towards migratory plans, but also to encourage the international public to adopt a more human approach to this issue.

The *Association Marocaine pour les études et les recherches en migration* (AMERM) was established in Rabat in February 1994 by a group of researching professors from different fields. Through the promotion of multi-disciplinary research on the migration phenomenon and developing research on the links between migration developments, this association establishes an autonomous space for scientific reflection on the migration issue.

The UNESCO chair 'Migration and Human Rights' was established in June 2001 at the *Université Hassan II Aïn Chock* of Casablanca. It comes from the network UNITWIN - UNESCO that aims to strengthen higher education in emerging countries and encourages cooperation between universities on an international level. This chair primarily promotes an integrated system of research, training, information and documentation in the migration domain emphasizing human rights.

The *Groupe de Recherches et d'Etudes sociologiques* (GRES), established in 1994, is an autonomous research laboratory at the Faculty of Humanities and Social Studies, in the *Université Mohamed V Agdal*. This facility carries out research and studies in all domains of social sciences, paying particular attention to certain topics, namely population migrations and movements.

Presently, we note that the fervent transition by migration research constitutes the beginning of a dynamism translated by the different intervening parties in public expertises. It currently needs to find real political will to substantially transform all these orientations. The resources allotted to this research remain weak and almost totally come from the state. This requires an active mobilisation of the politicians and civil society, maintaining a close relationship between migration, trade, financial, development and security policies. Clearly, the issue of human mobility can no longer be dealt with in an isolated manner.

While studying the same information, the various research entities show this isolation. This reflects a lack of coordination and synergy between the various groups and teams, characterised by a great parcelling, leading to the scattering of scientific production in this field.

Towards a Migration Science in Morocco

To understand the relevance of emigration in terms of positive contributions to Morocco, the scientific community must develop a real science of emigration (Boudou, 1998). This science should be capable of creating itself freely, distinguished from immigration science in the asymmetric correlation between emigration and immigration perceived in the relationships between the native and destination country.

The scientific research in Morocco, as a native country, should clarify the different hidden dimensions of the 'migration' issue, revealing the transforming relationships inside Morocco. It should highlight both the impacts and effects operating on the socio-economic structures and native populations and the political management of this data.

In order substantiate this reasoning, studies on immigration should become aware of all prevailing issues within migration research and, in matters of immigration science, question the way they are reproduced and the reasons for which they have been formulated. Since immigration studies are carried out exogenously, they primarily concern aspects regarding the host society, determined by security concerns, flow management, socio-economic integration, etc. Consequently, this creates a divergence and a gap in what should be considered major issues in emigration countries.

Nonetheless, this scientific step should not dissociate emigration science from immigration; it should instead allow a scientific prioritisation according to the hierarchy of the issues raised by each of the two societies, native and host, acknowledging a symbiotic correlation to these two sciences.

STUDIES ON THE EFFECTS OF EMIGRATION ON CERTAIN MOROCCAN REGIONS

It is necessary to pay attention to certain studies conducted in regions with a strong emigration potential. These studies have tried to analyse the emigration impact on the departure areas. Some of them have recorded these different impacts on the sociological conduct of the inhabitants and on household attitude changes. Others focus on geographic and spatial analysis of emigration's effects on the development of economic sectors and components. Some others have taken a greater scope, analysing the consequences of development on entire countries.

Despite the fact that these studies have not been considered globally, they especially concern the sector surveys in some areas. Since they are extremely localised, they allow a better understanding of regional migration phenomena and the heterogeneous migration behaviours. While it is true that many of these studies focus on rural areas, others have tackled the different changes due to emigration in urban areas.

Migration and Town Planning

In Morocco, like many migration habitats, international emigration has caused expansion for some towns as well as the creation of micro-urban centres. There are many explanations for this; one of them is that domestic migration caused an exodus of migrant families towards towns and urban centres (Lazaar, 1997). These families, mainly coming from villages and rural regional generally desire a better future that they hope to find outside their native places. This interference between domestic and international mobility proves difficult in demarcating the rural space with respect to the urban one.

Another element in urban growth is building sector development. This situation is actually the result of emigrant strategies oriented towards land property, particularly real estate. Even in the most remote rural areas, this emigrant tendency to invest in real estate properties illustrates the shocking progress of the built space (Berriane, 1993; Daide, 2003; Tamim, 1993).

The Role of Emigration in Social Vitalization

Emigrants' financial receipts demonstrate immigrations aid to many Moroccan regions. This is how we observe that the flow of emigrants' financial transfers, as well as their investments, particularly in the real estate and trade sectors, directly affect the expenses of their families and their consumption habits, which clearly evolve towards an urban model. [8]

Starting from this remark, in the native households, emigration has helped create a new social class, characterising the migrants, as well as their families, from the remaining population. This promotion in the social hierarchy has even enabled some families to acquire privileged social statuses, giving them access to benefits which, before any influence from migration, were reserved for the notables and bourgeoisie of the region.

The economic effects of emigration are not only observable on the families directly concerned since, through the effect of financial contributions, emigration also affects those who do not directly benefit (Benchrifa, 1997).

It is also extremely relevant to emphasise certain behaviours within the topic of social links caused by emigration when it becomes important in the apportionment of liabilities within the family cell. One side (emigrants) remits funds and, the other side (members of the family remaining in the country) is in charge of the management of these funds. This fact helps toughen the affective links of the emigrants with their families and their country.

MRE Action

The MRE's role is indisputable. Since they contribute to economic and regional Moroccan development, creating conditions favourable to strengthening that role is capital and it should represent more than a simple, casual measure.

The Role of the Funds Remittances

The question of fund remittances' impact, like the know-how transfer of migrant workers, is often behind the debate over the relationship between migration and development. Thus, it is important to examine it closely.

As far as Morocco is concerned, the financial transfers of Moroccans residing abroad have not failed to increase every year. In forty years, the volume of official remittances has multiplied drastically. The country is the fourth largest receiver of immigrant remittances in the world, representing the main source of currency in the kingdom together with proceeds from tourism and those generated from foreign investments (Godfrain & Cazenave, 2007). According to statistics from the Change Bureau, MRE financial remittances to Morocco have gradually increased during the last ten years, reaching 48 billion MAD at the end of 2006; this figure is now much higher because MRE receipts reached 55,053 billion dirham at the end of December 2007, an increase of 15.1 percent or over 7.22 billion dirham.

Compared to average receipts from 2002 to 2006 (i.e., 38.456 billion dirham) these receipts increased by 43.2 percent in 2007. Moreover, it should be noted that the financial flows generated by migration increase both the expatriate workforce and their distribution, depending on the host countries and/or regions, the socio-professional categories comprising them, their levels of activity, the nature of their employments, as well as their seniorities in the host countries.

These financial remittances from Moroccan workers abroad play a significant role in operating the macro-economic national economy. Their relevance seen on a regional, micro-economic level, recording a high emigration rate where they fulfil the basic needs required by households of these regions and supporting the economic weight of the social risks caused by poverty.

For a great number of Moroccan families, these remittances constitute a great contribution and source of survival, enabling them to escape poverty. Benefiting families employ the great majority of the funds for vital needs such as food, clothing and housing. These remittances are also used for current expenses relating to health care. They build or improve housing, purchase land or equipment (washing machines, television sets, etc.). Only a small percentage of these remittances are saved or invested in activities generating employment or revenue. This consumption, added to the investments related to education, represent 80–90 percent of the expenses covered by remittances. The outstanding 10–20 percent are a mix of official and unofficial savings and investments.

Some studies assessing the impact of MRE remittances on the lives of the population try to estimate the population escaping poverty thanks to these remittances.

TABLE 1. POPULATION SAVED FROM POVERTY THANKS TO CURRENT REMITTANCES[9]

DECILE	1 AGGREGATE POPULATION	2 POVERTY RATE OUTSIDE REMITTANCES	1*2 UNDER-PRIVILEGED POPULATION	3 POVERTY RATE REMITTANCES INCLUDED	1*3 UNDER-PRIVILEGED POPULATION	(1*2)-(1*3) SAVED POPULATION
10	2,797,712	100	2,797,712	100	2,797,712	0
20	2,796,033	66.2	1,850,974	64.7	1,809,033	41,940
30	2,795,664	27.7	774,399	25.1	701,712	72,687
40	2,807,828	2.9	81,427			81,427
50	2,786,963	2.2	61,313			61,313
60	2,796,998	2.8	78,316			78,316
70	2,792,469	0.4	11,170			11,170
80	2,799,162	1.1	30,791			30,791
90	2,795,030	0.6	16,770			16,770
100	2,797,141	0	0			0
Total	27,965,000	20.4	5,702,872	19	5,308,457	394,415

Source: National survey on the level of the household's life, 98/99.

Financial Remittances and Weakness of Production Investments

The impact of remittances on the economic development of the country depends on their uses and, namely, the quota destined to increase the production capabilities, i.e., the quota allotted to production investment.

An equally significant portion of emigrants' remittances can be allotted to profitable investments, namely for the creation of micro-projects generating direct employment. However, everyone agrees that the remittances allotted to profitable investments are weak, since family maintenance and community investments mobilise most of the emigrants' savings.[10]

In a survey conducted on Moroccans residing abroad in 2004 by Hassan II,[11] the conclusions confirmed this reality, since, according to this study, 40 percent of the projects submitted by the MRE do not exceed 500,000 MAD, while those which exceed 5 million dirham represent just 14 percent.

From this survey, we also see that the regions receiving the deposits are generally not those where investments are made. Globally, the MRE make their remittances in their native regions and where their families reside. The regions with a high emigration rate, such as Taza-al Hoceima-Taounate, Oriental, Souss-Massa-Draa and the region of Tadla-Azizal register the highest rate of deposits from national emigration. Between 38 and 66 percent of bank deposits here are composed of remittance. These regions are not necessarily those receiving most of the investments. The more dynamic regions of Morocco (which are less touched by emigration), such as the region of Grand Casablanca, Rabat-Salé and Marrakech, are financed.

The quota allocated to investments remains minimal with just 7.7 percent of the aggregate.[12] This investment is first applied to real estate properties and therefore not very profitable and without a great added value.

TABLE 2. SECTORIAL AND REGIONAL DEPLOYMENT OF THE INVESTORS IN PERCENT[13]

REGION/ PROVINCE	INDUSTRY	FARMING	TRADE	SERVICE	ALL SECTORS TOGETHER
Grand-Casablanca	8.0		7.7	8.6	6.3
Chaouia Ourdiga-Khouribga	12.0		19.2	25.7	16.0
Marrakech-Tensift -Al Haouz		24.6		2.9	7.1
Oriental	22.0	14.0	23.1	15.2	17.2
Rabat- Salé Zemmour Zaer-	6.0		11.5	8.6	6.3
Souss-Massa- Draa	8.0		30.8	22.9	15.1
Tadla-Azilal	10.0	61.4	7.7	14.9	23.1
Tanger- Tétouan	34.0			3.9	8.8
Total	**100.0**	**100.0**	**100.0**	**100.0**	**100.0**

Source: Survey MRE Investors Foundation Hassan II, 2004.

The MRE community increasingly chooses "services, neglecting the traditional sectors, such as farming and industry, considered less profitable." They further orient their projects towards trade (especially food) and often less profitable small shops. Consequently, a businessmen class, fully committed to the business development of their country, does not exist. Although trade holds a privileged place in the MRE investments, its increase was less than investments made in tourism, which recorded an increase of 138 percent between 1998 and 2005 and this falls within the context of the expansion of the service sector.

According to Hassan II, this growth is explained with the example of the financial costs of opening a small shop. During this last ten years, in fact, other service sectors, namely tourism, have drained a great part of the new investments.

We should note the appearance of a new category, however minor, of emigrants working in information technology (IT), as well as transports and stock exchanges.

Profitability of the Financial Remittances

According to a number of surveys carried out with MRE, the main obstacles their investments encounter in Morocco come from the Moroccan administration. In particular, the MRE point to slow administrative procedures. They also complain about corruption and pork-barrelling. The other constraints to investments involve finances and taxes. Access to financing is another obstacle cited.

This situation is due to little competition in the banking system, which is not designed to handle large activity. Banking facilities available to the population are weak, limiting opportunities to save funds and have access to credit in the remotest regions. These problems have generated much insolvency, causing a very weak repayment rate of granted credit.

Access to financial services and financial education are equally essential factors to unfreeze development of the funds remittances. Banks and financial institutions should be encouraged to simplify investment terms for Moroccan emigrants in order to remedy the difficulties, namely shortening the process and correcting bad estimations of the real costs of projects. In order to fight against the informal remittances and increase access to credit for the underprivileged, many strategies were explored to address emigrants' savings and revenue generating activities.

The banking network should also expand to cover the whole territory and implement those mechanisms that actually link remittances to the means to fund regional development, for instance, to micro-credit.

It is also necessary to complete these measures by reducing the cost of financial remittances. The goal is to encourage the banking sector and all remittances operators to reduce their costs.

Furthermore, public investment in the more underprivileged regions is required to encourage private investment in these regions. Public investments in Morocco are often too weak to provide favourable conditions for fragile investors like migrants. In order to allow the structuring of profitable investment projects, migrants need regulated markets, capital and heavy public investments.

RETURN OR 'INTRA-MIGRATION'?

Return as Probability to Achieve the Migration Circuit

The significance of the return issue stands on several levels, among which is native country development. Some projects and studies regarding Morocco focus on this issue in order to understand the prevailing characteristics prescribing this notion.[14] Despite the fact that these studies are not meant to be exhaustive, they nonetheless attempt to bring basic elements which might constitute the foundation of other studies, enabling them to expand upon the psycho-social factors and clarify the link between return and development.

For many expatriates, reinsertion into their native countries constitutes a vital step of the migration process. It is often part of the initial migrant project and is strictly connected to a successful relocation depending on an economically fruitful and constant reintegration. For the migrant, this means starting up a profitable project, enabling him to live fully safe and satisfied, avoiding the need to emigrate again.

Return can be solely undertaken by migrants without any assistance. In this context, the migrant relies on his/her own qualities and networks playing their roles since the migrant depends on a pattern of professional and family knowledge other than local and national institutions. Return may also be made through supporting programs developed by either international organisations or bilateral agreements between the host country and the native country. In both cases, the circumstances surrounding return projects often determine the elements of a successful reintegration of the migrant in his/her native country (Cassarino, 2007).

Alternative to the Final Return: 'Intra-Migration'

The mythos of the final return suggests that we question the pertinence of temporary migrations' contributions to development. In this frame, 'intra-migration' can be described as sequential and recurring movements alternating mobility within a space where the two societies, the native and host ones, merge in terms of crossroads. The means departure and arrival places of migration transcending borders enable migrants to preserve connections between their native societies and the host ones and allow them to be real catalysts of co-development. In this context, the projects started by migrants are entitled to be transnational, which is beneficial to the present and future economic situation.

Intra-migration is equally envisaged under another standpoint, one of circular migration within the frame of certain immigration. This final one lacks the power to set up the free movement of people, but attempts to allow legal movements and overcome illegal emigration. This falls within the scope of bilateral or multilateral agreements in the sector of manpower exportation. It meets the economic migration policies enforced by some European Union countries where worker selection procedures are diversified (e.g., systems of points) or quota policies or number caps like those applied by Spain, Italy, United Kingdom or Austria. Its aim is to eliminate the permanent aspect of the migration process, transforming the emigration candidates into temporary, working expatriates. These agreements control the migration flow, but also canalise and make the migrants' remittances profitable. However, this kind of migration's current structure leads us to believe that it does not meet the expectations of the native countries and are also discriminatory and do not serve the interests of the immigration countries.

Effort Synergy Inside and Outside Morocco

Cooperation and Co-development Programs

Morocco finds itself in a triple migration positioning, as an area of emigration, transit and immigration. However, it possesses an inability to solely manage the new circumstances that this imposes. Morocco's decision to open its borders to international trade liberalisation, counter to most old immigration countries' policies of closing to foreign workers, creating real cooperation and genuine co-development on either side of the Mediterranean, seems to be a good alternative to migration.

Since the development process lags behind the migration phenomenon in Morocco, more emphasis should have been given to developing the economy of the region, paralleling the migration transition, which began earlier than the economic development.

This situation leads us to question the link between co-development and migration flow management. Co-development should never represent a means to expel migrants back to their native countries and it should no longer be considered a means to contain migration flows. It is *impossible to ponder development outside migration flows.* The ways co-development impacts these flows is the same as for any development action: improving the life conditions in the emigration regions and reducing future departures by creating better conditions. This can only be envisaged in a more expanded time frame.

Morocco and its partners must attack poverty and establish resources of wealth and shared values, founded upon accrued economic integration, more intense political and cultural relationships, reinforced cross-border cooperation and a joint prevention of conflicts. The more tangible offers and preferential relationships are conditional upon the improvements made by Morocco in relation to economic and political reforms (e.g., sectorial policies, projects aids, programs aids, democratic conditions, regional integration, food safety, good governance) which may produce positive effects for all the various partners.[15]

However, cooperation can suffer from limitations and, therefore, may not reach the expected outcomes. Despite the efforts, some recent initiatives failed to achieve a real cooperative approach while consuming resources. The multiplicity of announced targets and the discrepancy between the discourse and the tangible problems which confront the countries of the southern shore looking to benefit from this cooperation must also be considered. The lack of intra-European coordination in some programs also complicates the actions of the beneficiary states.

Diaspora Implication and Associative Interconnections

Cooperation with NGOs consists of orienting emigrants' associations towards the development programs active in their native societies and associating them with local institutions (e.g., private and public corporate entities, territorial bodies, public entities and social interlocutors).

Because of their double membership, the MRE have succeeded, (through joint contribution) in structuring their actions to benefit Morocco. These actions first regard the local development and mobilisation of domestic savings, creating local services in the villages and districts, raising qualification levels and opening local groups. They are generally symbolic social investments (e.g., schools, wells for drinkable water, free health centres, etc.) and rarely economic (micro-projects). These forms of collective solidarity often express membership and attachment to the same identity group. They generally derive from a real dynamic of local social and transformational changes. The migrants' donations through various associations partially succeed in correcting the deficit in matters of public social investments, which, as mentioned above, are often inadequate in Morocco. These NGO actions are not limited to economic and social works, but also include cultural activities.

In general, the development networks, which build links with Moroccan migrants, are built on the basis of grades. At the upper level, the network of the OSIM (*Organisation de solidarité internationale de migrants*), and at the lower level, an aggregation of migrant groups, bearing micro-projects for the benefit of the native village, municipality or region.[16]

Despite the appearance of a new dynamic demonstrating the will of society to build a bridge of co-development between the host country and the native society, there are few actual examples of this practice in Morocco.

These cooperative programs should fall within the frame of an actual North-South partnership, which may change the methodology, allowing civil society operators from both sides of the Mediterranean to improve their tangible results in relation to development activities. This supposes different parties establishing a real partnership led by the same concerns: exchange dynamics, the need for diagnostics, feasibility studies, quality follow-up and assessment procedures, and capitalising on experiences. These solitary organisations of international migration (i.e., OSIM) should also improve their relationships between themselves and the other actors of cooperation and development.

Even if the obstacles are numerous (e.g., bad resource management, misappropriation of targets and means, etc.), they can be overcome every time the target possesses both the implementation of consistent political cooperation and development and mobilisation of internal dynamics.

Only an internal will can convert the current negative image of emigration into that of a source of positive benefits. The damaged and negative outcomes will not all disappear, but we should try to minimise them to foster the positive outcomes available to a society aware of the stakes and capable of collecting the ingre-dients for a successful migration strategy. A number of reforms must be pursued to achieve an amplifying effect of emigration's positive benefits. Also, Morocco should make its citizens abroad full partners, overcoming the pork barrel currently characterising relationships with them. Maybe, then, emigrants will be able to realise socio-economic integration with the country regardless of whether this happens on national or international levels.

Notes

1. Initially, it established the director of the Migration and Sur-veillance of the Borders as the Observatory of Migration. The missions granted to this Direction are two-level structured: the analysis of the network of the migrants' traffic at the national and international level and the operational support for the surveil-lance of the borders. As it regards the role of the observatory, it is the federation of all involved parties in the multi-disciplinary reflection on the migration issue and namely civil society and researchers. It also operates as a databank of the statistics at a national level. These two mechanisms mainly cover the security aspect of the migration issue.

2. Royal decree (dahir) implementing the Law no. 1-93 364 dated 6 October 1993, as amended and completed by another Royal decree no. 1-00-205 dated 19 May 2000 implementing the Law no. 11-00.

3. This body's powers are fixed by Decree no. 2-02-448 dated 17 July 2002.

4. Decree no. 2-00-1019 dated 11 July 2001 implementing the establishment of a permanent interdepartmental committee for scientific research and technological development.

5. It is governed by the provisions under Law no. 80-00, and replaces the National Centre for the Coordination and Planning of Scientific and Technological Research created by royal decree implementing law no. 1-76-503 dated 2 August 1976.

6. Provided by article 81 of law no. 01/00 under Royal decree 1600-1999 dated 19-05-2000, it is placed under the control of the gov-ernmental authority in charge of the higher education.

7. COOPI is an international association located in Italy, operating in the development field and AFVIC is a Moroccan association active in the defence of the immigrants' rights and the sensitisation against the dangers of illegal immigration.

8. The improvement of the lifestyle of the population in the rural regions, for instance, is particularly notable as it concerns the food trade with the proliferation of butcheries, groceries, cake shops and others. This is also noticed in respect of the clothing with the arrival of *prêt à porter* shops. Some other commercial activities are linked to the birth of new markets (souks) invigorated by the sale of materials brought from the European countries by emigrants during their holidays. It is primarily electronic equipment, kitchen tools, spare parts, etc.. If said contribution to the improvement of the life quality can be easily noticed in respect of the progress of the service sector, it is relevant to observe that this is not automatic in respect of farming, even if certain indicators show that the emigrants have become the vectors of the use and diffusion of innovation in this field.

9. The chart shows the detail by decile of population saved by poverty thanks to the contribution of these MRE current remittances.

10. According to the experts of the *Centre Marocain de Conjoncture* (CMC), the MRE remittances, having reached 47,833 billion DH in 2007, in respect of the economic plan remain underexploited. During the last year, the MRE have remitted 47,833 billion of dirham to the country. I.e., an increase of 15.1 percent compared to 2006. If the amount of the remittances is in clear progression, the impact, on its turn is not in line with the yearly pace of receipts increase. Letter from the *Centre Marocain de Conjoncture*, 'spécial investissement,' no. 187, January 2008.

11. This survey is supported by a methodological approach that consisted in seizing some official departments and banking entities. This approach obtained a list with the prefectures and provinces of the realm for about a thousand (1,003) Moroccan citizens having made investments. Fouad Sefrioui, *"Marocains de l'extérieur et développement,"* Foundation Hassan II, January 2005, p. 71.

12. In a study carried out within the scope of an M.R.T. program on the new strategies of investment and of spatial redeployment of emigrants in 3 native countries of the Mediterranean basin,

including Morocco, only 23.7 percent of all the emigrants interviewed living abroad and native of the northern area in Morocco have made various, small investments. These investments, albeit experiencing a certain diversification, are limited to food and clothing commerce and storefronts and craftsmen and industrial equipment. Lazaar, M'hamed, "La migration internationale et la stratégie d'investissement des émigrés," in Revue de la géographie du Maroc, Vol. 15, no. 1-2, 1993, p.175.

13. In this chart it is an assessment exclusively concerning the main project. This assessment is taken from the survey carried out in Morocco by the Foundation Hassan II. Fouad Sefrioui, above-cited, p. 100.

14. It is chiefly the MIREM project (collective actions of support to the reintegration of migrants coming back in their native countries are the three Maghrebi countries, i.e. Morocco, Algeria and Tunisia). This project, commissioned by EU and the European University Institute, was launched in 2005 and it is still ongoing. It aims at explaining the stakes typical to the return migration under a development perspective. Similarly, one can cite the interactive study made by the *Association Maroc Entrepreneurs* which, on 29 May 2006 was launched at 1,823 Moroccans abroad and 335 Moroccans who came back to their country, their aim is to understand the expectations of Moroccans in terms of professional opportunities and the social integration.

15. There are a number of regional programs: 'the dialogue 5+5' between Egypt, Libya, Algeria, Morocco, Tunisia, Malta, and Cyprus; and the MEDA program founding an economic and cultural partnership between EU and the PSEM. Moreover, there are also cooperation programs falling into a bilateral frame, such as the new *Programme indicatif de coopération* (PIC) for the 2006-2009 term, adopted following the 17th Mixed Commission for the cooperation between Belgium and Morocco (Brussels, 19 December 2005) and a partnership for cultural and development cooperation and a joint declaration relating to the French-Moroccan cooperation in economical and financial matters, both signed in July 2003. There are also inter-agency programs. Morocco benefits from a global project amounting to 3.8 M€ carried out by a French development agency, out of which 1.5 M€ is financed by the European Commission. This program supports the personal or collective technical and financial investments of the Moroccan Residing

Abroad (MRE), according to the spirit of co-development. It is also necessary to cite the project "Migration and Return, Resources for Development," which aims to promote the migration phenomenon by the International Organization for Migrations (IOM) with Italian aid amounting to 11 million dirham.

16. Among these different NGOs: Emcemo et Ecodel: the Euro-Mediterranean Centre of migration and development is an NGO, located in the Netherlands. Migrations et Développement: the actions of this Franco-Moroccan NGO, established in 1986 by the Moroccan immigrants settled in Marseille, focusing on the development of their native areas in the southern part of Morocco. Immigration développement, démocratie: is an association network born from the Moroccan immigration in France and in Europe. On the basis of the unofficial networks, these associations and these actors of the international solidarity are organized for coordinating their actions and revitalising the joint development with the southern part of Mediterranean region. Migrations et Développement Local: this federation groups together more than a hundred little associations for the local development of the Atlas region. Atime-Remcode: besides its work for the rights of the Moroccan workers, the major association of Moroccan immigrants in Spain holds a foundation dedicated to the international cooperation, Remcode. Le réseau Red Euromediterránea de Cooperación para el Desarrollo aims at encouraging the actions of local development in Morocco, starting from the experience acquired by the Moroccan immigrants in Spain. Unió de Pagesos-Pagesos Solidaris: the Catalan agricultural union Unió de Pagesos (Farmers Union) canalizes the professional migration of Moroccans wishing to work in the farming sector in Spain through initial hiring contracts. Codenaf: *Cooperación para el Desarrollo en el Norte de Africa* is the outcome of the initiative of Moroccan immigrants settled in Andalusia. Its outline meets the terms provided by OSIM. Joan Lacomba, "Migraciones y desarrollo en Marruecos," Ed. La Catarata, Madrid, 2004.

Chapter 6

MIGRANTS AND THEIR RIGHTS IN MOROCCO
– Khadija Elmadmad –

INTRODUCTION

Morocco's strategic position has always made it a migration country with its two elements of emigration and immigration. The country has also been a transit country. Moroccans have emigrated abroad since ancient times, just like the great Tangier voyageur and explorer of countries and continents, Ibn Batouta. Moroccans currently represent a real diaspora in many countries of the world.

Morocco has also been an immigration country, an asylum for numerous persons and populations from Europe, the Middle East and Sub-Saharan Africa. Throughout history and until today, emigration from Morocco and immigration to Morocco occurred for many reasons: finding jobs, escaping from persecutions and injustices or just living among populations of different cultures and other lifestyles. There have always been both voluntary and involuntary migrations.

As time passed, many populations which immigrated into Morocco integrated into the native Berber population and Morocco progressively became a real melting pot. Its population is now a mix of races, languages, traditions and habits. Many Moroccan family names show their foreign origins (Elmadmad, 1992). Islam and its principles of *hijra* and immigrant hosting have played a significant role in the integration of the different populations immigrated to Morocco (Elmadmad, 2002).

As of today, migration continues to be very important in Morocco. The country is still an emigration and immigration country. It is increasingly becoming a transit country. Irregular or illegal migration is more and more significant in the country: Today, Morocco faces irregular immigration of Sub-Saharan populations and a portion thereof also tries leaving to illegally settle abroad.

On the other side, Morocco has a long tradition with managing migration flows and migration law. This law has evolved along with migration flows. The country has ratified several international instruments related to migration and migrants. In 2003, the country adopted national legislation concerning migration. Governing the rights and duties of the legal, or regular, migrants in Morocco, this legislation addresses sanctions on illegal migration pertaining to the entrance and stay of foreign populations in the Moroccan Kingdom.

This paper shall regard the current situation of migration flows and migration policies in Morocco as well as the actors affecting matters of migration in their country.

THE CURRENT SITUATION OF MIGRATION FLOWS IN MOROCCO

Morocco has always been an immigration, transit and emigration country. Migration has quite a significant impact on the country.

Morocco: Immigration and Transit Country

Historically, Morocco was a country of immigration and asylum. For instance, the first King of Morocco, Moulay Idriss the 1st, descendant of Mohammed the Prophet, was a refugee from the Abbasid persecutions. He found asylum in Morocco around 785 A.D. Since the 14th century, Morocco has received several Jewish and Muslim communities, usually fleeing Europe or Andalusia. Later, during the 19th and the 20th centuries, it became a settlement for European occupants (mainly French and Spanish). It has been a country of asylum for Algerians escaping from French occupation, for Spanish people fighting against the Franco regime and for many European citizens escaping persecution in the socialist countries of Eastern Europe.

At various times, Sub-Saharan populations moved to Morocco. The country was crossed by migrants from Africa and Europe, or by those going to Europe, Asia and even America. Some among them settled down in the country while others simply passed through.

Today, the majority of immigrants are Sub-Saharan populations, illegally immigrating and, therefore, difficult to count. Most Sub-Saharan migrants merely consider Morocco a transit country, despite the fact that some of them stay in the country for many years.[1]

Sub-Saharan migration in Morocco is mainly characterised by a young population, coming from almost all African countries. It is primarily composed of men, but increasingly women, pregnant or accompanied by children, too.

The media of the country often report on illegal Sub-Saharan migration and arrests or tragic deaths in the Gibraltar strait and Atlantic Ocean. Most of the Sub-Saharan peoples crossing Moroccan borders come from Algeria with the goal of migrating to Europe through Morocco. They move and live in inhuman conditions, waiting for their trip to Europe and are often exploited by human smugglers and by Moroccan and Spanish ferrymen.

Several studies and surveys were made on illegal migration to Morocco. For instance, a seminar on illegal migration in Morocco was organized on April 29 & 30, 1999 by the Law School of Rabat, where Moroccan and foreign experts illustrated the data related to this migration (AMERM, 1999). While many of these studies regard the numbers, origins and conditions of moving, very few of these studies deal with legal conditions in Morocco.

Some interviews of the Sub-Saharan community settled in Morocco have demonstrated that most Sub-Saharan migrants do not work. However, some among them are active in informal sectors and most of them have temporary jobs while waiting to migrate to Europe.

Morocco as an Emigration Country

Emigration abroad has always existed in Morocco's history, but, during the 19th century, it intensified and shifted towards Europe. Commerce opening in Morocco during the second half of the 19th century generated an elite emigration to France and other European countries, mainly England and Gibraltar. The first Moroccan businessmen were all emigrants (Chigueur & Faleh, 1995). Before the migration to Europe, Moroccans flocked to the Middle East and West Africa.

Moroccan emigration to Europe is deeply marked by a colonial past. It has mainly developed since the 19th century and, more particularly, from the establishment of the Moroccan French Protectorate in 1912.

Following the country's independence in 1956, Moroccans emigration to France and, later, to other European countries grew at a regular pace until the '70s. The end of legal migration since 1970 has changed the characteristics of this migration and has altered the migrants' profiles. This migration always begins legally but only through familiar groups, so, more and more, it becomes an illegal migration.

The Moroccan community residing abroad (CME or MRE) has experienced a great evolution and its profile has changed a lot. In less than 15 years, it has witnessed a real demographic explosion. In 1993, 1,300,000 Moroccans were logged in consulate registers abroad. In December 2007, they were 3,300,000, not including children under 16 and illegal expatriates. *It is an emigration in full change.* In less than four decades, Moroccan emigration has deeply changed, namely on the account of:

- more globalization (Moroccan emigrants live on all continents, even if Europe prevails),
- increasing feminization (almost one out of two Moroccan expatriates is a woman),
- remaining in the residence country (with the appearance of second and third generations, born and socialised elsewhere than Morocco),
- emigration from all Moroccan regions,
- diversification of Moroccan expatriates' socio-professional profiles.

The new migration policies in Europe with a visa provision for Moroccans going to Europe have caused the development and increase of illegal Moroccan migration to Europe. Illegal migration has caused the appearance of new migrant profiles. Previously, the migrant was often a single, young, illiterate man or, at least, with very little professional training. Today, more single women, minors, educated and even highly qualified people migrate more than before. Illegal Moroccan emigration, made through the Gibraltar strait, frequently leads to human tragedies, often reported by the Moroccan media and documented by the associations working with migrants, like the *Association des Amis et des Familles des Victimes de l'Immigration Clandestine au Maroc* (Association of Friends and Families of the victims of the Illegal Immigration in Morocco) or the *Association des Travailleurs Marocains en Espagne* (ATIME) (Association of the Moroccan Workers in Spain).

Another kind of migration is expanding in Morocco: skilled migration. Even if migration by the Moroccan elite is not a new phenomenon, it has tended to develop with globalisation and it now extends to the whole society.

For instance, many specialized agencies and offices that organize the migration of Moroccan elite in Canada have been recently established in Rabat and Casablanca. Moreover, the annual lottery for migration directly organized by the American Ministry for Foreign Affairs, widely distributed in Moroccan papers, is more and more attractive to the young executives of the country. In 2008, Morocco was ranked as 8th in the world for the number of permanent emigration applications to the USA through the American immigration lottery relating.

Moreover, 2006–2007 saw the appearance of a new form of legal migration: circular migration. It involves mature, married women with children. They are chosen for seasonal work in Europe, namely Spain, and come back to Morocco upon termination of their circular migration contracts. For some researchers, this new form of migration, while simultaneously diminishing Moroccan illegal migration, violates certain fundamental rights of migrants, such as the right to live in his/her family or occasionally the social security right.

The final return of Moroccan migrants is increasingly rare as they settle in the host countries despite the great governmental efforts to encourage the Moroccan competences abroad to come back and MRE to invest in the country.

Migration Impact

Migration of Moroccans residing abroad (MRE) has a great economic impact on Morocco. Official statistics show that MRE remittances represent almost 10% of the country's GDP, a circumstance that might justify the governmental policy aimed at encouraging these remittances.

Migration of Moroccans abroad also has a social and political impact on Morocco. For instance, the King initiative, taken in October 2003, to grant more rights to women and revise the Moroccan Family Code (or Moudawana) to make it more egalitarian and more easily applicable abroad, was undoubtedly indirectly affected by the attitude of rejection adopted by certain expatriate women towards the ancient Family Code, considered unfair and too complex. The current Moroccan Family Code even includes some articles which are specific to the Moroccan community residing abroad.

Moreover, the Moroccan code for nationality policy to grant Moroccan nationality to children born to Moroccan mothers and foreign fathers was adopted because of complaints from women of the Moroccan diaspora. King Mohammed VI announced this decision in a speech given on July 30, 2005 at the Throne Feast. The proposal for the new code was presented on March 8, 2007 in the second chamber of the Moroccan Parliament on the same day as International Women's Day. Law no. 62-06 of March 23, 2007 enacted the code. It has met the expectations of all Moroccans, specifically the Moroccan men and women residing abroad.

The MRE spending their holidays in Morocco is a great event. Every year, more than two million MRE spend their holidays in the country data from the Change Bureau show relevant proceeds every year.

The impact Moroccan migration has in the host country is an economic, social and political one. In some cases, the Moroccan migrations, mainly in Europe, have contributed to the economic development of their host country. The MRE sometimes have a social impact in the foreign countries where they reside. For instance, couscous has become a French dish and some Europeans have started to arrange their houses with Moroccan lounges. From a political standpoint, the double nationality held by some Moroccans residing abroad gives them the chance to occupy high positions in their residence countries. For instance, the current French Minister of Justice is of Moroccan origin. Other ministers and parliament members of Western countries also come from Moroccan emigration, namely in Belgium, The Netherlands and Canada.

Relevant data suggests, since it is provided in the law, the double citizenship of Moroccan men and women will only increase. Subject to two distinct legal systems (the native country system and the one of the host country, with all implied consequences in terms of rights and duties), Moroccan men and women residing abroad become less foreign residents in their host countries and more full citizens. Even if they have not opted for the nationality of their residing countries, some democratic progresses enable Moroccan expatriates to take part in multiple forms of city life (e.g., right to vote and eligibility in local elections, election of trade union delegates, labour first degree judges, association rights, etc.), amplifying and making the exercise of residence citizenship more tangible.

Nonetheless, after 9/11, a certain Islam-phobia has developed throughout the world, especially in Western countries as well as the rise of distrust towards Muslims. The MRE were concerned, to a certain extent, by these international developments.

Foreigners living in Morocco have also affected the social and political life of the country. Every day life is marked by the phenomenon of illegal migration to Europe and especially by the flow of the Sub-Saharan in Morocco. Illegal migrants are present in several cities of the kingdom and come from many African countries (e.g., Congo, Ivory Coast, Mali, Senegal, Sudan, Somalia, etc.) and sometimes from Asian or Middle East countries (e.g., China, Bangladesh, Iraq, Palestine etc.). Certain districts in some Moroccan cities have become areas where many Sub-Saharan migrants reside, such as the district Taqaddoum in Rabat or neighborhoods of the university city in Oujda, a border city with Algeria.

On the other hand, the toughening of Moroccan policies regarding illegal migrants and the November 11, 2003 enactment of new legislation on migration (with its very repressive nature) is explained by the growth of illegal migration in the country and its occasional connections with terrorism and also by European pressure on the country to control its borders.

Laws Governing Migration

Legislation governing migration relates to immigration and emigration. It organizes the entries into and exits from the country, as well as foreigners' stays, sanctioning all non-authorized migration. Until November 2003, this system was governed by many scattered texts and the dated laws of the French Protectorate. Law no. 02-03 dated November 11, 2003 unified and 'decolonise' Moroccan migration law.

Moroccan law no. 02-03, relating to entrance and stay of foreigners in Morocco, illegal emigration and immigration, came into force at the date of its publication (November 20, 2003) in the official bulletin of the kingdom. This law is composed of 58 articles, 8 chapters and 3 titles ("Entrance and Stay of Foreigners in Morocco," "Criminal Provisions Relating to Illegal Emigration and Immigration" and "Temporary Provisions"). The law repealed all former provisions related to migration and, namely, the five main texts previously governing migration in Morocco. The *'dahir'* from November 15, 1934 governed immigration in the French area of the Sharif Empire. The *'dahir'* made September 17, 1947 related to measures and controls established in the interest of public security. Finally, the *'dahir'* of November 8, 1949 concerned the regulation of Moroccan workers' emigration.[2]

Law no. 02-03 establishes conditions by which foreigners may legally enter Morocco. Access into the country depends on the discretionary power of the Moroccan State. In article 4, the law clearly specifies that the competent authority can deny access to people who do not meet conditions imposed by the said law. Article 4 states, "the decision denying the access can be enforced ex-officio by the competent authorities in charge of border control." Law no. 02-03 conditions this discretionary power on the international obligations of the country, specifying in its first article that the law is "subject to the effect of the international conventions duly published."

To enter Morocco, Moroccan law on migration requires presenting a passport or travelling title (article 3). It details the control terms at the borders and specifies the conditions of entrance denial.

To enter the country, a foreigner must hold a valid travelling title, justify moving to the country and prove that he/she has adequate means to live (article 4, first par.). Entrance can be denied to any foreigner who may constitute "a threat to the public order" (article 4, second par.). The decision denying access to the country can be executed ex-officio and the foreigner who has been denied can be kept in rooms outside the penitentiary administration.

As it regards foreigners' stays, law no. 02-03 specifies that there are two titles of stay in Morocco: registration and residence certificates (article 5). The first title is given to foreigners residing in Morocco for more than three months. The second title is for people continuously residing in Morocco for 4 years. Articles 9 to 18 of law no. 02-03 fix the conditions to obtain these papers, giving information on the types of registration and residence papers and on the persons who are entitled to hold them.

As it regards migrants' circulation inside their country, chapter VII of law no. 02-03 relates to foreigners circulation in the kingdom, specifying that legal migrants can stay and circulate in the whole territory (article 4, par. 1). However, they cannot undertake profit-making activities without being duly authorized (article 40).

But law no. 02-03 has developed repressive aspects and provides various significant sanctions for all non-authorized migrations. Articles 42–56 of law no. 02-03 focus on infringements to the Moroccan regulation related to migration and, more specifically, illegal access and stays of individuals and legal entities. Article 42, for instance, provides for a fine of between 2,000 and 20,000 dirham (MAD) and/or imprisonment from one to six months for all persons entering, or attempting to enter, without valid travelling documents or staying in the territory beyond the term authorized by his/her visa. The penalty is doubled in cases of recidivism. Article 43 sanctions any stay without registration or residence paper with imprisonment from one to six months and a fine between 5,000 and 30,000 MAD. This penalty is also doubled in cases of recidivism. Foreigners not renewing their registrations or residence papers are punished with a fine between 3,000 and 10,000 MAD and imprisonment between one month and one year (article 43). Those aiding the entrance of illegal migrants are also punished (article 47). The first paragraph of article 52 provides for imprisonment between six months and three years and a fine 50,000–500,000 MAD for anyone who cooperates or helps a person enter the country illegally. This penalty may reach 10 to 15 years of imprisonment and a fine between 500,000 and 100,000 MAD.

The kingdom's jurisdictions are responsible for deciding all violations concerning illegal immigration or emigration even if the violation, or some elements constituting it, were committed abroad (article 56).

If the result of the transportation (the illegal entrance into, or exit from, the Moroccan territory) is a permanent incapacity, the penalty is imprisonment from 15–20 years. The penalty is a life sentence if it results in the death of human beings (article 52, paragraph 5 & 6).

Article 25 of law no. 02-03 states that expulsion can be decided by the administration if the presence of a foreigner in the Moroccan territory constitutes a serious threat to the public order. It is rendered against the foreigner by measure of the general director of national security and served upon him/her by police or gendarme officers, granting him/her a grace period to leave the territory. It can be executed ex-officio by the administration (article 28).

Article 26 of the law lists the foreign persons who cannot be subject to expulsion, such as foreigners residing in Morocco since the age of 6, foreigners residing in Morocco for more than 15 years, foreigners married for at least one year with a Moroccan spouse, pregnant foreign women or minors. In case of denial or an impossibility to expel, the foreigner is confined to the residence.

Article 34 of law no. 02-03 provides for rooms outside the penitentiary administration for keeping foreigners until their departure. A foreigner is informed of his/her rights after his/her transfer into these rooms.

Laws Protecting Migrants

A law protecting migrants in Morocco is included in the international tools (universal and regional) related to human rights and the rights of refugees and labour law ratified by Morocco as well as in the bilateral agreements and conventions (for establishment, manpower and social security) entered into by the country. Moroccan legislation related to the protection of migrants is mostly influenced by the international undertakings of Morocco and it regards the condition of foreigners in general and the protection of involuntary migrants or refugees, as well as of the expatriate workers.

We can count several tools for human rights adopted by Morocco which may be applied to protect migrants: an international treaty on economic, social and cultural rights dated December 16, 1966, an international treaty on civil and political rights signed on December 16, 1966, an international convention on the elimination of all forms of racial discrimination from

December 21, 1965, a convention on the elimination of all forms of discrimination against women held on December 18, 1979, a convention against torture and other cruel, inhuman or degrading treatment or punishments on December 10, 1984, a convention on the rights of the child held on November 20, 1989, an optional protocol for the convention on the rights of child on children's involvement in armed conflict dated May 25, 2000, an optional protocol to the convention on the rights of children concerning the sale of children, child prostitution and child pornography, from May 25, 2000.

For refugee protection, on November 7, 1956, Morocco confirmed the agreement executed by France in its name to accept and apply the Geneva Convention to refugees, originally signed on July 28, 1951 at the UN headquarters. Morocco has also ratified the January 31, 1967 protocol of this convention on October 4, 1967.

Decree no. 2-57-1256 dated August 29, 1957, fixed the application conditions of the convention related to the status of refugees dated July 28, 1951 (amended by decrees on October 8, 1970 and December 28, 1984). It is currently the main legislation of matters of asylum in Morocco.

Since its independence in 1956, Morocco has been a member of the International Labour Organisation (ILO); it has ratified several tools of this organisation. These tools represent an 'International Labour Code.' The ILO website lists the conventions ratified by Morocco. Several pertain to expatriates: Convention no. 4 of 1919 on women working at night, revised; Convention no. 29 of 1930 on forced labour and Convention no. 105 of 1957, abolishing forced labour; Convention n° 100 of 1951 on equal remuneration; Convention n° 138 of 1973 on minimum age; Convention no. 158 of 1982 on termination of employment; Convention no. 181 of 1997 on private employment agencies; and Convention no. 182 of 1999 on the worst forms of child labour.

Moreover, Morocco was the second country in the world to ratify the International Convention on the Protection of the Rights of All Migrants and Family Members, enacted by the United Nations on December 18, 1990. This convention went into force on July 1, 2003. For the time being, it represents a chart of all migrants' rights. Morocco is represented at the Committee for the Protection of the Rights of All Expatriate Workers set up by this convention.

On September 11, 2003, '*Dahir*', no. 1.03.194 enacted law no. 65.99 of the Moroccan Labour Code. Until that time, Moroccan labour legislation was scattered throughout several legal texts, mostly dating from the protectorate period. The Moroccan Labour Code was amended to take the provisions of the conventions adopted by the ILO and the tools employed by the Arabic Labour Organisation ratified by Morocco into account. The main provisions concerning expatriate workers are contained in Chapter V of this code entitled "Employment of Foreign Employees."

Morocco has also undertaken reforms of its family code in February 2004 and its nationality code in April 2007 to better regulate these domains and guarantee more rights to its community settled abroad, particularly to women and children born within mixed marriages.

POLITICAL ACTORS IN MATTERS OF MIGRATION

Moroccan migration policy is characterised by a multitude of actions and actors. It is composed of three types: MRE policy, policies to promote the rights of all migrants and policies fighting illegal migration.

The MRE Policy

The policies governing Moroccans residing abroad (MRE) consists of incitements to keep permanent links with the country and return every year for summer holidays and to contribute to its economic development through money remittances and investments. Governmental actors mainly lead this policy, as well as by high directives of King Mohammed VI.

Many are active in the MRE sector: the minister in charge of the Moroccan community residing abroad, the Foundation Hassan II, the Consulting Council for Human Rights and the Foundation Mohammed V for Solidarity and the new Council of the Moroccan Community Abroad (CCME), established on December 21, 2007.

This multitude of actors working for the same goals often creates great waste and redundancy. In most cases, MRE are not represented in the decision-making bodies involving them. This fact raises the question of the MRE right to vote. Many MRE NGOs profess this right.

The recent establishment of the Council of the Moroccan Community Abroad (CCME) does not seem to regulate this problem of political representation for the MRE or, more precisely, of their representation at all. This new decision-making body has highlighted the waste and diffused efforts. It has created a serious fracture within Moroccan diaspora by making unjustified and ungrounded selections of members and co-workers. This way of conducting itself has brought much criticism and negativity against this institution inside and outside of the country. For instance, inside Morocco, some experts have criticised the CCME's operation and, abroad, several members of the Moroccan diaspora have even organized demonstrations outside Moroccan embassies to protest the exclusions and unfairness of the council which is supposedly the voice of all MRE (Snassen, 2008).

The Promotion of Migrant Rights and the Fight Against Illegal Migration

Presently, non-governmental actors mainly lead the policy aimed at promoting the rights of all migrants. The national and international academic institutions and NGOs acting in this field mostly protect migrants' rights. Among the academic institutions active in this field of migrant rights promotion, we note the UNESCO Chair "Migration and Human Rights" and, among the NGOs defending migrants, we should mention *Inter Alia*, an association of 'migrations and rights' located in Rabat.

The other institutions engaged in the promotion of migrant rights in Morocco are the national associations for the defence of human rights; the *Croissant Rouge Marocain;* the MRE associations; some institutions affiliated with political parties; trade unions; some foreign NGOs, such as *CIMADE* or *Human Rights Watch;* some international organisations, like the International Organisation for Migrations (IOM); the CARITAS; and bodies of the United Nations, such as the UNHCR (United Nations High Commissioner for Refugees) or UNESCO.

The policies for fighting illegal migration are quite recent. They consist of adopting measures and actions against illegal migration, as well as establishing specialized institutions, such as the director of migration and border surveillance within the Ministry of Interior. Spain and other European Union countries foster this policy.

CONCLUSION

For better management of migration in Morocco, as well as other places, it is essential to ensure migrants' protection. However, hesitations and uncertainties characterise the actions and practices on this issue.

Moroccan law related to the entrance and stay of foreigners, irregular emigration and immigration has certainly unified the Moroccan legislation in matters of migration regulation by updating it; however, it remains limited in respect to the protection of migrants in Morocco. It does not provide judicial guarantees for illegal migrants, such as rights during arrests, appealing the expulsions or access to defence while in the penitentiary areas (Elmadmad, 2004). The expulsion of illegal migrants, quite hasty in general, often limits their rights to fair trials: lawyers and interpreters, translation of evidence, etc. This way of operating is contrary to provisions in the international instruments related to migrant rights that Morocco has ratified.

Law no. 02-03 does less to protect migrants than the Convention on the Protection of the Rights of All Expatriate Workers and Members of Their Families dated December 18, 1990, which Morocco was one of the first countries to ratify. Compared with the 1990 Convention, the Moroccan law on migration does not contain any specific provision for some fundamental rights of migrants, such as the right to family reunion or the social and cultural rights of immigrants in Morocco. Moroccan law is also silent on the political rights of migrants, namely, the voting rights of Moroccans residing abroad.

Notes

1. Surveys carried out in different moments and, namely, in 2004, by some researchers of the UNESCO Chair "Migration and Human Rights" and of the Doctorate specialized in "Migration and Law" of the Law School of Casablanca, as well as the meetings of the author with the Sub-Saharan in 2007 and 2008 have shown that the majority of the Sub-Saharan migrants living in Morocco do not intend to remain in Morocco, but want to go to Europe. Some refugees even hold UNHCR papers.

2. In Morocco, the term *dahir* refers to the decree enacted by the highest authority of the State, namely the King.

Chapter 7

— ◆◆ —

ILLEGAL MIGRATION IN LIBYA: PROBLEMS AND SOLUTIONS
— Bashir el Kot —

INTRODUCTION

The migration phenomenon dates to long ago in human history. People used to move from one place to another for many reasons: to look for food, for a safe place or for any other reasons. The freedom to migrate gradually decreased in the second half of the twentieth century. Most of the developed countries in the world began to impose restrictions to protect their societies from migrants, although they may accept highly-educated migrants in some fields. Thus, the problem of illegal migration came to the surface, and becomes the first problem in some countries.

This paper deals with several aspects of illegal migration in Libya:

- the situation of illegal migration in Libya;
- the effects of illegal migration on the Libyan society;
- Libyan efforts in combating illegal migration;

- cooperation between Libya and the EU to end the phenomenon of illegal migration;
- the possibilities of success and failure in solving the
  problem of illegal migration.

THE STATUS OF ILLEGAL MIGRATION
IN LIBYA

Libya is a North African country. Its area is very large (total area: 1.77 million sq km), with a small population of less than 6 million (about 3.3 people/sq km). Compared with the neighboring countries, its population is tiny. However, Libya is a wealthy country, exporting more than one million barrels of oil per day, while larger, nearby countries suffer from lacks of resources and economic problems.

Libya is indeed small. Its population is only 5 percent as large as its east-neighboring countries (Egypt and Sudan), 12.5 percent of adjacent countries to the West (Tunisia and Algeria), and 25 percent of the Southern countries (Chad and Niger) (Al Kut, 2008).

Libyan authorities estimate that the number of legal foreign workers is around 600,000, while illegal immigrants are estimated to number between 750,000 and 1.2 million. The authorities recognize that flows in and out of Libya are poorly controlled and not well known. It is estimated that between 75,000 and 100,000 foreigners enter Libya each year.

Libya is undeniably a destination country. Migration towards Libya is the result of a combination of factors: geographic (location of Libya, permeable borders), economic (Libya is economically attractive), political (negative effects of an open-door policy regarding sub-Saharan Africa), and administrative (lack of a global strategy on migration and border management). Libya has now emerged as a major transit country for illegal immigrants heading for Europe. According to available data, the recent trend shows a sharp rise in illegal immigration through the Sicily Channel and strengthening of the Libyan transit route.

The desert was the main route for 99.1 percent of the illegal migrants in Libya, 91 percent of them came from Southern borders, while only nine percent came from Northern areas. Only 3.3 percent of migrants came to Libya via air flights, and while 96.7 percent of them were captured by Libyan police, they continue to try. Winter is the favourite time for migrants to come to Libya as they can avoid the heat (60 percent); 19 percent of them come during autumn, 8 percent during spring, and only 3 percent during summer (Sawani, 2008). This information caused Libyan authorities to increase border control during wintertime.

The study also indicates that 44 percent of illegal migrants entered Libya with the help of gangs. Those gangs receive a certain amount from each migrant to enter Libya or to go to Europe, so it becomes a profitable trade in Libya. They provide transportation by trucks through the desert or by boats across the Mediterranean.

No one should expect any reduction in the number of migrants from Sub-Saharan Africa to Libya because push factors for migration continue to exist. The effects of poverty, civil wars and natural disasters, which all drive people from their homes, have only increased in these countries. Most migrants are fleeing poverty in countries like Niger, Chad and Mali or civil war as in Darfur. Some, like many Egyptians, simply come looking for work. Despite the specific reasons, the vast majority of Sub-Saharan migrants are escaping socio-economic conditions.

All these facts make Libya attractive for people from neighboring countries, either to find a job or to go through it to Europe because its coasts face the Maltese and Italian coasts. Migrants now come from many African countries (37 nationalities) other than adjacent ones. In fact, Egypt is now the main source of migrants, and North African countries supply a large source of illegal migration too.

The number of migrants changes from year to year according to Libya's current situation. They were about 569,000 in 1983, before new restrictions were placed on remittances abroad. In 1984, the official number was down to 263,100. More than 40 percent were Egyptians and 15 percent were Tunisians. The remainder came from a variety of other countries in Africa, the Middle East and elsewhere. In 1992, the foreign population was estimated at 2 million, half of them Egyptian, and 600,000 from other African countries as well as South Korea, the Philippines, Thailand and Vietnam. This higher figure probably reflects illegal immigration. In 2000 there were 570,000 migrants living in Libya, including 11,500 refugees. In that year, the net migration rate was - 0.4 per 1,000 persons. According to official statistics the number of foreigners in 2006 was 349,040 consisting of 250,073 males and 98,967 females. While Human Rights Watch estimated the number at one million. It is fairly certain that the official number underestimates the real number of foreigners.

According to a recent survey (Sawani, 2008), most migrants are young, less than 35 years old (84.8 percent). Most of them are single, with only 10.6 percent married. About 85.8 percent of migrants are males. This is due to the difficult ordeal of crossing the desert.

West African Countries are a large source for illegal migrants to Libya (58.7 percent). Roughly 36.4 percent come from Niger, 21.3 percent from Nigeria, 7.6 percent from Guinea Conakry and 3.8 percent from Senegal. The rest come from other West African countries like Mali, Gambia, Liberia, Ivory Coast, Burkina Faso, Sierra Leone, Guinea Bissau, Togo and Benin. The migrants from central Africa come in second place (22.6 percent)--specifically, Chad (15.6 percent), Cameroon (6.4 percent), Central Africa Republic (0.4 percent) and the Congo (0.2 percent). East African Countries come in third place with 18.1 percent, with Ethiopia at 9.4 percent, Eritrea with 8.1 percent and Zambia producing 0.6 percent of the total migrants to Libya.

THE EFFECTS OF ILLEGAL MIGRATION ON LIBYA'S RELATIONSHIP WITH NEIGHBORING COUNTRIES

Libya's relations with neighboring countries have been affected by the issue of illegal migration. There is no clear Libyan policy in the field of migration. Migration is sometimes influenced by the status of relations between Libya and its neighbors. When Libyan authorities want to put pressure on other countries, they often expel their citizens working in Libya. However, when relations with neighboring countries are good, Libya does not hesitate opening its borders to foreign workers. So, we can say the issue of migration is always affected by the quality of the relationships between Libya and its neighboring countries.

To a certain degree, ideological factors determine migration policy in Libya. In the 1980s, when Libya was preaching Arab unity, it welcomed Arab nationals to come to Libya. Laws were issued permitting any Arab citizen to hold what is known as "Arab Nationality," which gave him the same rights as Libyans.

We can predict that any man-made or natural crisis, including war, in any neighboring country could export thousands, possibly millions, of hungry or scared people to Libya.

Law number 6/1987 once gave any Arab citizen the right to enter Libya. This law later vanished from the books. Other laws organizing migration have since been issued. New laws do not tolerate illegal migrants or citizens helping them to break the immigration laws.

THE EFFECTS OF ILLEGAL MIGRATION ON LIBYAN SOCIETY

There is a lack of data on this topic. However, I, the author, can speak from personal experience as an eyewitness to these effects. For a time, I lived in a small city on the Libyan coast, 60 km west of Tripoli. While there, I saw how migrants create a serious security problem. As one sleeps, he expects someone to break into his house. The migrants live outside normal civil order. They made their own communities and laws. Some of them will murder Libyan citizens for their property. Many of those participating in this behaviour are Africans from the sub-Sahara. These actions resulted in bloody riots between the young generation and migrants in the capital, Tripoli, Zawia and other Libyan cities.

The other side of the problem, which I saw twice myself, is disturbingly demonstrated by bodies mingled with boat wreckage on the coast. These were people trying to cross the Mediterranean. This is a humanitarian situation. Migrants sacrifice their lives for a false dream.

Some organizations are asking Libya to commit to protecting the human rights of migrants as if Libya alone is responsible for these tragedies. Libya, itself, is a victim of this phenomenon. One can't speak of the human rights of migrants and keep a blind eye to innocent Libyans' suffering. Should Libyans be expected to pay this expensive price?

Economic and Political Effects

Libya, like most countries in the world has a significant percentage of unemployment. Migrants occupy most of the unskilled jobs. Libyans could not compete with them because of their willingness to work for cheap wages. Libyans also sometimes refuse to work in some jobs considered unsuitable for citizens or socially degrading.

The search for Libyan statistical studies that directly deal with this subject has proven fruitless. Some studies refer to ambiguous effects of migration, especially on the labor force, without giving details or accurate figures about these effects on all economic sectors. In 1975, the rate of foreign workers was 32 percent of the entire Libyan labor force. Later, in 1983, the rate reached 47 percent, a shocking number.

During the first decade of the age of the revolution (1969–1979) there were active plans for development. Things changed in the second decade. Oil prices went down and Libya expended a lot of its wealth on weapons and war, especially in Chad.

On the other hand, Libya opened its borders to Arabs and Africans to unite the Arab world and, later, African countries. This policy was one of the main reasons for increasing numbers of migrants in Libya. Migrants perceived Libyan slogans as an invitation to go to Libya.

In terms of GNP per capita, Libya ranks far ahead of all other African countries, thus acting as a pole of attraction for foreign labor, particularly for those workers from unstable and underdeveloped sub-Saharan countries. The Libyan economy is currently dominated by oil and gas and the public sector. Its main challenge is to promote growth of the non-oil sector, taking advantage of a vast unrealized potential for economic diversification, which is needed to reduce the unemployment rate currently estimated at around 25 percent.

Politically, most of migrants come from unstable countries like Chad, Niger and Sudan. They bring their conflicts along with them. In the past, Libya has become involved with some of these countries' conflicts (Chad, 1980s). Many mutual tribes along the borders of Libya may cause problems. Terrorist groups like Al-Qaeda could enter Libya disguised as illegal migrants.

Social Affects

Most of the migrants, especially sub-Saharan, have their own lifestyles. Some 69.6 percent of them say there is not any kind of connection between them and the Libyans. Libyans have a prejudice against some migrants from Nigeria and Ghana because migrants from these countries have committed crimes like killing, cheating and stealing. They may also carry diseases which may spread to others.

Some migrants may permanently stay in Libya. In the south of Libya, where many mutual tribes like the Tabo and Twareg exist, they may easily change their residence from Chad and Niger to Libya. That action could affect the structure of the sparse Libyan population in the south of the country.

LIBYAN EFFORTS TO COMBAT ILLEGAL MIGRATION

There is some collision between Libyan foreign policy which usually calls for open African borders and combating illegal migration. Some Africans understood this policy as an invitation to live in Libya. If Libya opens its borders for Africans, nobody can imagine the number of migrants who will come to Libya. However, we can note some Libyan efforts in combating illegal migration.

Laws Organizing Migration

We note that the Libyan authorities issued many laws organizing migration and work in Libya. These laws do not allow foreigners to work in Libya without an official work permit. On the other hand, Libya is a part of conventions with some African and Arab countries which give them the right to live and work in Libya (Sawani 2008). This is a contradiction in the Libyan foreign policy and it should be remedied.

Law number 456/1988 is one of these laws. According to this law, any Arabic citizen has the right to enter Libya and to have all the rights of Libyan citizens, including national service. This law is one of the procedures Libya took when it was advocating Arab unity. Later, the Libyan authority issued law number 403/2000 which allows the public sector or individuals to use African workers.

Later, in 2001, Libyan authorities issued law number 89 which required a visa for anyone to enter Libya. The law also made a budget for repatriation for those who enter Libya illegally or who are infected with diseases. This law reflects some changes in Libyan policy against migrants. In 2004, the cabinet issued law number 2 to amend law number 6/1987. The new amendment stipulates that Libyans who try to help migrants enter Libya illegally will be sentenced to ten years in prison and fined 1000 L.D.

Many laws have been recently issued to combat illegal migration to Libya. For example, law number 241/2004 forbade administrative jobs for non Libyans. Another, law number 125/2006, imposed strict control on outlets and borders and also allocated a budget for repatriating illegal migrants.

Border Control

Border control is significantly affected by the length of the borders (4,400 km of permeable borders with six countries, and 1,770 km of coastline), the geographical situation of border areas (desert in most cases) and the absence of demarcation in many locations. Libyan authorities seem to understand the serious problems it faces regarding the management of Libya's external borders, the need to dramatically increase the number of staff involved, to improve their training, to provide them with proper equipment, to develop international cooperation as well as to improve inter-service cooperation.

From 2003 to 2005, the Libyan authorities repatriated 145,000 illegal migrants of various nationalities, most of them from sub-Saharan countries. These repatriations continue with no end in sight.

COOPERATION BETWEEN LIBYA AND THE EU IN THE FIELD OF COMBATING ILLEGAL MIGRATION

There is a historical European responsibility for African poverty. So there are many European obligations in this field (Al-Kut, 2007). The first step in solving the problem of illegal migration must start in Libya, the main route of illegal migrants. Although few illegal migrants are Libyan, Libya is the favourite route for those migrants.

The Libyan-European history of cooperation in the field of migration is very small. Current cooperation between Libya and the international community remains limited, but Libya has gained an increasing understanding of the need to develop cooperation on migration issues.

The EU has given Libyan authorities considerable assistance to help them combat illegal migration. However, it does not seem sufficient to stop illegal migration. Bilateral cooperation exists only with Italy and Malta. Of these, Libya has considerably increased its cooperation with Italy in recent years.

In 2000, the two countries signed an agreement in Rome to fight terrorism, organized crime, drugs traffic and illegal migration. A September 2002 operational agreement in Tripoli later led to the establishment of a permanent liaison on organized crime and illegal migration between Italian police officers and the Libyan Security General Directorate in July 2003. The collaboration between the two countries extends beyond expulsions from the Lampedusa holding centre and includes constructing detention centres and developing return schemes in Libya.

In 2003, Italy financed the construction of a camp for illegal migrants in Gharyan 80 km south of Tripoli. For the 2004–2005 period, Italy allocated funds for two more camps: one in the city of Kufra, located in the south-east, close to the border with Egypt and Sudan and the other in the city of Sebha, in south-west Libya.

They also signed an agreement in 2004, while the Italian internal minister visited Tripoli, to cooperate in combating illegal migration. The Italian minister announced that Italy would provide equipment to Libya, including: 30 military vehicles, 2 aeroplanes, one IB 412 helicopter, 2 ITR 42 marine planes, and ships for 150 Libyan and Italian police to help patrol the Libyan coasts.

Before that announcement, between August 2003 and December 2004, the Italian government financially contributed to 50 charter flights from Libya that returned more than 5000 migrants to their origin countries, including some African countries like Egypt, Eritrea, Ghana, Mali, Niger, Nigeria, Sudan and Asian countries like Pakistan, Bangladesh, and Syria. From October 2004 to March 2005, Italian authorities returned more than 1500 irregular migrants and asylum seekers to Libya from the Lampedusa holding centre (Andrijasevic, 2008). Then, in December 2007, the Italian internal minister signed an operational convention to combat illegal migration with the Foreign Affairs Minister of Libya in Tripoli.

The IOM has also developed links with Libya and prepared a cooperative program for implementation. IOM signed an agreement on August 5, 2005 to open an office in Tripoli. Additionally, the EU has funded a regional project with the ICMPD (International Centre for Migration Policy Development). These actions have fostered cooperation between the EU and non-EU countries in the region, including Libya.

Migration has also become a priority area within the African Union and the informal '5+5' framework in which Libya participates.

The EU made unwise policy when it imposed an embargo on Libya during the final decade of the last century. This embargo forced the Libyan leadership to deal with other areas, even if some were made up of the poorest countries in the world, i.e., the Sub-Saharan countries. The price of this policy was a Libyan open-door policy for these countries. As part of its new pan-African policy, Libyan Authorities started to welcome Sub-Saharan Africans to work in Libya in the spirit of Pan-African solidarity. That also meant more black African migrated to Libya.

Later, after lifting the embargo, Libya especially responded to the policy of cooperation with the EU in regards migration. From the Libyan point of view, more cooperation between Libya and the EU may mean more intervention in Libyan local affairs and sovereignty. Some EU demands looked unreasonable. When the EU offered troops to Libya for monitoring the borders, Libya saw that as the EU looking to guard Europe because the EU cares about one thing: keeping Europe clean of black Africans who mostly come from Libya.

Despite this cooperation, we can say that cooperation between the two sides is generally less than required since the number of illegal migrants continues to increase.

THE POSSIBILITIES OF SUCCESS AND FAILURE IN SOLVING THE PROBLEM OF ILLEGAL MIGRATION

Nobody could assume that Libya has the ability to combat illegal migration alone, even if all Libyans stood in queue along the borders. A rich country with very long borders, a small population, surrounded by poor countries with huge populations—all these facts prove that Libya will be an easy target for migrants from the sub-Sahara and Egypt in the coming decades.

There are indications that those countries will continue to suffer from demographic booms, unemployment, and hunger. There is no place for them to export their problems except to Libya. Libya will not be able to defeat these waves of migrants without real assistance from another side; that side is the European Union. Because the next target of migrants after Libya is the EU. The EU has the ability to stand with Libya to combat illegal migration, not only for Libya's sake, but also to defend itself. Returning migrants to their countries of origin is an unsuccessful policy, because most migrants will try again. They have nothing to lose. The return trip is even by aeroplane.

We have to look for a real sustainable solution for this dilemma. We have to teach those migrants to produce their own food and to depend on themselves not on the ready meals from overseas. We have to do as a Chinese proverb says, "Instead of giving me a fish every day, teach me how to catch it."

This cooperation may take many forms:

- exchanging information between the two sides about migrant data in Libya and the EU;
- collecting data regarding the position of these migrants in their countries of origin in order to deal with the problem;
- coordinating efforts to help emigrant countries find projects that could feed them in order to lessen the causes of migration;
- establishing mutual committees between Libya and the EU to observe the migration issue and recommend solutions according to the situations;
- the two sides must share the costs of controlling migration, possibly through a fund for this purpose, with the EU providing the majority of the budget;
- coordination between the EU, Libya and the emigrant countries at many levels should also exist to deal with this issue.

Without cooperation between Libya, other Maghreb countries and the EU, the flood of migrants from Africa to Europe will never end.

Chapter 8

—◆—

IRREGULAR MIGRATION AND IMMIGRATION CONTROL IN THE MEDITERRANEAN
— Derek Lutterbeck —

INTRODUCTION

Since the beginning of the 1990s, irregular boat migration across the Mediterranean Sea has become an issue of growing concern in both EU countries as well as, increasingly, the countries on the southern shores of the Mediterranean. It is estimated that between 100,000 and 120,000 "boat people" try to cross the Mediterranean each year (ICMPD, 2004). Not only these numbers as such, however, but also the often-made association between illegal immigration and various social ills, such as over-burdened social welfare systems, rising crime rates, or even international terrorism, have led migration from the south to emerge as an ever more important policy challenge in European countries. Moreover, irregular migration across the Mediterranean has also become a serious humanitarian issue, as the would-be immigrants often travel in unseaworthy and overloaded vessels and accidents are frequent. The death toll among the clandestine migrants seeking to reach the EU by boat has been estimated in the hundreds if not thousands per year.

The countries on the southern shores of the Mediterranean, as well, have come to view irregular migration as a growing problem, as they have, in recent years, also become countries of transit and even of destination, in addition to being countries of origin.[1] The most important transit and destination country of the southern Mediterranean nowadays is Libya. According to the Libyan government, as many as 100,000 irregular immigrants from sub-Saharan Africa enter the country each year, and there are currently said to be more than one million undocumented migrants in Libya. These are considered to represent a growing strain on the country's welfare system, and with the different life-styles and traditions they bring, are viewed as seriously under-mining the country's internal stability (El-Kut, 2008).

This chapter looks at the main trends in irregular migra-tion across the Mediterranean over recent years and discusses EU countries' responses to the "migration crisis" in the region. It argues that while at the rhetorical level, European countries have been advocating a "comprehensive" or "global" approach to the migration issue, and have also been emphasizing the need to address the "root causes" of migration in the countries of origin, the core policy focus thus far has been on coercive and in particu-lar border enforcement measures. The article also addresses the main challenges which EU countries' border control efforts in the Mediterranean have been facing, as well as some the negative effects of these measures in terms of the human security of the would-be immigrants seeking to reach the EU from the south.

IRREGULAR MIGRATION ACROSS THE MEDITERRANEAN: ROUTES AND SOME FIGURES

Irregular boat migration across the Mediterranean Sea is a rather dynamic phenomenon, and since the beginning of the 1990s there have been considerable changes in the main routes used to cross the Mediterranean from the south. Throughout the 1990s, by far the most important entry gates along the EU's

Mediterranean borders were, on the one hand, the Adriatic route and in particular the Straits of Otranto, where Italy and Albania are separated by a narrow stretch of water of 70km, and on the other the Straits of Gibraltar, where the distance between the EU and the African continent is much shorter even, amounting to a mere 14 km. Along Italy's Adriatic coast, the largest number of arrivals occurred during the Kosovo crisis in 1999, when almost 50.000 would-be migrants and refugees were apprehended by Italian authorities in Apulia and Calabria. For the straits of Gibraltar, the peak was reached in 2001, with almost 15.000 interceptions of undocumented immigrants seeking to reach Spain from Morocco.

Over recent years, however, largely as a consequence of enhanced immigration control efforts of both Italy and Spain along their southern frontiers, these short routes have lost in importance relative to longer channels across the EU's southern borders (Lutterbeck, 2006). Since 2003, the Adriatic route is practically not used any longer, also as a result of the increasingly dense patrols of Italian security forces along the country's Adriatic coast and the far-reaching cooperation between Italy and Albania in this area. Instead, over recent years, the great majority of undocumented immigrants seeking to enter Italy have landed on Sicily or Lampedusa, with Libya becoming the main point of departure for crossing the Mediterranean. By 2004, more than 95% of all irregular immigrants intercepted along Italy's maritime borders were apprehended in or off the coast of Sicily. Similarly, the island of Sardinia has, in 2005, for the first time seen immigrants landing on its shores, although for this route the main point of departure seems to be Algeria and not Libya.

Another manifestation of the growing importance of the Central Mediterranean route through Libya and the Sicily Channel has been the sharp rise of irregular boat migration into Malta from 2002 onwards. While in 2000 and 2001, there were only very few sea-borne immigrants landing on Malta—24 and 57, respectively—in 2002, this figure jumped dramatically to more than 1,600. Since then the number of migrants arriving on the island has hovered between 1,500 and 2,500 per year. While these figures are, of course, low in absolute terms, given the country's small size and high population density, the impact of irregular immigration in Malta has arguably been higher than in any other EU country, and the migration issue is nowadays perceived as the country's most serious policy challenge (Lutterbeck, 2009; Lutterbeck & Calleya, 2008).

A similar shift from relatively short to longer routes has occurred along Spain's southern borders. While the "traditional" route through the Straits of Gibraltar remains important, there has, over recent years, been a clear diversion effect towards the Canary Island. The points of departure along this route have also increasingly moved southwards, from southern Morocco to Mauritania and then to Senegal. In 2006, more than three times as many would-be immigrants were intercepted on or off the Canary Islands than in the Straits of Gibraltar. Table 1 below provides an overview of arrivals of undocumented immigrants by boat in Italy, Spain and Malta since 2000.

TABLE 1. ARRIVALS OF IRREGULAR MIGRANTS BY BOAT IN ITALY, SPAIN AND MALTA, 2000-2007

YEAR	STRAITS OF GIBRALTAR	CANARY ISLAND	PUGLIA AND CALABRIA	SICILY AND LAMPEDUSA	SARDINIA	MALTA
2000	12,785	2,410	24,035	2,782		24
2001	14,405	4,112	14,639	5,504		57
2002	6,795	9,875	4,798	10,151		1,686
2003	9,794	9,382	314	14,017		545
2004	7,294	8,426	41	13,549		1,723
2005	7,066	4,715	107	22,842	8	2,416
2006	6,976	33,126	525	21,400	91	1,789
2007	5,579	12,478	nd	16,500	960	1,715

Sources: National ministries

Systematic data on the nationalities of irregular migrants crossing the Mediterranean by boat are difficult to come by, not least because the migrants often conceal their nationalities in order to avoid repatriation. The International Centre for Migration Policy Development (ICMPD) in Vienna has estimated that around half of all would-be immigrants crossing the Mediterranean are from southern and eastern Mediterranean countries, around 25 percent from Sub-Saharan African countries, and the remaining 25 percent from other, mainly Asian countries (ICMPD). According to available Italian data for 2006, the largest group were Moroccans, accounting for around 37 percent of all arrivals by boat, followed by Egyptians with around 20 percent and Eritreans accounting for some 12 percent. In the case of Malta, by far the most important country of origin of seaborne immigrants in 2007 was Somalia (42 percent), followed by Eritrea (24 percent), and Ivory Coast (5 percent).

A significant development in the Maltese case has been the growing number of arrivals of immigrants from the west African coast, in particular Ivory Coast and Mali, since 2007, whereas previously practically all would-be immigrants had come from East African countries. It appears that that this, too, has been the result of a displacement effect: with increasingly effective controls by Spain off the Canary Islands and along the West African coast, the migratory flows seem to have been diverted from the Atlantic route via Mauritania or Senegal towards the Canary Islands—where there has indeed been a considerable decline since 2006—to the Central Mediterranean route via Libya. Again, this diversion effect shows how "plugging" one "hole" in the EU's outer perimeter often leads to enhanced pressure on other parts of its external borders.

Finally, it should also be note that while irregular boat migration across the Mediterranean has generally attracted great media attention, and there seems to be a rather wide-spread perception of EU countries being "invaded" by immigrants seeking to reach the EU from the African continent, clandestine migration by boat accounts for only a small fraction of the overall volume of undocumented immigration into southern EU countries. In most southern European countries (apart from Malta) estimates are that only between 5 and 10 percent of all irregular immigrants have crossed, or attempted to cross, the country's borders in a clandestine manner (Baldwin-Edwards, 2007). It is commonly agreed that by far the largest number of undocumented immigrants are so called visa-overstayers, i.e., persons who entered the country with valid travel documents and then remained in the country even though their visas had expired. Regardless of the relatively minor importance of irregular border crossings, however, as following sections will show, a core focus of EU countries' efforts to prevent irregular immigration has been on upgrading EU countries' Mediterranean borders.

PREVENTING IRREGULAR MIGRATION ACROSS THE MEDITERRANEAN: THE PREDOMINANCE OF BORDER CONTROL

In view of the growing "migration crisis" in the region, European countries have been advocating a broad range of policy measures aimed at curbing the flow of boat people across the Mediterranean. Over recent years, EU countries have in particular been calling for a so-called "comprehensive" or "global" approach to migration, which should not be confined to border control measures to prevent illegal entries but should also include, for example, development assistance to the source countries of migration, or the opening up of certain channels for legal immigration, so as to relieve "pressure" on illegal channels. The migration-development nexus, in particular, has become a core focus of high-level discussions between EU and African countries, as evidenced, for example by the recent Euro-African Ministerial Conference on Migration and Development held in Rabat in July 2006, or the EuroMed Ministerial conference on Migration which took place in Algarve in November 2007.

However, despite EU countries' rhetorical commitment to a such a comprehensive approach to migration, and the seemingly growing recognition that in the long run the migration issue can only be effectively tackled by addressing the "root causes" in the countries of origin, the main policy focus thus far has remained on more security-oriented measures, and in particular the strengthening of border controls along the EU's southern borders.[2] The issue of 'visibility' seems to be key here: just as the most visible form of irregular immigration—clandestine border-crossings by boat—has attracted the most attention, despite its rather marginal importance in terms of numbers, it is the most visible form of immigration prevention—border control measures—which has been the EU's predominant response to the "migration crisis" in the Mediterranean.

Over recent years, EU countries have thus been devoting large financial and human resources aimed at upgrading the EU's Mediterranean borders, while hardly any specific policies on migration and development have thus far been implemented, at least not at the EU level.[3] This bias towards border control measures is also evident, for example, in the funds allocated for the different items of the EU's migration policy. For the period 2007-2013 the External Border Fund received a total of EUR 1.82 billion, making border control by far the largest spending item of the EU's overall migration policy.[4] The sum also more than double the amount (EUR 700 million) which has been made available for structural assistance (in areas such as the environment or transport) to countries neighboring the EU under the recently launched Neighborhood Investment Fund.[5]

One EU country which, over recent years, has sought to direct its development assistance more towards the main source countries of migration is Spain. In 2006, the Spanish government, confronted with a rapid rise of immigrants from sub-Saharan African countries arriving on the Canary Islands, launched the so-called *Plan Africa*. According to this plan, Sub-Saharan Africa is to become the priority area for Spanish development assistance—whereas traditionally the main focus was on Latin America.[6] However, while *Plan Africa* has overall led to an increase of development assistance to the African continent—in 2006, it amounted to 400 million EUR, including contributions to multilateral organizations—critics have pointed out that that the bulk of measures contained in the plan are not development aid as such, but are rather aimed at strengthening African countries' capacities to control their borders, and at strengthening cooperation in repatriating irregular migrants back to their countries of origin. Thus, while officially presented as a development project, aimed at addressing the "root causes" of migration in the countries of origin, the *Plan Africa*, as well, seems largely control-rather than development-oriented. The Oxfam representative in Spain has called it a Spanish plan *in* rather than *for* Africa.[7]

At the same time Spain has also been spending large sums of money aimed at strengthening the country's Mediterranean borders. For example, in Ceuta and Melilla, the two Spanish enclaves on the North African coast, Spain and the EU spent around EUR 60 million the construction of several kilometers-long perimeter walls consisting of two parallel fences hedged by barbed wire entanglements and equipped with electronic sensors, to prevent irregular immigration into the two cities. More significantly, in the late 1990s, the Spanish government initiated the construction of a vast coast control system (so-called SIVE—Sistema Integrado de Vigilancia Exterior) along the country's southern coast. The EUR 200 million-worth system is composed of fixed and mobile radars, infrared sensors as well as boats, helicopters and airplanes which are being deployed along the country's Mediterranean coast in order to prevent boats carrying immigrants from reaching the country's shores.[8] Moreover, in 2007, the Spanish Ministry of Defence announced the launching of a satellite-based surveillance system to monitor the Mediterranean and the West African coast, which would be able to identify boats transporting migrants towards Spain and the Canary Islands. The price tag for this system is expected to amount to some EUR 325 million (*Diario Sur*, 6 April 2007).

As these examples illustrate, strengthening the EU's Mediterranean borders has also involved the increasing use of military technology and hardware for border and immigration control purposes—a development often decried by human rights and immigrant support organizations as unacceptable "border militarization." A particularly contested measure in this regard has been the growing involvement of European navies, and thus of military security forces, in the prevention of migration across the Mediterranean. In both Italy and Spain, for example, the respective navies have been deployed in a growing number of anti-immigration operations. Critics have in particular pointed to the unsuitability, and indeed dangerousness, of using warships for immigration control purposes.[9] This was underscored by the to date most serious accident involving a warship of the

Italian Navy deployed on an anti-immigration mission during the (second) Albanian refugee crisis in March 1997. The Italian warship, whose task was to prevent departures from the Albanian coast towards Italy, collided with a boat transporting Albanian migrants, resulting in the death of some 100 Albanians.

FRONTEX

The EU's predominant focus on border control measures has also been manifest in the setting up, in 2005, of the EU border control agency FRONTEX based in Warsaw. The principal task of FRONTEX is to coordinate the activities of the border control forces of EU member countries, which continue to bear the main responsibility for controlling their frontiers. While FRONTEX has its own budget and staff, it (thus far) does not have its own assets and operative personnel for carrying out border control operations. For joint EU operations, FRONTEX thus relies entirely on the assets and personnel provided by EU countries. As a consequence, it is also heavily dependent on the (political) will of the member states to contribute to any given operation.

In 2006, FRONTEX launched its first operations in the Mediterranean and Atlantic. Thus far, FRONTEX has concentrated its activities in three sectors of the Mediterranean/ eastern Atlantic: off the Canary Islands, it has been carrying out Operation Hera under Spanish leadership; in the central Mediterranean, Operation Nautilus has been conducted under the auspices of Malta, and in the eastern Mediterranean, Greece has been running Operation Poseidon. In 2007, so-called Rapid Border Intervention Teams (RABIT) were created within the framework of FRONTEX. These teams are drawn from a pool of experts from the member states, which are trained by FRONTEX, and which can be deployed in situations of emergency. The first RABIT exercise was carried out in late 2007. The growing importance attributed to FRONTEX can be seen in the rather dramatic budget increases it has witnessed over recent years. While the initial budget allocated to FRONTEX in 2005 was 5 million EUR, this was increased to 70 million in 2008.

However, FRONTEX's operations, at least those in the Central Mediterranean, have been quite slow to start, and have remained rather limited in scope. In Malta, which has been the main contributor to, as well as the main beneficiary of, the FRONTEX operation in this part of the Mediterranean, this has given rise to considerable frustration, as the country has felt let down by the EU in coping with the rapid rise of irregular migration towards its shores. Not only budgetary constraints, but also uncertainties revolving around Libya's participation—which given its role as a main transit country is generally seen as crucial—have been the main reasons for repeated delays of FRONTEX's operations in the Central Mediterranean. The first operation in 2006, for example, was launched only in October—when the "migration season" was practically over—after EU officials had for months tried—unsuccessfully—to involve Libya in these efforts (Bussutil, 2007). In 2007, Frontex's operations started earlier, in June, but as Libya still refused to participate, Italy also pulled out, arguing that the operation could not be successful without Libya's contribution (*Times of Malta*, 13 July 2007). Moreover, due to budgetary constraints, the mission had to be halted entirely at the end of July, and it only resumed in mid-September, although this time with Italian participation (*Times of Malta*, 10 September 2007).

Moreover, while Malta has put all of its—very modest—assets at FRONTEX's disposal, the assets provided by other EU countries to FRONTEX's maritime patrols in the central Mediterranean have been very limited. In 2007, for example, other EU contributions were limited to two German helicopters and an occasional presence of a Greek and a Spanish vessel as well as an Italian patrol aircraft, although in the second part of the operation Italy also agreed to send three Navy vessels.[10] EU countries have generally been reluctant to provide the usually most needed patrol boats, as this entails the "risk" that the country providing the vessels will remain responsible for migrants rescued or intercepted at sea. As a result, at least according to Maltese officials, the Maltese Navy has been responsible for 90 percent of the surface coverage in Malta's search and rescue area, even in the framework of FRONTEX's operations (*Times of Malta*, 28 July 2007).

While FRONTEX is set to play an increasingly prominent role in controlling the EU's outer borders, and there are plans to transform into an autonomous body with its own assets, the agency has also met with considerable criticism, not only from pro-immigrant organizations, but also from bodies such as the UNHCR. Critics have in particular highlighted that FRONTEX's main focus has been on deterring and preventing illegal immigration as opposed to rescuing would-be immigrants in situations of distress. Indeed, FRONTEX' director, Ilkka Laitinen, has himself emphasized that FRONTEX's main task was to protect the EU's external borders and not to carry out search-and-rescue missions in the Mediterranean (*The Sunday Times*, 8 July 2007). Another criticism often made of FRONTEX is that it lacks democratic accountability and parliamentary oversight. Thus, while the European Parliament has oversight over the agency's budget, FRONTEX's operational planning and analysis is kept secret and is removed from any parliamentary control (Carrera, 2007).

Cross-border Cooperation

It is generally agreed that effective border controls in the Mediterranean—as well as elsewhere—require close collaboration not only between EU but even more so between countries north and south of the Mediterranean. The arguably thus far most significant example of successful cross-border cooperation in immigration control in the Mediterranean has been the collaboration between Italy and Albania, which was initiated in the aftermath of the Albanian refugee crisis of 1997. From 1997 onwards, Italy (as well as the EU) established a number of police assistance missions in Albania—most of them along the country's Adriatic coast—with the aim of supporting the Albanian police in combating migration and human trafficking from its shores towards Italy. These missions have involved activities such as joint patrols along the Albanian coast, training, the provision of technical equipment, and intelligence sharing.[11] An important element of this collaboration has also been the repatriation of undocumented migrants who have been caught by Italian authorities from Italy back to Albania.[12] Arguably as a result of this close collaboration between Italy and Albania, the "Adriatic route," which throughout the 1990s was one of the main entry gates for undocumented immigrants seeking to enter the EU, has nowadays become largely obsolete.

Spain, as well, has made considerable efforts to engage more closely with its southern neighbors in preventing undocumented migration from the African continent towards Spain and Europe. For example, since 2004 Spain and Morocco, despite the traditionally difficult relationship between the two countries, have been carrying out joint patrols along Morocco's northern and western coast, and Morocco has also been showing a greater willingness to collaborate with Spain in the field of readmission of uncommented migrants intercepted in Spain. In return for its participation in these immigration control activities, Morocco has received considerable financial and technical assistance from both Spain and the EU. More recently, Spain has also been expanding such joint operations to countries further south such as Mauretania and Senegal, again in the form of joint maritime patrols and close collaboration in returning intercepted migrants. This increasingly close cooperation between Spain and these countries has probably been one of the main reasons why irregular migration from the West African coast towards the Canary Islands has declined sharply—by around 60 percent—between 2006 and 2007, with current trends pointing to a further reduction (*Diario Canarias*, 30 July 2008).

From an EU perspective, the most "problematic" country in this regard, at least until very recently, has been Libya. Even though since 2002, Libya has become one of the main transit countries for irregular immigrants seeking to enter the EU from the south, EU countries have found it difficult to enlist Libya into their immigration control efforts. Libya's main argument for refusing to cooperate with FRONTEX has been that that the EU has thus far not provided sufficient support to Libya in policing the country's vast southern borders (*The Sunday Times*, 1 July 2008). Moreover, Libyan officials have considered measures such as joint EU-Libyan patrols along Libya's coast as incompatible with the country's sovereignty (Al Kut, 2008).

Between Italy and Libya, by contrast, there has been increasingly close collaboration in recent years, although here too there have been considerable ups and downs and several diplomatic crises between the two countries over the migration issue. Italian policy-makers have regularly accused Libya not only of failing to prevent boats carrying irregular migrants from leaving its coast, but also of actively "dumping" Sub-Saharan migrants on its shores. On the other hand, the two countries have begun to collaborate in different ways in preventing migration from Libya towards Italy. Since 2000, the two countries have signed several agreements on joint measures to combat irregular immigration, and Italy has also funded the construction of several immigrant detention camps in Libya (European Commission, 4 April 2005). In December 2007, an agreement was signed providing for joint operations between the two countries, as well as for the delivery of patrol boats and other equipment from Italy to Libya (*La Stampa*, 29 December 2007). This was followed, in August 2008, by the signing of the Treaty on Friendship, Partnership and Cooperation between Italy and Libya. Even though the main objective of the treaty is to settle differences between the two countries stemming from colonial times, a core focus is on cooperation in preventing illegal immigration (*Corriere della Sera*, 30 August 2008). The most significant—and most contested—step thus far in the deepening collaboration between Italy and Libya in migration control came in April 2009, when Libya for the first time agreed to take back undocumented immigrants who had been intercepted on the high seas by Italian naval vessels.

While the emerging cooperation between Italy and Libya has officially been declared as "historic," and as a model to be followed by other European countries, the policy has however also been sharply criticized by UN bodies and various human rights organizations alike. UNHCR, Human Rights Watch and other organizations have pointed out that pushing back intercepted migrants to their point of departure is incompatible with the Geneva Refugee Convention, as potential refugees are thus effectively prevented from lodging an application for political asylum.

Border Externalization

While a core focus of European countries' efforts to prevent irregular immigration has been on border controls, this has not only involved a strengthening of EU countries' Mediterranean borders as such, but also what could be called an increasing externalization of border control, i.e. the moving of border and immigration controls outward from the external borderline of EU countries towards the transit and source countries of migration. The collaborative efforts between EU and southern Mediterranean countries as described above, can be seen as one example of such border externalization. Other forms have also become increasingly important over recent years. For example, instead of merely patrolling their coastline and territorial waters, countries such as Italy and Spain have increasingly been carrying out immigration control operations in international waters, in particular through the deployment of their navies, or even in the territorial waters of southern Mediterranean countries as described above. The strategy of externalizing border and immigration controls has also been evident in measures such as the provision of technical equipment for border management to transit countries of migration, the deployment of immigration liaison officers, the conclusion of readmission agreements and related policies.

Critics often point to the (highly) problematic nature of this strategy of outsourcing border and immigration controls, in particular from a human rights and refugee protection perspective. With regard to cooperation with the countries of the southern Mediterranean in this area, it can be noted that most of them do not have adequately functioning systems of asylum and refugee protection. Libya has been considered particularly problematic in this regard, not only because of its generally poor human rights record, but also because it has not signed the Geneva Refugee Convention. In some countries of the region, human rights organizations such as Amnesty International, have also reported rather widespread human rights abuses of immigrants. Enlisting these countries as gatekeepers in the EU's anti-immigration efforts, while often considered essential in order to achieve effective border controls, thus also raises serious human rights concerns.[13]

EFFECTS OF BORDER CONTROL MEASURES

What have been the effects of EU countries' border control measures as described above? European policy makers usually argue that these efforts should achieve two main objectives: on the one hand to curb the flow of irregular migrants across the Mediterranean, and on the other to reduce the death toll of would-be immigrants seeking to reach the EU from the African continent. However, with regard to neither of these two objectives, can the balance sheet thus far said to be a positive one.

Given the clandestine nature of the phenomenon, it is of course impossible to assess the actual volume and evolution of irregular migration across the Mediterranean. The only available data (at least in part) are interceptions of would-be immigrants, and these might or might not be a reliable indicator of the actual number of migrants seeking to cross. Interception figures, however, show a rather clear trend: between 1993 and 2006, the total number of interceptions in the two most important southern European destination countries—Italy and Spain—rose continuously and more than ten-fold, from about 5,000 to almost 70,000. The year of 2007 has at least by some policy makers been seen as a turning point, as in both Italy and Spain the numbers of interceptions declined considerably. While in Italy it dropped by about 35 percent, Spain saw a reduction by as much as 50 percent compared to 2006, a development which at least officially has been seen as a sign that EU countries' border control activities in the Mediterranean are indeed proving effective. However, while in Spain and the Canary Islands this downwards trend has continued into 2008, in the Central Mediterranean (Italy and Malta), there has again been a massive increase in irregular migration in 2008. As already mentioned above, this seems to have been the result of a diversion effect away from the Atlantic route to the Central Mediterranean route though Libya and the Channel of Sicily.

More generally, it can be argued that EU countries have been successful in closing down, or at least considerably limiting, certain channels for irregular immigration—typically in areas where there has been close collaboration with the country on the other side of the border, such as in the Adriatic between Italy and Albania, or between Spain and Mauretania or Senegal along the West African coast. Practically always, however, closing down or limiting one channel has also led to a diversion effect towards other routes, without a clear impact on the overall volume of irregular immigration. As already mentioned previously, in the case of Italy this has involved mainly a diversion of the migratory flows across the Adriatic towards the Central Mediterranean route, and in Spain from the Straits of Gibraltar towards the Canary Islands, and most recently, from the latter also towards the Central Mediterranean crossing.

In most if not all cases, these displacement effects have also come at a considerable human cost, as the new routes have typically been much longer and thus also more dangerous than the original entry gates used by the would-be migrants. This has been reflected in the growing death toll in the Mediterranean. Along Spain's southern borders, for example, the number of reported deaths of clandestine migrants rose from 66 in 1999 to more than 1000 in 2006, with the actual death toll most likely being much higher. A similar increase in the number of deaths has been reported in Italy, with the shift from the Adriatic route to the crossing through the channel of Sicily. Thus, ironically—or even cynically—while EU countries' border control measures are often explicitly justified with the need to prevent the loss of life at sea, the overall effect of these measures has been exactly the opposite, in that they have increased the dangers for the would-be immigrants attempting to each the EU by boat.

Other perverse side-effects of EU countries' enhanced border control activities have also been highlighted by human rights organizations. For example, one consequence of the increasingly severe punishment of persons (allegedly) involved in human trafficking or smuggling has been that nowadays practically none of the boats carrying irregular immigrants across the Mediterranean are driven by experienced pilots but rather by one of the migrants themselves. Needless to say, this too has increased the risks for clandestine immigrants seeking to cross the Mediterranean from the south.

Conclusions: Towards a new Mediterranean barrier

Throughout history the Mediterranean has been viewed both as a bridge as well as a barrier, as a sea bringing the peoples and countries along its shores together or as dividing them apart. The current "migration crisis" in the Mediterranean, and in particular EU countries' policy responses to the crisis, suggests that, at least at least in this regard, the Mediterranean is nowadays first and foremost a barrier between north and south. It is a line of separation between highly industrialised, prosperous and stable countries to the north, and countries to the south which are plagued by poverty, demographic imbalances and various domestic and regional tensions, not unlike the border between the US and Mexico. It is a barrier because the possibilities of legally migrating from south to north are nowadays, with few and minor exceptions, practically non-existent. The Mediterranean barrier is also particularly manifest in EU countries border enforcement measures aimed at preventing unwanted migration from the African continent, including by military means.

The main difference, perhaps, to a "traditional" barrier is that the contemporary Mediterranean barrier is sustained not only by unilateral action by the countries along the northern shores, but increasingly also by collaborative arrangements between the countries north and south of the Mediterranean. The Mediterranean divide is thus not really a (civilizational) "fault line" à la Huntington, where the north and south are diametrically opposed, with little scope for cooperation across the divide. Rather it is a relatively collaborative barrier where the countries of the southern shore are increasingly also taking part—or better, are being enlisted—in the EU's efforts to prevent movements of people from south to north.

However, while this growth in cooperation across the Mediterranean can at least in certain ways be seen as a positive development, and as indicative of stronger cooperation and a "rapprochement" between the countries north and south of the Mediterranean, it too has its dangers. The risk is not only that through ever more intense border control measures the would-be immigrants are forced towards more dangerous routes across the Mediterranean, but also that migration management is increasingly being externalized towards countries with a poor human rights record and inadequate refugee protection, thus jeopardizing both the rights and security of the migrants, including potentially genuine refugees, seeking to reach the EU from the south.

Notes

1. Among southern Mediterranean countries, Egypt and Morocco are currently the most important countries of origin of irregular immigration into the EU. Libya, by contrast, is almost exclusively a country of transit and destination.

2. See. e.g., CeSPI (Centro di Politica Internazionale) and SID (Society for International Development), *European Migration Policy on Africa—Trends, Effects and Prospects*, 2006, available at: http://www.sidint.org/migration/html/publications.html, or Michael Collyer, "Towards Mediterranean Migration Management 2008?" Developing Discourse and Practices," Real Insituto Elcano, 2.6.2008.

3. The only concrete measure implemented by the EU so far in this context seems to have been the setting up of an immigrant employment and training centre in Mali (CIGEM—Centre d'Information et de Gestion des Migrations).

4. For an overview of the different items of the EU's migration policy, see "European Migration Policy Receives Funding," *Europa World*, 15.12.2006, available at: http://www.europaworld.org/week289/europeanmigration151206.html

5. Commission of the European Communities, Communication to the Council and the European Parliament on Strengthening the European Neighbourhood Policy, Brussels, 4 December 2006 COM(2006)726 final.

6. An overview of *Plan Africa* can be found on the website of the Spanish Foreign Ministry at: http://www.maec.es/es/Home/Paginas/20060605_planafricaingles.aspx.

7. Asociación Pro Derechos Humanos de Andalucía, *Derechos Humanos en la Frontera Sur 2006*, January 2007.

8. The system is described on the website of the Spanish Guardia Civil: http://www.guardiacivil.org/prensa/actividades/sive03/index.jsp.

9. On the role of the Italian Navy in preventing irregular migration via sea, see Fabio Caffio, *L' Italia di fronte all'immigrazione clandestine via mare*, Rome, 2005. Since May 2006, the Spanish Navy has been carrying out Operacion Noble Sentinela between the Canary Islands, Cap Verde, Senegal and Mauritania.

10. Author interview with officials of Armed Forces of Malta, 5 October 2007.

11. In the late 1990s, some 300 Italian police and coastguard officers were deployed in Albania in the framework of these police assistance programs.

12. In 1999 alone, some 18,000 irregular migrants, including third country nationals, were repatriated from Italy to Albania.

13. On all of these issues see, e.g., Amnesty Internacional, *Frontera Sur. El Estado da la espalda a los derechos humanos de los refugiados e inmigrantes*, 2006, available at: http://www.amnesty.org/es/report/info/EUR41/008/2005. Asociación Pro Derechos Humanos de Andalucía, *Derechos humanos en la Frontera Sur 2006. Informe sobre la inmigración clandestina durante el año 2005*, 2006, available at: http://www.apdha.org/index.php?option=com_content&task=view&id=175&Itemid=32. Human Rights Watch, *Stemming the Flow: Abuses Against Migrants, Asylum Seekers and Refugees*, 2006, available at: http://www.hrw.org/reports/2006/libya0906/.

Chapter 9

WHEN RIGHTS AND DUTIES COLLIDE: THE CHALLENGE FACING MALTA IN THE FIGHT AGAINST IRREGULAR MARITIME MIGRATION
– Patricia Mallia –

INTRODUCTION

Irregular maritime migration presents a challenge which calls upon States to consider principles other than policing and interdiction since the core of the activity lies on *persons* on the move, therefore requiring consideration of issues of human welfare and dignity. At the same time, States have security interests and are entitled to take any action in accordance with international law, which will minimise the risk caused thereby. In this area therefore, the rights of States and duties of those same States towards individuals meet and often collide.

The facts surrounding the phenomenon of irregular migration and the trafficking and smuggling of migrants by sea are well-known, and have been amply discussed elsewhere.[1] Equally documented, albeit not so clearly-defined, are the various applicable legal regimes which surround this trend. This contribution aims to separate the different regimes, often apparently conflicting, in a bid to clarify the various rights and duties with which a State is presented. Although reference is made to the situation facing Malta,[2] this article is relevant to all States facing a similar challenge—and therefore highlights the need for cooperation amongst States, primarily, amongst Member States of the European Union.

This contribution is written with a non-legal readership in mind, in a bid to make clear some of the complex legal principles applicable in this area.[3]

SETTING THE FACTS STRAIGHT

Prior to the main discussion it is imperative to set straight certain misconceptions regarding core issues. The first of such clarifications relates to the fact that migrant arrivals by sea are often perceived as being wholly made up of asylum-seekers or else, entirely composed of economic migrants. This point is not merely academic; on the contrary, it is crucial as it influences State policies and reactions to such arrivals. The consideration of this mixed influx of arrivals must be placed at the forefront of any cooperative exercise to curb irregular migration. While human rights apply equally to all individuals, (including the migrant smugglers)[4] the smuggled migrants also enjoy a further protection under the umbrella of refugee rights owing to the fact that they may be genuine asylum-seekers.[5] The consideration of this mixed influx of arrivals must be placed at the forefront of any cooperative exercise to suppress migrant smuggling.

Another point which must be highlighted at the outset is that there is a distinction between the undisputed duty to rescue those in distress at sea and the subsequent processing of any asylum claims that may be made by those rescued. In other words, fulfilment of the duty to rescue does not necessarily imply that the same State must therefore disembark those rescued. Again, this point is made because of its impact on the conduct and reaction of States when faced with irregular migrants on board vessels in need of rescue.

OVERLAPPING LEGAL REGIMES—LAW OF THE SEA, HUMANITARIAN CONSIDERATIONS AND SEARCH AND RESCUE OBLIGATIONS

The law of the sea, predominantly regulated by the 1982 United Nations Law of the Sea Convention (LOSC),[6] lays down a framework which gives coastal States various rights over the different maritime belts adjacent to their coasts. In the overview that follows it will be noted that the LOSC therefore may be described as providing 'opportunities' for State action. The next section on Humanitarian and Human Rights considerations, on the other hand, may more aptly be described as providing 'constraints' on State action.

The aim of this section is to give a very basic overview of State powers in the various relevant maritime zones since permissible State action in relation to vessels laden with migrants is determined by the location of the vessel. In other words, State action differs according to the maritime zone in which the vessel is situated. A general rule is that a State's powers are stronger in the maritime zones closer to its coasts and diminish the further away one proceeds from those coasts. In this regard, the internal waters of a State (that is, ports and harbours) constitute the maritime area in which the State is best placed to exercise jurisdiction over persons situated and events occurring therein. Indeed, internal waters are assimilated to the land territory of a State and therefore, the coastal State enjoys full sovereignty in this zone.

Following on from the internal waters is the territorial sea which extends over a belt of sea to a limit of 12 nautical miles measured from the baselines of a coastal State.[7] This zone is seen as an extension of a State's territory and therefore, sovereignty exists in this zone also and the coastal State is given legislative (article 21 LOSC) and enforcement jurisdiction (Article 27) over vessels in the territorial sea. However, the quality of sovereignty over the territorial sea differs from that which exists in the internal waters and the differentiating factor is what is known as the right of innocent passage existing in the territorial sea regime.

This right is enjoyed by ships of all States and refers to the free and uninterrupted passage across the territorial sea of a State or proceeding to or from the internal waters of a State.[8] Passage must however be 'innocent,' meaning that it must not be 'prejudicial to the peace, good order or security of the coastal State.'[9] The provision then goes on, in Article 19(2), to provide a list of activities purporting to define instances of a breach of the coastal State's peace, good order or security. Of relevance for our purposes is article 19(2)(g) which presents, as a non-innocent activity, 'the loading or unloading of any ... person contrary to the ...immigration law and regulations of the coastal State.'

In the case of non-innocent passage the LOSC (article 25(1)) allows the coastal State to 'take the necessary steps to prevent passage which is not innocent' and it may also temporarily suspend innocent passage in certain areas of its territorial sea if this suspension is essential for the protection of its security (Article 25(3) LOSC). Indeed, the EU Commission's 2007 Staff Working Document, 'Study on the International Law Instruments in Relation to Illegal Immigration by Sea' states that:

> A ship which has the intention to disembark passengers in contravention of the coastal state's immigration laws cannot benefit from [the right of innocent passage]. The coastal state has the right to escort such a ship to the high seas or proceed with arrests.[10]

In the contiguous zone, a zone adjacent to the territorial sea (of not more than 24 nm from the baselines), a State is given the faculty to act against irregular maritime migration since article 33 LOSC gives specific power to the coastal State: it may exercise the control necessary with respect to two functions: to prevent and to punish the infringement of customs, fiscal, immigration and sanitary regulations within its territory or territorial sea. It is important to note that the contiguous zone is not part of the territorial sea and freedom of navigation of all ships exists therein. This therefore has an effect on the quality and extent of the coastal State's powers within this zone.

The high seas is composed of that vast area of ocean space[11] which 'is open to all States' (article 86 LOSC) and where the so-called freedoms of the high seas apply.[12] The main principle applying in the high seas is that of flag state exclusivity whereby, save for a few exceptions, ships are subject to the exclusive jurisdiction of the flag State while on the high seas (article 92(1) LOSC). This obviously causes problems when dealing with ships sailing under the so-called flags of convenience which States either do not have the will or the resources to control such vessels. Indeed, many crime-committing vessels are either stateless (that is, not registered in any State) or else, are registered under flags of convenience.

There are however certain exceptions laid down in the LOSC and others in international agreements, whereby non-flag State actors are permitted to act, usually on the basis of consent of the flag State. In default of such agreement between the flag State and the State wishing to take enforcement action, the LOSC only permits non-flag State action in a limited number of instances: the suppression of the slave trade (Article 99), piracy (Article 100 *et seq*), illicit traffic in narcotic drugs and psychotropic substances (Article 108) and unauthorized broadcasting (Article 109).[13] However, these provisions are relatively weak and of questionable effectiveness in view of the current maritime security scenario. It is for this reason that the international community has stepped in to fill such jurisdictional gap. Examples of major international interventions have come in the form of the Convention for the Suppression of Unlawful Acts against the Safety of Maritime Navigation,[14] the Migrant Smuggling Protocol[15] and also the recent international action spearheaded by the IMO and the UNSC to fight piracy and armed robbery off the Coast of Somalia.

Although not mentioned in the LOSC, no analysis of zonal jurisdiction would be complete without mention of the so-called 'SAR zone' and the responsibilities of States within such zone. Following the adoption of the International Convention on Maritime Search and Rescue (SAR Convention),[16] the IMO divided the world's oceans into 13 areas in each of which the countries concerned have delimited search and rescue regions.

A SAR region is defined in the Annex to the SAR Convention as an 'area of defined dimensions associated with a rescue co-ordination centre within which search and rescue services are provided.'[17] This area defines which State has primary responsibility for coordinating rescue operations in response to a distress situation. Each region has an associated Rescue Coordination Centre (RCC)[18] The SAR Convention provides, in paragraph 3.1.6.4 of its Annex, that it is the States' responsibility to cooperate with other RCCs to identify the most appropriate place(s) for disembarkation of persons found in distress at sea.

A fundamental duty of contracting States Parties to the Convention is that of cooperation in the conduct of search and rescue operations. Chapter 3 of the Annex states that '[p]arties shall co-ordinate their search and rescue organizations and should, whenever necessary, co-ordinate search and rescue operations with those of neighboring States.'[19] They are also required, unless otherwise agreed, to authorize 'immediate entry into or over its territorial sea or territory of rescue units of other Parties solely for the purpose of searching for the position of maritime casualties and rescuing survivors of such casualties.'[20] There is also an obligation, imposed by Chapter 2.1.1 of the Annex to the SAR Convention that, on receiving information that a person is in distress at sea in an area within which a Party provides for the overall coordination of search and rescue operations, the responsible authorities of that Party are to take urgent steps to provide the most appropriate assistance available.

Malta has a vast SAR zone, spanning an area of approximately 250 000 square kilometres, an area linked to its flight information region. This has a direct impact on its international obligations regarding search and rescue, as shall be mentioned hereunder.

Of course, no legal framework can be seen in a vacuum as one regime constantly influences the other. In this regard, it must be stressed that the above discussion only relates to a State's powers under the LOSC and that the broader picture shows that a coastal State has concurrent obligations incumbent upon it. It is for this reason that humanitarian and human rights considerations may be described as constraints on State action as, irrespective of the powers under the law of the sea regime, States are bound notably the obligation of *non refoulement*, which applies, at the latest, once the vessel has reached the territory of the coastal State. Thus, 'people flows' invoke the ever-struggling dichotomy between human rights protection and the protection of national security.

The doctrine of *non refoulement*, enunciated in Article 33(1) of the 1951 Convention relating to the Status of Refugees prohibits the expulsion or return ('*refouler*') of a refugee (or asylumseeker)[21] 'in any manner whatsoever to the frontiers of territories where his life or freedom would be threatened on account of his race, religion, nationality, membership of a particular social group or political opinion.' Looking momentarily at the situation in the Mediterranean, it is for this reason that Italy's practice of returning rescued migrants to Libya raised a certain amount of international alarm.[22] It is true that Libya may not be a place of persecution for such migrants, however, due to its lack of ratification of the Refugee Convention, there is no guarantee that Libya will not *refoule* such individuals to such place of persecution.[23] In other words, Libya may hold itself not to be bound by the *non refoulement* obligation and this is a risk that the international community should not be prepared to take.

Besides this, it is generally recommended that the status of rescued persons is best determined by the appropriate authorities on land.[24] Therefore, a State would therefore be held to be in breach of the *non refoulement* principle were it to intercept and turn back a vessel to the borders of persecution—or arguably, to a non-Party State to the Refugee Convention—without reviewing any asylum claims made on board the intercepted vessel.

SEARCH AND RESCUE

Moving on now to consider the rescue scenario, a preliminary point must be made: rescue at sea is different to the act of maritime enforcement amounting to interception, differing in both intention and purpose. However, the two sometimes overlap, and disembarkation is common to both processes.[25] Interception is an exercise reserved to State authorities and is an exercise of a programme of maritime enforcement. However, interception may pre-empt the need for a rescue.[26]

The duty to rescue those in distress at sea is enshrined in Article 98 LOSC and may be regarded as part of customary international law.[27] The terms of Article 98 impose obligations on both the flag and coastal States in this regard, obligations which also impact ships' Masters. The provision dictates that every State is to require the Master of a ship flying its flag, insofar as he can do so without serious danger to the ship, crew or passengers, to render assistance to any person found at sea in danger of being lost and to proceed with all possible speed to the rescue of persons in distress once informed of their need of assistance and insofar as such action can be reasonably expected from him.[28] Furthermore, every coastal State is to promote the establishment, operation and maintenance of an adequate and effective search and rescue service, and to cooperate with neighboring States to this end.[29]

Although the duty to rescue has been repeatedly emphasized in international documentation 'what the lawmakers systematically had in mind were classic shipwrecks and sailors surrounding whom no attendant legal problem was suspected. Nationals of any given State, they could expect to be repatriated from the rescue ships' first port of call. In the case of asylum-seekers, however, repatriation must be ruled out. Whose responsibility they should become is something on which international law is practically silent.'[30] International legal norms therefore, are faced with developments unforeseen at the time of their drafting; nevertheless, these same international norms are the only ones which apply in these new scenarios.

Until recently, nothing in the international legal regime indicated what was to occur once the rescue had been effected. The obligation to rescue therefore, presented the problem of what happened after the actual rescue operation, which only terminated once the rescuees were delivered to a place of safety.[31] This is currently the dilemma facing Mediterranean States at the moment, with disagreements primarily between Italy and Malta on this issue.[32]

RECENT AMENDMENTS TO THE
INTERNATIONAL REGIME

IMO Assembly Resolution A.920(22) on the Review of Safety Measures and Procedures for the Treatment of Persons Rescued at Sea of 2001 called for a review of existing treaties and IMO instruments and for appropriate action to be undertaken within the context of an inter-agency group. The intended result of such review was *inter alia* that survivors of distress incidents would be given assistance, regardless of nationality or status or circumstances in which they are found; that rescuing ships would be able to deliver the survivors to a place of safety; and that survivors, regardless of nationality or status (including undocumented migrants, asylum-seekers, refugees and stowaways) would be treated, while on board the vessel, in the manner prescribed in the relevant IMO instruments and in accordance with relevant international agreements and long-standing humanitarian maritime traditions.

There was a general recognition that *lacunae* existed in both the International Convention on the Safety of Life at Sea (SOLAS)[33] and SAR Conventions in relation to the disembarkation of persons rescued at sea and the requirement of bringing them to a place of safety.[34] In this regard, an important distinction drawn early on in the deliberations was that there were two issues which, although related, had to be kept distinct. These were the purely SAR aspect of rescuing persons in distress at sea regardless of their nationality, status or circumstances and the concomitant necessity of delivering them to a place of safety under the SOLAS and SAR Conventions, and the related but distinct considerations of the status of the persons after the rescue when other related international instruments would subsequently have to be taken into consideration.[35]

On 20 May 2004, the IMO Maritime Safety Committee, during its 78th session, adopted amendments to the SOLAS and SAR Conventions concerning the treatment of persons rescued at sea, and/or asylum-seekers, refugees and stowaways, together with Guidelines on the Treatment of Persons rescued at Sea.[36] The SOLAS Convention obligates ships and thus flag States to render assistance to those in distress at sea, and the SAR Convention obliges coastal States to assist persons in distress at sea.[37]

The Guidelines provide general guidance to ship Masters, governments and RCCs. The purpose of the Guidelines is stated as being that of providing 'guidance to Governments and to shipmasters with regard to humanitarian obligations and obligations under the relevant international law relating to treatment of persons rescued at sea.'[38] They sum up in a nutshell, the main effect of the amendments to the SAR and SOLAS Conventions:

> Specifically, paragraph 1-1 of SOLAS regulation V/33 and paragraph 3.1.9 of the Annex to the SAR Convention, as amended, impose upon Governments an obligation to co-ordinate and co-operate to ensure that masters of ships providing assistance by embarking persons in distress at sea are released from their obligations with minimum further deviation from the ship's intended voyage.

As realized by the MSC in adopting the amendments, the intent of new paragraph 1-1 of SOLAS Regulation V/33 and paragraph 3.1.9 of the Annex of the International Convention on Maritime Search and Rescue, 1979, as amended, is to ensure that in every case a place of safety is provided within a reasonable time. The responsibility to provide a place of safety, or to ensure that a place of safety is provided, falls on the Government responsible for the SAR region in which the survivors were recovered.[39]

To this end, SOLAS Regulation V/33.1.1 runs as follows:

> Contracting Governments shall co-ordinate and co-operate to ensure that masters of ships providing assistance by embarking persons in distress at sea are released from their obligations with minimum further deviation from the ships' intended voyage, provided that releasing the master of the ship from the obligations under the current regulation does not further endanger the safety of life at sea. The Contracting Government responsible for the search and

> rescue region in which such assistance is rendered shall exercise primary responsibility for ensuring such co-ordination and co-operation occurs, so that survivors assisted are disembarked from the assisting ship and delivered to a place of safety, taking into account the particular circumstances of the case and guidelines developed by the Organization. In these cases the relevant Contracting Governments shall arrange for such disembarkation to be effected as soon as reasonably practicable.[40]

Currently, therefore, the State in whose search and rescue area the rescue takes place bears the main responsibility for the rescue and disembarkation of rescuees.[41] This is not, however, a solution which has met with the approval of all Contracting Parties. The Maltese delegation, supported by only a few delegations, did not agree with placing the final responsibility of accepting persons rescued at sea on the Contracting Government responsible for the search and rescue area in which the rescue took place. It feared that this arrangement would encourage the trafficking of illegal migrants, since the vessels carrying them would simply have to enter the closest neighboring SAR area and call for assistance. The Contracting Government of that SAR area would then have to come to their assistance and effectively provide them with a place of safety.

A recent circular of the IMO's Facilitation Committee (FAL.3/Circ.194, 22 January 2009), recognising the important of common ground between States as to the administrative procedures used in the disembarkation of persons rescued at sea, has identified a number of 'essential principles' which it is recommended that member States should incorporate into their administrative procedures for disembarking persons rescued at sea. Coordination between the SAR services of the States concerned is the first principle mentioned, to be followed by the fact that screening and status determination procedures are to be carried out after disembarkation to a place of safety. Cooperation with the State of disembarkation for return or repatriation and also, respect for international principles of protection are also listed. However, the central principle relates to the fact that all parties involved must:

...cooperate in order to ensure that disembarkation of the persons rescued is carried out swiftly, taking into account the master's preferred arrangements for disembarkation and the immediate basic needs of the rescued persons. The Government responsible for the SAR area where the persons were rescued should exercise primary responsibility for ensuring such cooperation occurs. If disembarkation from the rescuing ship cannot be arranged swiftly elsewhere, the Government responsible for the SAR area should accept the disembarkation of the persons rescued in accordance with immigration laws and regulations of each Member States into a place of safety under its control in which the persons rescued can have timely access to post rescue support.[42]

UNDERSTANDING THE AMENDMENT AND THE DUTY OF THE EUROPEAN UNION

The general obligation imposed upon States is one of coordination and cooperation. The obligation of the State in whose SAR area the assistance was given is to exercise primary responsibility for ensuring that such coordination and cooperation occurs so that disembarkation occurs and a place of safety is provided. However, this begs the question of what happens in default of agreement. The new provision may not therefore, be clear enough in its terms, as it still fails to stipulate a State of disembarkation. The amendment is rather more focussed on the duty of coordination and cooperation amongst States. To interpret the spirit of this amendment as imposing an automatic duty of disembarkation upon any one State is both irresponsible and incorrect. Unfortunately however, until—unless—the duty of cooperation is given teeth this new legal regime will not meet the aims of the drafters.

There is urgent need for a solution to this problem to be being found at the European level, especially due to the ever-increasing incidents of disputes between States, notably Malta and Italy, with regard to the rescue of irregular migrants in Malta's search and rescue area but situated close to Lampedusa.[43]

This is a situation which has been brought on by entirely licit actions—Italy, on the basis of international agreements to which it has acceded to (i.e., the amendments noted above) maintains that the rescuees are to be sent to Malta due to the fact that the rescue was effected in Malta's SAR zone. Malta, on the other hand, equally rightly, maintains that since it has not accepted this amendment (which, incidentally, it is entirely within its right not to accept) the established position applies, that is, that rescuees are to be taken to the closest safe port. This is problem engendered by conflicting regimes which must, for the sake of good international relations, State security and more importantly, safety of migrants, be settled without delay.

Apart from the IMO Conventions, there are other international agreements which aim to assist in the fight against migrant smuggling and also, migrant trafficking. These documents, primarily the Migrant Smuggling Protocol,[44] tackle this aspect of organized crime by permitting, with flag State consent, non-flag State action over vessels carrying irregular migrants on the high seas.

The Migrant Smuggling Protocol aims to fight the crime of migrant smuggling by creating a framework for legal and judicial cooperation while ensuring the protection of victims and respect for their inherent rights. The Protocol is especially interesting, not only because it recognizes that migrant smuggling requires universal criminalisation and a consequent cooperative framework for its prevention but, also because it contains a section on migrant smuggling by sea, to be found in articles 7 to 9.[45] These latter provisions are based on article 17 of the Convention against Illicit Traffic in Narcotic Drugs and Psychotropic Substances[46] and are drafted in conformity with the LOSC. The general obligation in Part II stems from the overriding duty to 'cooperate to the fullest extent possible to prevent and suppress the smuggling of migrants by sea, in accordance with the international law of the sea.'[47] However, noteworthy as this—and other—instruments are, they understandably fall short of settling the issue of disembarkation.

Relevant legal principles and practical procedures are now helpfully laid out in a document produced jointly by the IMO and UNHCR in a bid to further amplify upon the relevant obligations of the Master and the relevant coastal States so as to ensure prompt disembarkation following a rescue operation.[48] These, together with the 2004 amendments and associated Guidelines, present a hope for future resolution of disembarkation situations; a solution based on the pre-requisite of cooperation and coordination of all parties concerned, being both States and non-State actors. However, by failing to specify a particular State which is obliged to permit disembarkation and process any asylum claims made, it may be said that the refugee protection perspective and sharing of responsibilities in this regard has not been adequately catered for. Indeed, due to the fact that such protection perspective is outside the remit of the IMO as such it seems that agreements to this end would have to be concluded possibly within a regional ambit, such as that of the European Union.

One of the main aims of the EU is the establishment of an area of freedom, security and justice without internal borders guaranteeing freedom of movement to citizens of the Union and non-citizens alike. Precisely because this freedom is also guaranteed to non-citizens of the Union, '[t]his in turn requires the Union to develop common policies on asylum and immigration, while taking into account the need for a consistent control of external borders to stop illegal immigration and to combat those who organize it and commit related international crimes.'[49] The fight against illegal immigration in the EU sphere is thus firmly rooted in the development of a common and comprehensive asylum and immigration policy. The European Union has produced a vast amount of documents and policy papers over the years, however, a number of Member States, notably, Malta, Italy, Spain and Greece, feel that the EU must be more pro-active and attentive to their immediate needs. To this end, the recently-unveiled EU pilot burden-sharing project offers a step—even if minimal—in this direction.[50]

CONCLUSION

As mentioned at the outset, irregular immigration presents a conceptual challenge to any State: security interests and the sovereign right of a State to control access to its territory come face to face with fundamental principles of protection. Individuals will always seek to leave their own countries and enter States in an irregular manner, be they persons who are attempting to flee conflict, persecution, or natural disasters as well as those seeking to circumvent migration and border controls, often in order to improve their economic circumstances. Some States are harder-hit than others, and Malta has been harder-hit than most, being the southern-most border of the European Union.

Malta's failure to accede to the IMO amendments of 2004 has been discussed above and its stance is understandable. Unless and until the duty of cooperation is given a firm and concrete application in International Law, Malta cannot be expected to accede to a rule that cannot be sustained with its present resources while letting other countries off the hook through its hardship. On the other hand, what is being considered are *persons* on the move—persons with human rights and who travel in the poorest and most dangerous of conditions. A solution must be reached, and this solution cannot be reached by one State alone, nor can one State alone be burdened with the 'solution.' And so we return to the crux of the matter—the duty of cooperation and coordination.

A number of examples of material cooperation exist in international law (to name but a few: the bilateral ship rider agreements concluded between the US and various Caribbean States and the so-called Aruba Agreement[51] in the field of maritime drug smuggling; ship boarding arrangements in the context of the Proliferation Security Initiative,[52] the enforcement jurisdiction mechanisms laid out in the Convention for the Suppression of Unlawful Acts against the Safety of Maritime Navigation and lastly, the recent initiatives taken by the IMO and the UNSC in the field of piracy and armed robbery off the coast of Somalia).

In this respect, Malta's calls for burden-sharing are commendable as they embody the materialization of the recent approach focussing on cooperation in international law. This cannot be the only route however. The duty of cooperation goes beyond the duty of good faith but it is a distinct and independent legal obligation with a specific legal content. It is augured that the European Union will forge ahead in this journey, catalysing concrete application to the duty of cooperation amongst its Member States.

Notes

1. A useful selection of documents is as follows: UNHCR, 'Refugee Protection and Migration Control: Perspectives from UNHCR and IOM' Global Consultations on International Protection (31 May 2001) EC/GC/01/11; For general information on migrant smuggling definitions see: A Schloenhardt, *Migrant Smuggling: Human Trafficking and Organized Crime in Australia and the Asia Pacific Region* (Martinus Nijhoff, The Netherlands 2003) Chapter 1; JE Lake, WH Robinson, LM Seghetti, 'The Complexity of the Challenge' (29 March 2005) CRS Report for Congress, Border and Transportation Security; J van Selm and B Cooper, 'The New Boat People: Ensuring Safety and Determining Status' (MPI, Report) (January 2006) 59; S Ginsburg, 'Countering Terrorist Mobility: Shaping an Operational Strategy February' (February 2006) Migration Policy Institute Report.

2. The situation relating to Malta is indeed dire: in 2008, for the first time, the number of immigrant arrivals exceeded the local birth rate.

3. This contribution takes into consideration events occurring up to September 2009.

4. Note that most irregular migrant arrivals are smuggled migrants.

5. UNHCR, 'Refugee Protection and Migration Control: Perspectives from UNHCR and IOM.' Global Consultations on International Protection (31 May 2001) EC/GC/01/1, paragraph 2. See also: UNHCR, 'Interception of Asylum-Seekers and Refugees: The International Framework and Recommendations for a Comprehensive Approach' (9 June 2000) EC/50/SC/CRP/17, paragraph 2.

6. Montego Bay, 10 December 1982, entered into force 16 November 1994, 1833 UNTS 3; 21 ILM 1261.

7. See LOSC articles 2(1)(2), 3. Note that this sovereignty extends also to the air space overlying the territorial sea.

8. LOSC articles 17, 18.

9. LOSC Article 19.

10. Commission Staff Working Document Commission (EC) 'Study on the International Law Instruments in Relation to Illegal Immigration by Sea' (Staff Working Document) SEC (2007) 691, 15 May 2007, 691, paragraphs 2.1.2-2.1.4.

11. It is interesting that the high seas are not geographically defined; rather, article 86 describes the high seas as 'all parts of the sea that are not included in the exclusive economic zone, in the territorial sea or in the internal waters of a State, or in the archipelagic waters of an archipelagic State.' Note that the EEZ in not relevant for immediate purposes save insofar as the high seas regime (articles 88—115 LOSC) is made applicable to this zone by article 58(2) LOSC.

12. These freedoms are laid out in a non-exhaustive list in article 87 LOSC and include, for example, the freedoms of navigation, over-flight, fishing and scientific research.

13. It should be noted that the right of 'hot pursuit' and the notion of 'constructive presence' also provide for increased activity on the high seas. See LOSC article 111.

14. Vienna, 10 March 1988, entered into force 1 March 1992, 27 ILM 668; 1678 UNTS 201.

15. Protocol against the Smuggling of Migrants by Land, Sea and Air, Supplementing the United Nations Convention against Transnational Organised Crime (Palermo, 15 November 2000, entered into force 28 January 2004) 40 ILM 384 (Migrant Smuggling Protocol).

16. Hamburg, 27 April 1979, entered into force 22 June 1985, 1405 UNTS 97.

17. Chapter 1, paragraph 1.3.4.

18. Chapter 1, paragraph 1.3.5.

19. Paragraph 3.1.1.

20. Paragraph 3.1.2.

21. This guarantee of protection does not refer solely to 'declared' refugees. In this way, *non refoulement* obligations fall upon a State once an asylum claim is made, irrespective of whether the person seeking asylum has been declared a refugee or not. See in this regard: UNHCR, *Handbook on Procedures and Criteria for Determining Refugee Status under the 1951 Convention and 1967 Protocol relating to the Status of Refugees* HCR/IP/4/Eng/REV.1 (UNHCR 1979; re-edited, Geneva, January 1992) paragraph 28; EXCOM Conclusions: No. 6 (XXVIII)—1977 paragraph (c); No. 79 (XLVII)—1996, paragraph (j); No. 81 (XLVIII)—1997, paragraph (j); UNGA Resolutions: UNGA, A/RES/52/103 (9

February 1998) paragraph 5; UNGA A/RES/53/125 (12 February 1999) paragraph 5; UNGA A/RES/55/74 (12 February 2001) paragraphs 6, 10; G Gilbert, 'Is Europe living up to its Obligations to Refugees?' (2004) 15 EJIL 5, 966.

22. See for example, the Human Rights Watch report 'Pushed back, Pushed Around' (2009). Available at: http://www.hrw.org/sites/default/files/reports/italy0909web_0.pdf.

23. Regarding the prohibition of 'chain *refoulement*' (i.e. causing a person to return to another place from which *refoulement* occurs) see P Mathew, 'Legal Issues concerning Interception' IARLJ Conference 2002, 95.

24. UNHCR, 'Background Note on the Protection of Asylum Seekers and Refugees Rescued at Sea' (18 March 2002) paragraphs 23-24, (final version as discussed at the expert roundtable *Rescue-at-Sea: Specific Aspects Relating to the Protection of Asylum-Seekers and Refugees,* held in Lisbon, Portugal on 25-26 March 2002). See further: TA Aleinikoff and V Chetail (eds), *Migration and International Legal Norms* (The Hague, TMC Asser Press, 2003) 143-144.

25. A Brouwer and J Kumin, 'Interception and Asylum: When Migration Control and Human Rights Collide' (2003) 21 Refuge 4, 11.

26. UNHCR, 'Background Note on the Protection of Asylum Seekers and Refugees Rescued at Sea' (18 March 2002) paragraph 18, (final version as discussed at the expert roundtable *Rescue-at-Sea: Specific Aspects Relating to the Protection of Asylum-Seekers and Refugees,* held in Lisbon, Portugal on 25-26 March 2002) paragraph 26 states in this regard that 'the responsibility [for admitting asylum-seekers] accruing to the flag State would be stronger still, where the rescue operation occurs in the context of interception measures.'

27. This duty is also provided for in other international instruments such as: Salvage Convention 1910; SOLAS 1925; HSC 1958; SOLAS 1960; SOLAS 1974; SAR 1979, Annex; Salvage Convention 1989. Note also the ILC's view that this duty is also part of general international law: UN Doc A/3179 (1956) regarding the proposed draft of Article 12 of the 1958 HSC. See also R Barnes, 'Refugee Law at Sea' (January 2004) 53 ICLQ 1, 49.

28. LOSC Article 98(1).

29. LOSC Article 98(2).

30. 2 Refugees 21 (February 1984) cited in LB Sohn and JE Noyes, *Cases and Materials on the Law of the Sea* (Transnational Publishers, New York, 2004) 98.

31. Generally, the rescuing ship cannot be considered to be a 'place of safety.'

32. 'Italian frigate takes migrants to Sicily after Malta refusal' *The Times* (Malta, 11 May 2009); 'Malta insists it is not responsible for all migrants in its search area' *The Times* (Malta, 27 May 2009). Available at: www.timesofmalta.com.

33. London, 1 November 1974, entered into force 1 May 1991, 1184 UNTS 3; 14 ILM 959.

34. FAL 30/9 (24 October 2002) paragraph 9.

35. COMSAR 6/22 (8 March 2002). See also: MSC 75/11/2 (11 March 2002) paragraph 7.

36. MSC.167(78).

37. FAL 32/22 (25 July 2005). An amendment to the FAL Convention relating to persons rescued at sea was also adopted to be included in Section 2—Arrival, Stay and Departure of the ship. This amendment requires public authorities to facilitate the arrival and departure of ships engaged in the rescue of persons in distress at sea in order to provide a place of safety for such persons. (See FAL 31/9/Add.1 (25 March 2004) for text of amendments).

38. *Ibid* paragraph 1.1.

39. Guidelines, paragraphs 2.4-2.5.

40. A synonymous provision exists in the SAR Convention placing this obligation on Contracting Parties to the Convention. See Annex, paragraph 3.1.9.

41. MSC 78/26 (28 May 2004) paragraphs 16.48-16.54.

42. FAL Circular, para 2.3.

43. In February 2009, Italy and Libya concluded a Friendship, Partnership and Cooperation Treaty with Libya and in May 2009, Italy began a process of interdicting vessels at sea and returning the migrants thereon to Libya without any granting any possibility screening for potential asylum claims. Although this approach led to a decrease in the numbers of migrants undertaking the hazardous voyage across the seas, these push-backs prompted

widespread criticism as a clear violation of international law, and more specifically, of the *non refoulement* obligation.

44. This Protocol supplements the United Nations Convention on Transnational Organised Crime (Palermo, 15 November 2000, entered into force 29 September 2000) 40 ILM (2001) 335 (CATOC). A very useful guide to the interpretation of the Migrant Smuggling Protocol is UNGA 'Report of the Ad Hoc Committee on the Elaboration of a Convention against Transnational Organized Crime on the work of its first to eleventh sessions, Addendum: Interpretative Notes for the official records (*travaux preparatoires*) of the negotiation of the United Nations Convention against Transnational Organized Crime and the Protocols thereto' (3 November 2000) A/55/383/Add.1.

45. Note especially article 8 which contains provisions on the particular measures that can be taken.

46. Vienna, 20 December 1988, entered into force 11 November 1990, UN Doc E/CONF.82/15; 28 ILM 493.

47. Article 7.

48. IMO and UNHCR, 'Rescue at Sea: A Guide to Principles and Practice as applied to Migrants and Refugees' (2006). This document has no legal force; it is merely intended as a useful reference guide in which all provisions from the various relevant international instruments are laid out, thus providing a central source of reference for obligations and definitions in international maritime and refugee law in the context of rescue at sea.

49. Tampere European Council, 15-16 October 1999, Presidency Conclusions, point 3.

50. See I Camilleri, 'EU pilot burden sharing project' *The Times,* (Malta, 5 June 2009); I Camilleri and C Busuttil, 'Resettlement offers total just 100 migrants' *The Times*, (Malta, 23 September 2009).

51. Agreement concerning cooperation in Suppressing Illicit Maritime and Air Trafficking in Narcotic Drugs and Psychotropic Substances in the Caribbean Area (San Jose, Costa Rica, 10 April 2003, not yet in force) Available at: http://www.state. gov/s/l/2005/87198.htm.

52. See for example: Agreement between the Government of the United States of America and the Government of Malta concern-

ing cooperation to Suppress the Proliferation of Weapons of Mass Destruction, their Delivery Systems, and Related Materials by Sea (Washington, 15 March 2007, entered into force 19 December 2007). Available at: http://www.state.gov/t/isn/trty/81883.htm. The text of other similar agreements are to be found at: http://www.state.gov/t/isn/c27733.htm.

Chapter 10

—◆—

MIGRATION, DEVELOPMENT
AND POLICY COHERENCE IN THE
MEDITERRANEAN REGION
— Ivan Ureta —

Migration has written the history of humanity. Social, political and economic development and growth couldn't have happened without this exchange of ideas, people and financial resources (De Lucia, 2006; Moch, 1995). All the great moments of humankind's history correspond to population movements from peripheral areas to central areas of intellectual, artistic, commercial, political and economic power. These 'crowded places,' these 'melting pots,' provided, and still provide, an essential and valuable force in terms of creativity, competition and entrepreneurship. However, despite the evidences, migration issues have become a major topic worldwide given the wide array of problems attached to this multifaceted phenomenon, although, beyond this complexity, there is a common denominator: human beings. Max Frisch said of the period in which Switzerland needed hands to shore up its economic growth during the '60s, "[they] were summoned as workers but came as human beings" (Coulson 1998:155).

Behind figures, statistics, charts and forecasts, we are 'dealing' with human beings not with numbers. It is easier, however, to manage social problems after deleting and expunging names and biographies. To elaborate on this, it would be illuminating to quote Finkielkraut (2001; 5) who wrote:

> To accept the idea that all people in the world form a single humanity is not, it is true...What distinguishes mankind from most other animals is precisely the fact that he does not identify with others of his kind. A cat for a cat has always been another cat. A man on the other hand must fulfil a set of Draconian conditions.

In fact, Finkielkraut points out Levi Strauss's observation on the 'inclusive humanity' concept, which appeared very late in the literature (Levi Strauss, 1983; 329). It seems like a paradox, but The Universal Declaration of Human Rights in article number 13/2 expresses that "everyone has the right to leave any country, including his own, and to return to his country." As Ban Ki-moon said during the 60th anniversary of the declaration, "[the] Declaration was the first global statement of what we now take for granted—the inherent dignity and equality of all human beings" Since 1948, the world has changed enormously and, despite the universality of these principles, Some consider them good for generating political influence. Still, the prevalence of the French saying *"deux poids, deux measures"* and the distinction between sameness and otherness (Bauman, 2001) rule the way human migration issues are treated.

Today, the Mediterranean region is witnessing some developments dealing with humanitarian problems, economic inequality and injustice. The Mediterranean area has played a leading role in the cultural evolution of the Western world. Over the centuries, the Mediterranean has been a cultural, social, economic, and religious vehicle for the communities living on its shores. However, the deep-seated differences between countries and cultures have also been at the origin of great tensions and conflicts. The European Commission reports the difference in income between Europe and the Mediterranean countries was

1:12 in 1999 and will increase to 1:20 in 2010 if no measures are taken to support the economic development of our partners, whose population of 220 million in 1995 will exceed 300 million in 2010 (Mold, 2007). In addition, it seems likely that environmental immigration could become one of the most important problems, which European governments should face by 2020 (Solana and Ferrero-Waldner 2008). Thus, it is likely that the Euro-Mediterranean region will continue to be a problematic area due to human mobility. Given the precedent scenarios, it is necessary to point out that the current global economy and international flows of information are not controlled by states. Given the current importance of migration and mobility, the 2009 Human Development Report has been dedicated to this theme. It will surely lead public debate over a great number of approaches for decades to come.

An Overview on Migration Processes and Theories

Nobody knows how many migrants are in the world. According to U.N. estimations, at the beginning of the 90s, there were between 120-130 million international migrants and refugees (Assogba, 1995) compared to 70 million at the beginning of the 60's. Nowadays, the proportion of international migrants and refugees is about three percent of the world's population, or, according to UN estimations (2007), roughly 200 million displaced persons worldwide. Most migration remains internal. International migrants are almost a quarter the number of internal migrants (+/- 740 million) and less than 30 percent of international migrants go from developing to developed economies. For example, only 3 percent of African migrants live beyond their countries (UNHDR, 2009).

These nuances are not explained and presented to the public opinion in OECD countries. On the contrary, migration is seen and used by political forces, not always by parties linked to extremist, right-wing positions, as a very important argument to profit (Castles and Miller, 2003: 36; Santamaria, 2002; Ureta

2009). In more industrialized countries, given these misconceptions, public opinion overwhelmingly subscribes to the idea that migration is triggered by extreme poverty. This fact can cause compassion and sympathy when immigration is not a strongly present event. This initial compassion drastically diminishes as soon as 'visible migrants' living close to a population. Using Bauman's language (Bauman, 2005), these perceptions change from the *mixophilia* to the *mixophobia*.

Commonly, public opinion is easily influenced with simplistic cause and effect explanations. Infrequently, average citizens question the accuracy of the information they receive. More often, they accept poverty as the primary reason. This leads to ideas like "these people escaping from their homelands will take our jobs and will jeopardize our welfare system and cultural identity." These views belong to a determined belief system attached to romantic sentiments regarding old notions of the nation state (Castles and Miller, 2003). They do not belong to the 'reality' of a globalized environment (Castells, 1997).

We must note that it is not the poorest people of a society who do the majority of migrating (Skeldon, 2003). According to the Global Commission on International Migration (2005; 5), "Migrants have often been amongst the most dynamic and entrepreneurial members of society, people who are prepared to venture beyond the confines of their own community and country in order to create new opportunities for themselves and their children." Nevertheless, it is very difficult to trace a universal taxonomy for migrants since many evident and 'blurry' factors play important roles in defining migratory projects.

Although not the purpose of this paper, it would be interesting to do a summary survey on the main theories dealing with migration issues, even though a comprehensive critical study has already been done by Douglass Massey, et. al. (2000). It is necessary to say that there is not a common and accepted framework to study migration as a unified discipline (Massey et. al., 1994 and Massey et. al. 1993). In spite of that lack, there are four main groups of theories. First, there are economic theories, then, the historical-structural approaches, third, the migration systems theory and, finally, the transnational theory (Castles and Miller, 2003).

The first group of theories generally say that, according to available scientific literature, quality of life is a major driving factor to push individuals beyond their regional or national boundaries (Pei-Shan, 2001; Basu, 1992; De Jong and Fawcett, 1981; Varady, 1983). Accordingly, individuals would act on push-pull factors and guided by their autonomous decision, which follows a cost-benefit analysis. Therefore, the decision to migrate seems to be a rational choice (Castles and Miller, 2003: 22). However, revisionist economists like Amartya Sen, in showing his opposition to the neo-classical economic doctrines, described how the theory of rational choice has radical restrictions (Sen, 1977).

Moreover, it is possible to find an additional obstacle regarding this group of theories, as far as quality of life (Sen and Nussbaum, 1993) can be analysed as an objective-subjective factor. Brock (1993: 98) wrote, "The question of whether accounts of a good life are objective or subjective is, then, an explicitly normative issue about what is the correct or most justified substantive theory of a good life."

It is difficult to deny that this group of theories contributes to the understanding of migratory processes. The complexity of the phenomenon, being wider, requires some other explanatory patterns. Partially contrary to the first theories, the historical-structural approach, which has been developed since the 70s, stresses theoretical fundamentals using elements of Marxist political-economic theory where asymmetrical relationships constitute a central part. Authors like Saskia Sassen highlight the fact that the combination of objective elements such as poverty or distortions in the local labor market, combined with emerging ideological stimulus would induct migratory processes (Sassen, 1988: 9). This ideological stimulus relates to the presence of FDI (ODA as well), which need an increasingly need a cheap labor force. As Castles and Miller (2003: 25) explain, migration has been seen as a method of mobilizing cheap labor force and to maintain privileged positions of control over less developed countries (Cohen, 1987). Although this historical-structural approach also has some possible difficulties, mainly in terms of generalising migratory processes, it may still be acceptable to explain some migratory processes.

Thirdly, by accepting the complexity of international migration, the migration systems theory offers an interdisciplinary approach, highlighting the importance of cultural, economic or even political links between sending, transit and destination countries. This theory is partially illuminating because it explains how migratory flows are affected by the interaction of three specific realms or structures which operate at macro, micro and meso levels. This interaction functions by intertwining formal, informal and 'facilitating' factors like the political economy, law, interstate relationships, social networks (Boyd, 1989) and the 'migration industry.' This theory has been reshaped in part by Jennissen (2007) introducing four factors (economic, social, political and 'linkages') that work as causality chains within the frame of the international migration system.

Finally, the transnational theory has the elements to become one of the most important theoretical approaches to understanding migration related issues, but mainly explaining current and future human mobility based on the deterritorialization of nation states (Basch et.al., 1994). This mobility, this new interpretation of space, time and territory brings with it the concept of 'transmigrant' (Glick-Schiller, 1999) and the transnational model of citizenship (Castles and Miller, 2003: 45). Obviously, this theory has an implicit risk: challenging traditional, national identities based on strong systems of collective beliefs. Although these transnational communities can have an institutional form like the multinationals operating worldwide, they can adopt the form of more or less formal communities of transmigrants: transnational communities which are connected with communities based on countries of origin, promoting social movement and developing a certain kind of power.

After this survey, it is important to check, observing current political and economical facts, how these theories affect the present and future of international migration in terms of policy making, development policies and, most important, policy coherence among partners sharing the same region: the Mediterranean.

THE MEDITERRANEAN: SPACE FOR COMMUNICATION AND EXCHANGE FROM 1995 TO 2005

The Mediterranean area recovered prominence after the second world war, especially after the Rome treaty. Since then, the region has become an area of political experimentation based on multi and unilateral interests. Economic reasons justified the creation of the European Union. These economic reasons then established the ground for successive political initiatives. It is necessary to note that without sharing this economic, or economist, vision, the European Union would not have had its *raison d'être*. This point is important to understand how international politics evolved until 1995 and from then onwards.

As Calleya (2004: 2) stressed, "the growth of regional arrangements since the end of the Cold War is partly due to the fact that great powers and regional powers welcome the opportunity to participate in collective security and cooperative frameworks in which the costs of foreign policy actions are shared among several actors." Within this trend and wave of optimism (Schumacher, 2004, 89; Rudolph, C. 2003: 603), several groups formed: the 5+5 initiative, the Council of the Mediterranean launched by the Maltese government, the Mediterranean Forum initiated by the Egyptian Government, the Italian-Spanish proposal to flesh out a Conference for Security and Cooperation in the Mediterranean (CSCM), the Arab Maghreb Union (AMU, 1989) and, finally, the Euro-Mediterranean Partnership led in 1995 by the European Union (Calleya, 2004: 4).

The Barcelona Process, or European Mediterranean Partnership was created with the goals of breathing new life into the unifying aspect of the Mediterranean, boosting democratic involvement, upholding human rights and safeguarding regional security. Regional initiatives and multilateralism were also encouraged in an attempt to overcome the traditional bilateralism which had characterised the region until then. Arguably, the Barcelona conference was inspired by a desire to promote interaction and cooperation in the Mediterranean. The need arose to strengthen the political dialogue by drafting a treaty in which the economic and financial component would integrate social, cultural and human components. Since the beginning, there were some pessimistic voices, like Bichara Khader's, quoted by Sonia Felipe (2005) claiming possible failures of the Barcelona Process, "this Summit will not disembark on any concrete agreement, although it will give a place to certain means that assure the continuity of the Barcelona Process in itself."

Despite it all, and recapping slightly, the philosophy behind the Barcelona Process may be said to encompass three issues: politics and security, economic and financial issues and social, cultural and human aspects.

The first issue, security is a fundamental issue, which can actually determine the operative scope of the second and third ones. This discourse on security finds very fertile ground in the current economic system based on trading states as Rudolph (2003; 603) stated, "power is increasingly based on Ricardian notions of comparative advantage, factor mobility and free trade" (Rosecrance 1986). In addition, economically speaking, the free trade area will, by 2010, be the most ambitious objective (Miller and Mishrif, M, 2005).

Nevertheless, these first three issues do not consider the migratory issue as a fundamental process regarding the stability of the whole Mediterranean area. These first moments of general optimism and mutual trust probably contributed to later, negative international migration issues.

Over the next five years the international situation changed and migration and security issues demanded increasing attention (1999-2004). During the session of the European Council at Tampere (15–16 October 1999), four main intertwined factors were revealed as critical for the future of the Euro-Mediterranean region: 1) a common EU asylum and migration policy, 2) a genuine European area of justice, 3) a union-wide fight against crime, and 4) stronger external action (European Parliament, 1999). As for migratory issues, the fourth pack of measures highlighted the importance of managing migratory flows, especially points 22, 23 and 24 (European Parliament, 1999):

22. The European Council stresses the need for more efficient management of migration flows at all their stages. It calls for the development, in close co-operation with countries of origin and transit, of information campaigns on the actual possibilities for legal immigration, and for the prevention of all forms of trafficking in human beings. A common active policy on visas and false documents should be further developed, including closer co-operation between EU consulates in third countries and, where necessary, the establishment of common EU visa issuing offices.

23. The European Council is determined to tackle at its source illegal immigration, especially by combating those who engage in trafficking in human beings and economic exploitation of migrants. It urges the adoption of legislation foreseeing severe sanctions against this serious crime. The Council is invited to adopt by the end of 2000, on the basis of a proposal by the Commission, legislation to this end. Member States, together with Europol, should direct their efforts to detecting and dismantling the criminal networks involved. The rights of the victims of such activities shall be secured with special emphasis on the problems of women and children.

24. The European Council calls for closer co-operation and mutual technical assistance between the Member States' border control services, such as exchange programmes and technology transfer, especially on maritime borders, and for the rapid inclusion of the applicant States in this co-operation. In this context, the Council welcomes the memorandum of understanding between Italy and Greece to enhance co-operation between the two countries in the Adriatic and Ionian seas in combating organized crime, smuggling and trafficking of persons.

By reading these three paragraphs, it is possible to detect when, at the level of the European Union, migratory issues started to shift from the domain of 'low' politics to the realm of 'high politics.' After Tampere, these policies acquired full significance and 'justification' after the attacks of 9/11 occurred. The precedent multilateralism based on optimism and a multicultural approach, changed slightly, returning to precedent models of bilateral proximity (Thieux, 2005). This probably blocked consolidation of the Barcelona process because the achievement of such results requires concerted policies of cooperation and non competition.

In 2003, the European Neighbourhood Policy (ENP) was created in parallel with the Barcelona Partnership, generating not only expectations, but also uncertainties. The internal consistency of this Mediterranean project has much to do with the consistency of the interaction between previous policies of this area: NATO's Mediterranean dialogue, the '5+5' and also the initiative known as *Broader Middle East and North Africa (BMENA)* or, again, the Free Trade Area (FTA) planned for 2010.

The Hague Program (2004-2009) gave continuity to the points established in Tampere, describing a master plan divided into 10 points. Four out of these points relate to migratory issues. This means that international migration debate reached its height. Adding to this, on October 3, 2005 FRONTEX (European Agency for the Management of Operational Cooperation at the External Borders of the Member States of the European Union) became operational.

During 2005, the Barcelona Summit reviewed the results achieved since 1995 in terms of economic and financial cooperation. All the association treaties with Algeria, Morocco, Tunisia, Israel, Jordan, Egypt, and Lebanon were operational. The ones with Syria and Palestine were in the final stages, and Cyprus and Malta joined the EU. The Barcelona negotiations basically focused on farming trade, migration and social affairs.

Clearly, the development of social events in the Mediterranean migratory context is a source of serious concern. Only fairly recently did the debate shift and focus on migration and development.

The dialogue stemmed quite naturally from the events of the past few years. Special emphasis was placed on political and economic reforms rather than on social, cultural and intercultural communication reforms. Thus, after more than 10 years of effort, the economic gap between the EU and its Mediterranean neighbors has three critical characteristics: (1) it appears to be one of the most marked, (2) has widened, and (3) is causing virtually uncontrollable migratory movements.

The Anna Lindh Foundation for dialogue between cultures started in 2005, with the expressed goal of mitigating such effects. This represents a step forward in the development of cultural exchange in the Mediterranean region. Then, in 2004, Euromed, a non-governmental platform, was created by civil society, to bring together non-governmental organisations in the Mediterranean area. The risk exists, however, that these demonstrations in favour of culture and intercultural communication will spawn a language of their own—a sort of *culturalist* jargon, scarcely compatible with the equally necessary reforms in the economy.

Critically, we note that the objectives of the Euro-Mediterranean partnership scarcely materialised. This is plainly shown by the three points listed above and one of the main reasons could be related to the study of migratory phenomenon as a consequence, not studying the deep, interlinked causes. Therefore, migration represents a necessary indicator of the effectiveness of a political project, at any level, through a simple attractiveness/effectiveness analysis.

MIGRATION AND PUBLIC OPINION

As explained earlier, migratory political dialogue started to be more present in governmental agendas from 1999 onwards. This presence has had a clear impact on Europeans' public opinion regarding this issue. Using data published by the Eurobarometer, I constructed a multivariable quantitative analysis to understand to what extent the increasing political measures regarding migration-related issues had on Europeans' opinions (Ureta, 2009). Although the original research looked for correlations or discontinuities among five variables (terrorism, security, migration, crime and employment), the graphic below shows how the migratory issue evolved from 1999 to 2007 (and 2008).

GRAPHIC 1. MIGRATION AND PUBLIC OPINON, EUROPE

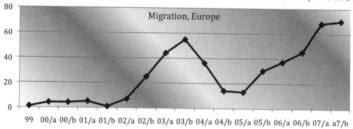

Source: Eurobarometer. Elaborated by the author.

It is evident that migratory related issues started to be a main driving factor from 2002 onwards, but they specially peaked in 2006-2007. This is just a snapshot of Europe in general, however, by examining individualized studies in really stressed countries like Spain, Italy or Malta, the evolution appears much more evident and consistent. What is clear from this point of view is that migration started to be seriously discussed from 2006 onwards.

GRAPHIC 2. MIGRATION AND PUBLIC OPINION, SPAIN

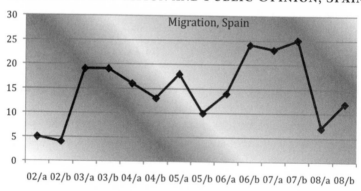

Source: Eurobarometer. Elaborated by the author.

GRAPHIC 3. MIGRATION AND PUBLIC OPINION, ITALY

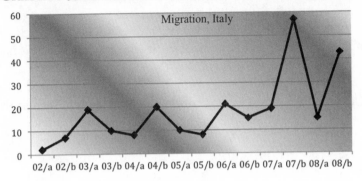

Source: Eurobarometer. Elaborated by the author.

GRAPHIC 4. MIGRATION AND PUBLIC OPINION, MALTA

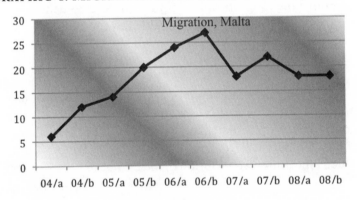

Source: Eurobarometer. Elaborated by the author.

Together with this increasing debate on migration issues, scholars and politicians began discussing another complex concept, 'Migration and Development,' at the beginning of the new century.

As Hein de Haas has pointed out (2007), the academic dialogue on this interdisciplinary and crucial topic has tended to swing back and forth like a pendulum, moving from developmentalist optimism in the '50s and '60s, to a structuralist and neo-Marxist pessimism and scepticism over the next two decades, on to the nineties when scepticism became absolutely rooted. On the other hand, from 2001 and onwards, a new wave carrying a growing number of publications regarding migration and development generated an optimistic spirit within both academic and non-academic realms.

Concerning its exact scope and meaning, in 2001, the Danish Ministry of Foreign Affairs, commissioned a study related to the present and potential links between migration and development (Nyberg-Sorensen, Van Hear, Engberg-Pedersen, 2002). One year later, in January 2002, the new Danish government announced a decision to enhance and empower links between its aid and refugee policies as part of the overall focus on poverty alleviation.

So, as recognised by the European Parliament, "countries and international organisations increasingly perceive migration as a phenomenon whose positive impacts in development nexus is one of the central issues being examined by the Global Commission on International Migration (GCIM)" (2005). As a consequence, we can point to a wide array of international conferences regarding this problem: the July 2006, Euro African Conference in Rabat (its continuation was actually developed at the General Assembly of the United Nations), the Global Forum on Migration and Development held in Brussels (2007) or the elaboration of the Comprehensive European Migration Policy (CEMP), which represented a conclusion of the European Council (2007).

Some other top-level discussions took place both at the United Nations (September 2006) and at the EU Council (October 2006). Both drew attention to the relationship between remittances and economic growth in the country of origin, regarding a policy of integration in its several forms. As a result, a new sphere of action opens up, which, in order to avoid useless voluntarism, must be planned rationally and responsibly to pursue a concrete objective in the short, medium and long terms.

The question is how all these political intentions and developed, scholarly debates find a common path to improve the overall situation based on principles of action in policy coherence and cooperative methods.

YES, AID—BUT...

International aid and cooperation policies amongst more developed countries and less developed countries have played a strategic role on inter-state relationships during the second half of the twentieth century and, more intensively, during the past three decades. Economic, political, social and moral concerns were also main justifications for states to commit to crusades against poverty, inequality and injustices throughout the world. However, after decades of international aid, and despite some achievements, the current situation is not very positive.

Concerning the African situation, Riddell (1987, 1999 and 2007) presents six challenges regarding conventional donor views. First, the amounts of aid provided to Africa are not based on Africa's poverty needs and the gap between aid needs and the aid provided is widening. Second, donor commitments to poverty reduction in Africa are not new; they are severely weakened by divisions among donors and large gaps remain between the rhetoric of support for poverty alleviation and the reality of sectorial aid allocations. Third, there are serious doubts about whether the development model within which aid funds are located can 'deliver' the growth and employment generation required. Fourth, though donors have given increasing prominence to aid which reaches the poor directly, there are doubts about the scale and effectiveness of such aid. Fifth, the growing emphasis donors place on the results and effectiveness of aid risks shifting aid towards the less poor. Sixth, aid donors have recently tended to place less emphasis on politics, self-interested elites and asset distribution in helping to solve Africa's poverty problems

Thus, the fifteenth Annual Human Development Report (2005) was titled "International Cooperation at a Crossroads; Aid, Trade and Security in an Unequal World" As recognised by the authors of this document, "human development is faltering in some key areas, and already deep inequalities are widening" (2005:2). Although, since the 1990s, there has been a consensus concerning development, "unfortunately, the consensus has yet to give rise to practical actions--and there are ominous signs for the decade ahead. There is a real danger that the next 10 years, like the last 15 years, will deliver less for human development than the new consensus promises" (2005:3).

Continuing the UN's position, "international aid is one of the most effective weapons in the war against poverty. Today, that weapon is underused, inefficiently targeted and in need of repair. Reforming the international aid system is a fundamental requirement for getting back on the track for the MDGs" Consequently, the UN describes three conditions to provide effective aid (2005:7):

- It has to be delivered in sufficient quantity to support human development. Aid provides governments with a resource for making the multiple investments in health, education and economic infrastructure needed to break cycles of deprivation and support economic recovery.
- Aid has to be delivered on a predictable, low transaction cost, value-for-money basis.
- Effective aid requires *country ownership*. Developing countries have primary responsibility for creating the conditions under which aid will yield optimal results.

Within this realm, we observe that the great increase of international aid coincides with the boom of international migrations and with worldwide globalization processes. In a way, international aid policies have to deal with these social, political, economic and even new cultural transformations and social changes as well.

As a result of the precedent scenario, international migration flows have reconfigured conventional approaches on local and even national development, given that remittances are playing an important role. This fact has been appreciated by multilateral agencies, governments and NGOs, but we must note that there are correlated problems along with this fact: diasporas, circular migration, brain circulation and brain drain. Of course, in this plight, contemporary manifestations have been developed, for example, the UN Development Millennium Goals.

Migration and development is a concept fundamentally related to an economicist approach where remittances are the main engine to stimulate development. Quoting Ratha (2003), worker remittances have emerged as a major source of external development finance in recent years and this approach is not explicative of socio-economic problems (Kachani, 2005). By linking migration and development exclusively to remittances flows, developmental issues are constrained to financial and monetary restrictions or access and a static, deterministic *ethos*. Thus, officially recorded remittances received by developing countries exceeded USD 126 billion in 2004, but we have to observe that the actual size of remittances, including both officially recorded and unrecorded transfers throughout informal channels, was larger. For example, according to the World Migration Report released by the IOM (2005:269), "in 36 out of 153 developing countries, remittances are larger than all capital flows, public and private. In many countries, they are larger than their earnings from the most important export item."

Following this argumentative thread, current beliefs concerning migration and development assume that the links between these two correlated aspects offer a significant potential for furthering development goals. Obviously, migration and development is not an isolated issue. It is intimately related with official development policies. Therefore, there is a huge international movement which believes that this fact is absolutely relevant for future collateral aspects: international relations, fights against poverty or security.

The precedent scenario allows us to now reflect on an important issue regarding the future of international relations between European countries and the Maghreb. As pointed out by Kofi Annan (UNHLD, 2006):

> International migration constitutes an ideal means of promoting co-development, that is, the coordinated or concerted improvement of economic conditions in both areas of origin and areas of destination based on the complementarities between them....Countries can cooperate to create triple wins, for migrants,

for their countries of origin and for the societies that receive them. (The) potential benefits [of international migration] are larger than the potential gains from freer international trade.

Thus, co-development should pursue a non-zero-sum game. Analysing current migration policies and the economic environment, it is unlikely that these intentions and theoretical perspectives will be a means to an end, however.

REINFORCING OUR PALISADES: INTENTIONS vs. POLICY COHERENCE

The European Union is the main aid donor, representing 56 percent of the world's total, which means 47.6 billion euro in 2007. According to the EU's forecasts, this aid would rise to 66 billion euro by 2010 and to 90 billion euro by 2015 (European Commission, 2007). Spain, a main party in current Euro-Mediterranean politics seems to follow this path. By 2007, Spanish aid reached an ODA/GNI ratio of almost 0.41 percent. Authorities expect this number to grow to an ODA/GNI ratio of 0.72 percent by 2012. Conversely, despite this evidence, the Spanish model of aid giving should concentrate more on qualitative factors rather than quantitative figures (Tezanos, 2008). Spanish aid is still politically oriented and conditioned by two main issues: commercial interests and migration related issues.

This brings us to the question of what this trend signifies. It may represent a noble commitment to help less prosperous countries, or it implies renewed examples of servitude and dependence.

The paper started with a brief overview on migration theories, and presented four main models. What seems likely is that academic efforts aiming to reach a higher understanding on migration issues do not have huge repercussions on policy-making processes. The first and second group of theories (economic theories and the historical-structural approach) are much more understandable to the larger majority. That is because their arguments are very close to a cause-and-effect or action/reaction explanatory model. For political communication, it is important to correctly use these mechanisms and take advantage of them in order to reach a higher consensus. Using these predominant thoughts, traditional views say that improving socio-economic and political conditions through development cooperation will reduce North-South migration flows (Rotte, R-Vogler, M and Zimmermann, K.F. 1997). Likely, the reason behind political gestures of increasing economic, technical and financial aid is the hidden hope that migratory flows will curb.

If this view is plausible, all the effort and noble intentions could be ruined due to a particularly strict policy regarding international migration, and, chiefly, migrants. These punishing policies, which started to criminalize this phenomenon, were evident after 9/11 (Fekete, 2001; Chapkis, 2003) and strengthened since 2006. Clearly, this punishment affects, irregular, clandestine, illegal and regular migration equally. As has been pointed out by Içduygu (2007; 142), what seemed a paradox, especially before the current economic downturn, is that the European Union's policies of blocking and preventing migration targeted 'illegal' migration, but their economies need the participation of those of newcomers.

More intensive policies devoted to controlling migration flows were issued since 2007. Surely, the blue card (23rd October 2007) started to mark a new rhythm in 'managing' migratory flows. Given that European countries attracted mainly non-skilled migrants (85 percent, according to the European Commission, 2007), a new policy was launched to overturn this trend. The USA, conversely, attracts 50 percent skilled migrants. This initiative was contested since it would worsen situations of brain drain in less developed countries. While this measure may prove positive, it could also penalize migrants since the blue card aims at reinforcing the idea of circular migration.

In addition, and reinforcing all the previous policies which went into force, the European Pact on Immigration and Asylum was approved on October 15, 2008. This was actually the banner issue of Sarkozy's election campaign in 2007. Given the importance of the migratory challenge within the European region, Sarkozy probably thought that, by leading this initiative, France could regain its dominant position in the region. The pact was articulated into four main pillars: legal migration, illegal migration, asylum policies and foreign countries.

In July 2008, a refurbished Barcelona Process emerged and the Union for the Mediterranean requested attention to failed tasks. The three points which characterized the Barcelona Process became four since International Migration demanded customized attention. This occurred when the economic downturn started to be recognized by major governments. As soon as economic perspectives started to darken, migration issues gathered momentum in the public discourse and the response was clear during the 2009 European Parliamentary elections.

CONCLUSION

As was said before, policies regarding migration seem 'inspired' according to the first and second groups of theories where economy utility is the main driving factor, especially for industrialized countries. A report by the Frontex (2009:8) analysed the impact of the economic recession on illegal migration. These sources show that by 2009 illegal immigration figures dropped by 47 percent. This fact entails two subsequent factors: less availability of work and stronger border control and migration policies. These two causes affect the inflow/outflow amount of illegal migrants and, finally, this means that there would be a reduction of remittances, FDI and ODA in third countries.

Considering this scheme raises some questions. First, political institutions are dealing with migration-related issues following postulates represented by the two first groups of migration theories above. Secondly, if these theories explain a kind of auto-regulation regarding migratory flow dynamics, it would not make sense to strengthen repressive migration policies. In addition, it seems strange that the Frontex is predicting a reduction of humanitarian aid for third countries when before it presented just the opposite.

It would be extreme to say that this economic downturn has been 'designed' and 'implemented' to regulate sharp problems like international migration, which was creating episodes of social conflict. However, considering that these two precedent factors are contradictory, an offensive against international migration seems to be a properly orchestrated plan to safeguard European welfare systems and their economic and commercial interests. In the end, the economic downturn, attached to strong migratory policies has, at least in the short term, produced expected results. In this case, policy coherence has not led the EU's political decisions regarding the interests of southern Mediterranean partners. It is likely that this situation could encourage bilateral relations instead of presenting the EU as a multilateral mediator. This could cause an important loss of credibility.

Chapter 11

Defining the Role of the European Union in Managing Illegal Migration in the Mediterranean Basin: Policy, Operations and Oversight
– Alina Khasabova and Mark Furness –

Introduction

Illegal migration is a controversial, emotive issue that reso-
nates in European society, media and politics.[1] Increasingly,
illegal migration has been portrayed as an urgent security threat
because of its supposed relationship with organised crime and
terrorism. Misinformation about illegal migration is widespread,
while politicians have seized upon its tractability with voters.
EU member governments have deployed various measures to
fight illegal migration, including militaries and paramilitaries
to protect land and sea borders, high-tech data collection and
storage and readmission agreements with third countries. These
national responses to border enforcement and illegal migrant

management have proved relatively effective in reducing success-ful clandestine border crossings. And yet, the individual efforts of member states are unlikely to continue efficiently protecting Europe's frontiers as global push and pull factors increase. In recent years, it has become more accepted in most member states that an increased EU dimension in managing illegal immigration and enforcing external borders has more potential effectiveness, particularly since the Schengen agreement removed most inter-nal border controls.

Although the EU's precise role in managing illegal migra-tion is not yet clearly defined, its main function is threefold: improving policy efficiency through encouraging conformity of member state legislation; helping to reduce the security threat by providing common assets to support member state border control operations; and ensuring controversial policies and prac-tices are conducted legitimately, according to both the rule of law and standards of conduct generally regarded as acceptable by European public opinion. To meet these three objectives, the EU operates on three levels: policy, operations and oversight. At each level the EU helps member states coordinate and inte-grate their existing efforts. The EU's primary role is to act as a policy 'clearing house,' improving policy efficiency by providing member states with an institutional environment in which to coordinate their policy preferences. At the next level, the EU aims to improve border management by facilitating operational cooperation among member states and third countries through agencies such as FRONTEX and EUROSUR. At the third level, the EU oversees member states' adherence to European and international human rights conventions, especially in regard to their bilateral relations with third countries and their activities enforcing border control.

At the policy and operational levels, the EU dimension has been effective at improving the efficiency and effectiveness of border management. While there is still no common EU migra-tion policy, member states (and EFTA states) have engaged in a coherent policy debate at the EU-level, most have signed the Schengen agreement, and there is a common understanding of what constitutes illegal migration to Europe. The European

Commission is continuing to work towards defining common policies and practices for all EU member states. This process has been complemented and reinforced by the creation and increasing participation of the EU's newly-established common agencies for border and migration management, enhancing the effectiveness of existing national efforts. Although certain short-comings on these two levels remain to be addressed, in general the increasingly common approach to enforcing European immigration laws has achieved some success in reducing the numbers of illegal migrants to Europe.

However, a number of concerns can be raised regarding the oversight level where the EU endeavours to ensure legitimate practices, especially with regard to bilateral cooperation between member states and Mediterranean partner countries. The tendency of national governments, specifically those with strong preferences in this issue, to partake in bilateral cooperation agreements with Southern and Eastern Mediterranean governments outside the system supervised by the EU, has raised issues regarding the consistency of some bilateral partnerships with European and international human rights law (Human Rights Watch, 2006; Baldwin-Edwards, 2006). While the task of overseeing EU member state agencies is complex enough, the challenge of ensuring standards are maintained in Mediterranean partner countries as well is even greater, especially as attempts to encourage Mediterranean partner governments to implement EU governance standards under the Euro-Mediterranean Partnership (EMP) have been considered as interfering in the internal affairs of sovereign countries.

The oversight of illegal migration cooperation would, therefore, be best addressed within an institutional framework that enables all interested countries (Southern and Eastern Mediterranean, as well as European) to participate in the formulation and implementation of policies and practices. What is required is a common set of standards and practices, reached through mutual agreement and reflected in a code of practice to be incorporated in readmission and bilateral agreements. These standards would be maintained under the supervision of a joint oversight body comprised of officials from Mediterranean and EU member countries. Although such a body would not have the ability to sanction, it would be able to examine breaches and issue reports. Such an arrangement would create more efficient and legitimate cooperation in the management of illegal migration through a common set of standards; better distribution of responsibility among non-EU and EU Mediterranean countries and non-Mediterranean EU members; and mutual oversight, rather than EU-only supervision.

The 'Barcelona Process: Union for the Mediterranean' (UPM), launched in spectacular fashion by French President Nicolas Sarkozy in Paris on July 13, 2008, could provide the over-arching institutional framework for overseeing the management of illegal migration in the Mediterranean basin. The proposed UPM promises a much greater level of shared decision-making than has taken place since 1995 under the EMP. The UPM's biennial summits, co-presidency and joint secretariat have the potential, if implemented fully, to introduce more 'joint owner-ship' to Euro-Mediterranean relations. The UPM's project-based structure promises much in terms of enabling progress in areas of common interest. A Euro-Mediterranean illegal immigra-tion oversight project, jointly designed and implemented and managed as part of the UPM could enable more coherent, legiti-mate and, in the long run, more effective Mediterranean-wide approach to illegal migration management.

SOME FACTS ON ILLEGAL IMMIGRATION TO THE EUROPEAN UNION

As a result of increased global migration, intensified push factors in origin countries and attractive pull factors in desti-nation member states, Europe is experiencing increasing legal immigration, which is paralleled by illegal immigration pres-sure as border controls tighten. Due to the clandestine nature of the phenomenon, reliable data on undocumented residency in EU countries is lacking and estimates vary widely. Estimating annual flows is more difficult still. Most rely on estimations of total numbers, which are in turn based on a range of disparate and often non-corroborating sources. Much of the available official information is several years old. A European commission collation of member state border control data showed that in 1997 699,393 people were refused entry to 15 EU countries. This number had risen to 1,105,206 refused entries in 2001, the vast majority of whom were Moroccan citizens trying to enter Spain (European Commission, 2004). A late 1990s study based on the numbers of irregular migrants apprehended estimated that between 350,000 and 500,000 illegal migrants travel to the EU every year, joining an existing population of up to 8 million undocumented residents (Salt, 2000). A more recent OECD estimate puts the total number of illegal migrants at around 1 percent of the EU's population, rising to 4 percent in southern European countries (roughly 4.5 million total) (OECD, 2007). Interestingly, data on legal migration is also a matter of interpretation. A recent report notes that official European figures count 5,635 migrants from Arab countries and Turkey registered in the EU, while the consulates of origin countries count 8.177 million. Some of this number are illegal migrants for whom registration with their home countries' embassies offer a meagre form of protection (CARIM, 2007). Such statistical discrepancies do not help objective analysis of a politically sensitive issue.

The figures on illegal migration across the Mediterranean are also somewhat patchy.[2] A study conducted by the International Centre for Migration Policy Development (ICMPD) estimated that 100,000–120,000 irregular migrants cross the Mediterranean every year, of which 55,000 are citizens of Mediterranean partner countries, 35,000 are of sub-Saharan origin and 30,000 come from other regions, such as Asia (Simon, 2006). The most commonly used route for illegal migration is from Libya to Sicily, Malta or nearby islands. It carries over 80,000 migrants per year, making Libya the primary departure and transit country (ICMPD, 2004). Recent data from FRONTEX counts 1,230 arrivals in Malta and 7,889 in Lampedusa from January to August 2007, rising to 2,187 and 17,302 for the first seven months of 2008.[3]

Existing research does point to some important and often overlooked facts about illegal immigration to the EU. First, only a minority of undocumented residents in member states entered the EU illegally. Illegal immigration across the Mediterranean by sea has attracted the most dramatic headlines. As one report put it, 'on arrival they make a far bigger impact than those who slip across land borders [...] Every time a party of wretched Africans is filmed landing ashore, it shows the public that illegal migrants are still coming'[4] However, clandestine entrances into EU territory, especially by sea, but also by land or air, constitute only a small percentage of total illegal immigration. The vast majority of undocumented immigrants residing in member states enter the EU legally and then overstay their visas (Sciortino, 2004, OECD, 2007). According to the Italian Ministry of Interior, only 10 percent of undocumented residents in Italy in 2002 arrived illegally by sea, 15 percent entered the country illegally by land and the majority, 75 percent, overstayed short-term visas. In 2004, illegal arrivals by sea were estimated at approximately four percent of the entire undocumented population, increasing to 14 percent in 2005 and 13 percent in 2006 (Coluccello and Massey, 2007).[5] It should also be noted that the main irregular migratory flows originate in Eastern Europe, rather than in Southern Mediterranean countries, suggesting that an increased emphasis on Europe's Southern borders is only a partial solution to the multifaceted problem of illegal immigration (European Commission, 2004).

Second, official concerns have been raised regarding facilitated illegal immigration as transnational, organised criminal activity. It is often assumed that the same transnational organised criminal groups that facilitate illegal migration may use their experience to coordinate and finance other cross-border crimes. This has been illustrated by the experience of Turkey, a major transit country for illegal immigrants and drugs into cities in Italy, France, Germany and the Netherlands.[6] It is, however, difficult to precisely define the extent of the relationship between organised crime and illegal migration. There is no reliable data on the number of illegal immigrants involved in organised crime during, or prior, to their residency in the EU. While EUROPOL cites intensive involvement of organized crime groups in illegal migration, this relationship may not be as developed as perceived

(Europol 2007). In Spain, smuggling or trafficking of migrants by organised transnational criminal groups has not been the major mechanism of migration. More than 75 percent of illegal residents in Spain did not rely on help from others in making their journey (Baldwin-Edwards 2002).

Furthermore, the link between illegal migration and transnational organised crime does not usually progress beyond trafficking of the migrants themselves. Although it is not unknown for people smugglers to be involved in other forms of organised crime (such as drugs and arms smuggling, international automobile theft, or counterfeiting), such connections are rare. Most people traffickers supply the sex industry and are small, loosely affiliated organisations that rarely fit the conventional portrayal of organised criminal groups (Kaizen and Nonneman, 2007). Even when organized transnational criminal groups are involved, the nature of these groups is not hierarchical or sophisticated, but rather based on loose, often temporary, collaborations (Monzini et al., 2004; Coluccello and Massey, 2007). Researchers have also noted that illegal migration facilitated by organised criminal groups is much more common across Europe's Eastern borders than across the Mediterranean (Pastore et al., 2007).

It is important to differentiate between the phenomena of migrant trafficking and smuggling. UN Protocols on trafficking in persons and smuggling migrants make a distinction between the two concepts. Smuggling is defined as an act in which the state's borders and admission regulations are violated, while the phenomenon of migrant trafficking infers the infringement of migrant rights and freedoms (UN 2007). In the latter case, the migrants involuntarily become associated with transnational crime. Neither FRONTEX nor EUROPOL make much of the fact that in many cases illegal migrants are themselves victims of transnational crime, and that the relationship between the two groups is not always that collaborative. Many of those who are smuggled by organised criminal groups have to pay for the service with long-term, poorly salaried menial labor or, in the case of many women, forced prostitution (ICMPD, 2001).

Thirdly, media attention has engendered a widespread perception of poorly controlled borders that present a serious security problem for Europe (Lavanex, 2006). Since the shock of September 11, 2001, fears have been raised that organised criminal groups may attempt to smuggle not only economic migrants and refugees, but also potential terrorists (Demleitner 2008, Sarrica 2005). This fear has profoundly influenced border management policy in the EU, especially since the March 2004 Madrid train bombings (Widgren et al, 2005). The threat extends to all EU member states since internal EU border controls were lifted, and policy makers often speak of 'terrorism' and 'illegal migration' in the same breath.[7] However, the little research that exists on a link between terrorism and illegal migration suggests that the relationship is rather tenuous, especially as highly risky and unpredictable asylum and illegal migration routes are unlikely paths for bringing terrorists into the EU. Terrorists do not normally need to risk a one-way trip to Spain or Italy in an unseaworthy boat (Guild, 2003).

THE POLICY LEVEL: THE EU AS A 'CLEARING HOUSE' FOR MEMBER STATE INTERESTS

Concerns about intensified illegal immigration pressure and poorly enforced physical borders that may serve as gateways for terrorists and transnational criminal groups affect government policy because they resonate with European voters. Nevertheless, effective management of illegal migration flows in a 27-member EU is beyond the capabilities of individual member states, and a community dimension to support national responses is required. EU-level involvement has the potential to generate a more coherent and efficient response to the problem of illegal migration. While the precise role of the EU in this issue is not yet clearly defined, its principal function is clearly to help improve efficient and legitimate management of the problem through the 'communitarization' of the EU's external borders. These tasks are to be achieved through coordinating member state policies, supporting operations at the member state level and overseeing bilateral partnerships between individual EU member states and Mediterranean partner countries.

The extent to which the EU dimension should supersede the actions of individual national administrations in managing the illegal migration problem has been widely debated. A number of researchers have noted the inability of national administrations to effectively control their external borders. They argue that migration policy should be decided at the EU level and implemented by common European border control agencies instead of national services (Monar 2006). Accordingly, the emergence and development of Justice and Home Affairs (JHA) at the EU level, specifically in regard to its competencies in illegal migration and cross-border crime prevention, has been welcomed as a potentially effective and necessary response to increased migration pressure on the EU member states (Monar 2006, Lobkowicz 2002). However, the extent to which the management of illegal migration should be taken over by common EU action is debatable. An important question is whether the EU could better deal with this particular problem than national border control services, coordinating their activities through EU-level institutions and organizations where necessary. At least one scholar who addresses this question has argued that limited EU participation, which does not extend beyond policy coordination and facilitation of member state cooperation, is likely to be the most effective EU approach possible (Mitsilegas et al., 2003).

Some EU member states feel the pressure of illegal migration in the Mediterranean more than others. Southern EU member states, where most trans-Mediterranean migrants enter the EU, not surprisingly, have stronger opinions on the issue. Spain, Italy and Malta have long emphasized the need for joint action on illegal immigration and border control. This would allow for a more effective burden-sharing mechanism among EU members.[8] One of the central tasks of the commission is to facilitate this common understanding by identifying the policy priorities of EU member governments and working out a solution that all can accept. The commission has emphasized that a successful response to illegal migration would be possible only under the condition of expedited and deepened cooperation based on common understanding of key issues among member states (European Commission, 2005b). External shocks can help. In response to discussions in the council following the events of September 11, the commission voiced its intention to 'address the issue of illegal immigration with a comprehensive approach' and to create a joint EU illegal immigration policy (EC, 2001a). Focusing on illegal immigration from African countries, the commission saw the need for a coherent, collaborative and balanced approach. It identified strengthened cooperation among member states and partnerships with countries of origin and transit as the principal objectives and priorities to manage illegal immigration (European Commission, 2005c).

The EU's primary institutional function is to acts as a policy 'clearing house' for member state preferences for policy responses on any given issue. The EU improves policy efficiency among member states by providing an environment in which they can coordinate their bargaining. Common policies and more efficient decision-making are developed through negotiation. Normally, intra-EU bargaining is a structured process in which extreme member state preferences are reconciled or bought with side payments, pork-barrelling or old-fashioned political pressure. Out of this process emerges a common position, sometimes after marathon negotiating sessions involving member state and community-level officials. Member states raise important issues (either formally in the European Council, or less formally when they see fit) which are incorporated in a union-wide discussion involving stakeholders. Sometimes debate takes place openly and is widely reported. Sometimes it takes place behind closed doors. Policy issues often reach the implementation stage when the commission prepares a communication to the Council and Parliament based on consultation with member governments and its calculation of what an acceptable common position would be.

The common EU position on migration that has emerged from this bargaining process is contained in several policy documents and declarations. These include the 2005 'Global Approach to Migration' which prioritised Africa and the Mediterranean. A commission memo from 2007 declares Europe's intention to develop an integrated approach to migration:

> [One that] strikes the right balance between labour
> market shortages, economic impacts, social con-
> sequences, integration policies and external policy
> objectives. In addition, it highlights that the concerns
> of EU citizens in this area need to be addressed. This
> approach fully respects the competencies of Member
> States and does not confer new powers to the EU.[9]

Similarly, the 2005–2010 Hague Programme, which is directed towards making the EU an "area of freedom, security and justice" stresses the need to use community-level resources and economies of scale to support member states in managing migration, including their agreements with third countries.[10]

Common EU positions on the management of migration in the Mediterranean are evident in the 1995 Barcelona Declaration; the EMP's so-called 'fourth chapter' of cooperation on migration, social integration, justice and security introduced at the 2005 10th Anniversary Summit in Barcelona; and the May 2008 communication proposing a union for the Mediterranean (European Commission, 2008c). At the policy level, precedence is given to deepened partnerships, active engagement and enhanced dialogue with key origin and transit countries. Bilateral cooperation between EU members and Mediterranean neighbors is considered the backbone of the fight against illegal migration, to be stiffened with community resources where necessary. The EU reserves the responsibility of ensuring legitimacy standards are maintained for itself (European Council, 2007).

Specifically, within the overall framework for cooperation with Mediterranean partner countries, the EU emphasises developmental projects and policies as long-term solutions to mounting migration pressures (Joffé, 2008). The aim is to facilitate dialogue and integration among the relevant parties, while the EU oversees transnational parties. Within the Barcelona Process framework, the EU endeavours to foster cooperation and prosperity by promoting political and economic reforms, sustainable development and trade liberalisation. Targeting root causes of emigration in origin and transit countries is regarded as the long-term solution for illegal migration and emphasis is put on reducing immigration into Europe through development support for partner countries (Joffé, 2008). Since September 11, 2001, security concerns have risen to the forefront and the view that illegal migrants are a security problem has been a major influence on the implementation of European policies. EU member states less affected by the problem have not objected to Southern EU members' renewed focus on securing their borders so long as the link between migration flows and political and economic reform in Mediterranean partner countries is clearly acknowledged.[11] This rhetorical link has been ignored by European and Mediterranean partner governments in practice, which have focussed on securing their borders in the short term (Schumacher, 2008).

THE OPERATIONAL LEVEL: FACILITATING AND COORDINATING MEMBER STATE OPERATIONS

At the operations level, the EU aims to improve the efficiency of integrated management of the member states' physical borders by facilitating information-sharing and operational cooperation and by rendering assistance to the existing activities and programs of national agencies. Essentially, the EU offers support when the illegal migration problem surpasses individual member state capabilities (de Vries, 2007). To this end the EU has established communal agencies and institutions that are intended to provide organisational support and assist in technical cooperation among interested parties. The European Agency for the Management of Operational Cooperation at the External borders of the Member States of the European Union, better known as FRONTEX, both coordinates and supports member state operations. The European Surveillance System for Borders (EUROSUR) coordinates national border surveillance systems. The EU does not intend for these agencies to supplant the existing efforts and assets of the member states, but rather to make available a 'common tool box' to address member states' day-to-day operational needs (European Commission, 2005 b).

An important tool in the box is the principle of information availability, which allows competent member authorities access to migrant and asylum information. The Schengen Information System (SIS II), the Visa Information System (VIS) and EURODAC function as cross-border systems that enable authorities to access personal data. SIS is an EU-wide information system containing 'alerts' regarding certain third-country nationals, who may be refused entry into, or stay within, a member state. The SIS program facilitates informational interchange between national agencies and makes police and judicial cross-border cooperation in criminal matters easier. The VIS program allows member states to exchange information on short-stay visas and is intended to contribute fighting illegal immigration by supporting the common visa policy and checks on the visa applicants. Finally, EURODAC was established as a fingerprint database allowing officials to identify applicants who have formerly entered the EU without the necessary documents or those applicants who may have been previously convicted and/or detained.

These information inventories collate data gathered by the national agencies of individual member states as well as facilitating technical cooperation among member government agencies. Great emphasis is placed on the availability and synergy of technical instruments and border surveillance methods since integrated actions are likely to improve the efficiency of member states' border enforcement activities. The EU's role in this area is centred on amalgamating or 'pooling' the material resources of member states and making them easily available. It is important to note, however, that participation in these, as well as all other EU-organised coordination projects, is voluntary and at the discretion of individual national governments. The EU exercises little real power over the extent to which national agencies participate in these programmes, and the commission has recently acknowledged that all three of the systems discussed above are under-exploited. Many member states maintain separate, but similar, lists, resulting in duplication, overlapping and possible operational conflicts (European Commission, 2005 b). This may change if the commission's 'border package' information system comes into force. However, this programme has met with considerable scepticism from experts who question its technical feasibility and its potential for intrusiveness (Guild et al,, 2008).

FRONTEX is designed to support national governments in circumstances requiring increased technical and operational assistance. While recognizing that responsibility for border control and surveillance lies within the competencies of member states and acknowledging that national agencies will continue their individual efforts, FRONTEX facilitates practical cooperation by providing technical support and expertise. FRONTEX is not designed to respond to emergencies, but to help member states implement well-planned, regular patrols.[12] In cases of member states facing 'urgent and exceptional situations resulting from a mass influx of illegal immigrants' and requiring assistance at their external borders, FRONTEX is authorised to deploy the Rapid Border Intervention Team (RABIT). The 'toolbox' for RABIT is the Central Record of Available Technical Equipment (CRATE), which collects information from surveillance assets belonging to member states. This information is voluntarily put at RABIT's disposal for a limited period of time and upon request from another member state.

Similarly, EUROSUR's central function is clearly to facilitate voluntary cooperation based on the existing member state instruments where member states deem EU involvement will improve the effectiveness and efficiency of border management activities. EUROSUR is intended to prevent unauthorised border crossings and increase the security of the EU by helping prevent cross-border organised crime. The objective of this system is to 'support the member states in reaching full situational awareness on the situation at their external borders and increase the reaction capability of their law enforcement authorities' (European Commission, 2008 b)[13] EUROSUR is to be incorporated into existing member state surveillance systems and is intended to provide a common technical framework for daily cooperation and communication between national authorities. In the future, EUROSUR will even replace national surveillance with a community-wide radar and satellite system (European Commission, 2006 b).

Although EUROSUR and FRONTEX are relatively new to border policing and illegal migration management, they have already reduced the number of successful clandestine crossings into Southern European states. During the first eight months of 2007, 72 percent fewer immigrants crossed to the Canaries and 41 percent fewer reached the countries of the central Mediterranean compared to the previous year.[14] Specifically regarding FRONTEX, in 2006 and 2007, approximately 53,000 persons were apprehended or denied entry at the border by the agency, more than 2,900 false or falsified travel documents were detected and 58 illegal migration facilitators were arrested. In joint operations with FRONTEX (Hera, Agios, Minerva and Poseidon), 34,905 illegal migrants were intercepted and 9,671 were diverted (European Commission, 2008a).

The quantifiable results of FRONTEX have been described as 'impressive' by the Commission and consequently the agency has received a large increase in funding, from 41 million euros in 2007 to 70 million euros in 2008.[15] Nevertheless, the agency is new and its future evolution is not yet clear. Although FRONTEX has been established as a support mechanism for member states and as a 'common toolbox' to provide operational assistance upon request, to date, only a modest use of equipment has been made. The potentials of CRATE have not been fully exploited and so far no member state has requested a RABIT team. Furthermore, even though FRONTEX's mandate is currently only to support member states, the commission's long-term recommendations for the agency envisage a major expansion of its competencies, including the ability to conduct operations with third countries (Jeandesboz, 2008).

Finally, in order to address the overburdening of certain states, the EU has established the External Borders Fund with a budget of 1820 million euros for 2007–2013.[16] The Fund is a financial solidarity mechanism to support member states that incur heavy financial burdens and to spread that burden around the EU. The money is allocated on the basis of criteria that assess the burden of each state to control external borders. While some structural obstacles hinder its effectiveness, the fund has the potential to offer financial relief to overburdened member states, especially in Southern Europe. It remains to be seen whether lessening financial pressure will create a favourable environment for complying with human rights regulations.

THE OVERSIGHT LEVEL: MONITORING MEMBER STATES' PARTNERSHIPS WITH THIRD COUNTRIES

The EU's role at the oversight level is to ensure that member state responses to illegal migration are conducted in accordance with European and international human rights conventions, especially with regard to national border enforcement practices and bilateral relations with third countries. Beyond this legal framework, the legitimacy of European border protection is also defined more subjectively by various means, including media coverage, expert opinion, public responses to specific incidents and broad trends, and ultimately by voters' responses to government policies.

From a legal point of view, the oversight of member state border enforcement is, at least in theory, relatively clear. The European Court of Human Rights in Strasbourg is tasked with enforcing European human rights law. Although the European Convention on Human Rights and Fundamental Freedoms does not deal directly with illegal migration, courts in Europe and elsewhere have interpreted its general provisions in a way that protects people who are either expelled or prevented from arriving in Europe. Two well-established protections have been established. The first is that no one should be returned to a country where they face the risk of torture or cruel, inhuman or degrading treatment (Phuong, 2007). Second, although member states have the right to protect their own borders and are not legally responsible for deaths or injuries indirectly caused by increased border protection measures, they do have an obligation to take appropriate steps to prevent deaths when there is reason to believe that a particular life is at risk (Spijkerboer, 2007). While the European Court of Human Rights has established the right of member states to refuse access to their territory, it has emphasised that any measure they adopt in exercising this power must comply with human rights obligations (UK Parliament, 2006).

BILATERAL COOPERATION WITH THIRD COUNTRIES: THE ITALY/LIBYA EXAMPLE

Several EU member states have stepped outside the EU framework and have developed their own bilateral illegal migration combating arrangements with third countries. Readmission agreements between EU members and third countries are intended to facilitate the removal of illegal immigrants from European territory. These agreements require neighboring countries to readmit their own nationals as well as nationals of another country who transited the neighboring country on the way to the EU. In return, neighboring countries get financial help with the costs of accepting and possibly resettling illegal migrants (Baldwin-Edwards, 2004). A second form of cooperation is operational, where EU member state border control agencies work closely with their counterparts in third countries. These bilateral arrangements exist in varying degrees of formality and have entailed cooperative relationships between European and Mediterranean partner security services, some of which have poor records in upholding international human rights standards (Lutterbeck, 2006). While these arrangements have not necessarily raised the number of deaths at sea or the possibility of unsavoury incidents, such as the shootings at Ceuta and Melilla in October 2005, they have raised the difficulty of transparently dealing with such incidents when they occur.

A good example of bilateral anti-illegal migration cooperation comes from the Italian government. Influenced by internal political developments and pressure exerted by the electorate, Italy has entered into cooperation with Libya under a framework of numerous bilateral agreements for curbing illegal migration and joint patrol of the Libyan coastline. Libya and Italy signed an agreement to fight terrorism, organised crime and illegal migration in 2000 and established a permanent liaison in 2003. The Italian government reportedly provided substantial financial support to a Libyan migrant detention camp and has proposed creating more Libyan holding centres (Hamood, 2006). In return, Libya has tightened its border controls in recent years, arresting and deporting thousands of would-be migrants to

Europe (Trucco, 2005). The partnership has been credited with a number of successes, such as preventing approximately 40,000 undocumented people from leaving Libya in 2005 and 2006.[17]

Italian and Libyan cooperation has attracted the attention of human rights groups. Human Rights Watch has raised concerns about Libya's record in upholding international human rights standards in border management. Libyan authorities have been accused of arbitrary arrests, physical abuse, lengthy and arbitrary detention in poor conditions and forced deportations without allowing opportunities to seek asylum, all of which violate Libyan and international law (Human Rights Watch, 2006). More recently, Human Rights Watch has warned that Italy may be guilty of violating the fundamental principles of international refugee law because would-be asylum seekers detained at sea by joint coastal patrols have been subsequently deported from Libya (Human Rights Watch 2008). The Council of Europe's Commissioner for Human Rights has raised questions about the return of some 1600 aliens who landed on the Italian island of Lampedusa in 2004 and 2005, describing these removals as intransparent since they were not independently monitored. 'Although I heard no allegations of official violence in connection with expulsions,' wrote the Commissioner, 'I did suggest to the Minister of the Interior that the presence of an impartial outside observer might help to ensure full respect for human dignity—and protect Italy's good name in this area' (Council of Europe, 2005).

The Italian/Libyan relationship is not the only case for concern. Similar incidents of human rights violations have been noted in other bilateral partnerships and unilateral efforts. Questions have been raised regarding the adherence of the Spanish and Moroccan border management authorities to international human rights principles.[18] Greek migrant reception centres were harshly criticised by the UN Human Rights Commissioner and Italy and Germany's proposal to set up migration and refugee detention camps in southern Mediterranean countries has been criticised as incompatible with international human rights conventions (Weinzierl, 2007; Assembly of Western European Union, 2006). On the southern side of the Mediterranean, NGOs and human rights organisations continue to condemn existing legal provisions and practices, arguing that they give rise to serious humanitarian problems and tend to marginalise and repress illegal migrants (Fargues 2005, p. 28).

EXISTING EU OVERSIGHT MEASURES

The potential for bilateral agreements to breach European human rights law has been recognized in Brussels. The Assembly of the Western European Union has noted that, on many occasions, cooperation between EU member governments and their Mediterranean counterparts has been conducted at lower levels of accountability and human rights compliance, and the WEU has warned that relying on Mediterranean partner countries to serve as protective barriers against migratory flows could lead to increased incidences of major human rights violations (WEU, 2006, pp. 30-31).

The EU has begun to address oversight issues by creating working groups, regulations and funds designed to monitor compliance with international human rights regulations. In 1998, the commission established the High Level Working Group on Migration and Asylum (HLWG), a group consisting mainly of justice and home affairs officials in cooperation with individual member state institutions. The HLWG was tasked with drafting guidelines on a coherent framework approach on the issue of visa facilitation to cover migration, security and external relations. Specifically, it reviewed multilateral, European and bilateral agreements and existing policies in the field of asylum and immigration to coordinate EU policies. The ARGO program, operational from January 2002 until December 2006, intended to encourage migration policy harmonization and the uniform application of community law. The program was targeted not only to European member states, but also to third countries since funding was only provided for projects involving at least one foreign state. Through ARGO, the EU encouraged transparency in the actions of national authorities, especially in relation to the member states activities in third countries. Bilateral partnerships were thus monitored and evaluated by the EU in order to ensure compliance with relevant human rights laws. These efforts were aimed at both overseeing member state compliance with international human rights principles and harmonising EU policies to minimise the potential overburdening of certain states.

Establishing a standard legal framework for member states to manage illegal migration has only recently become a priority area for the European Commission as the member states themselves have come to accept that community-level oversight has certain advantages. In September 2005, the commission adopted a proposal for a directive on common standards and procedures for member states returning people staying illegally in the EU to their 'country of origin, transit or another third country, whether voluntary or enforced' (EC 2005, p. 13). In July 2006, the commission adopted a communication on illegal migration policy priorities in an effort to strike a balance between European security and the basic rights of individuals. This document reaffirmed the importance of cooperation between EU member states and third country governments. It also called for 'a common understanding of integrated border management to cover the full spectrum of border management activities,' including 'the identification of best practices for an integrated border management model' (EC 2006). In June 2008, the European Parliament adopted a directive on the return of illegal immigrants after a compromise was struck with the European Council. The directive approves deportation but sets down minimum standards, including voluntary departure periods, a maximum detention period of six months, and access to legal aid for poor migrants.[19]

The EU has also partly addressed human rights concerns arising from the increasingly militarised bilateral relations between EU member governments and their South Mediterranean counterparts by proposing policies to incorporate human rights protections into everyday operations. The European Commission's regulation establishing a community code on the rules governing the movement of persons across borders provides a legal framework, taking relevant human rights principles into account, for member state cooperation with third countries.[20] Articles of the regulation deal directly with border surveillance, refusal of entry and implementation of controls. It clearly outlines the procedures that should be, or may be, taken by member states in regard to migration issues. Of particular importance, and difficulty, is the task of legally supervising member states' surveillance of maritime borders. In this area, the need for common, comprehensive European regulation becomes more immediate since operations at sea, especially those taking place in extra-territorial waters (the high seas and territorial waters of third states) tend to be governed by international legal instruments, rather than by purely national ones.[21]

While these EU-level initiatives are undoubtedly a step towards more efficient and transparent management of illegal migration under the rule of law, they nonetheless still fail to fully incorporate and supervise all existing national illegal migration policies in the Mediterranean region. There is a clear need for more structured, permanent and institutionalised oversight of bilateral partnerships.

Nevertheless, it is unlikely that Southern and Eastern Mediterranean partner governments will passively accept Europe's lead in these matters. The situation becomes more delicate regarding the oversight of readmission agreements and other forms of bilateral cooperation between EU member governments and their Mediterranean counterparts. These agreements bypass EU institutions and sidestep Brussels because it has no jurisdiction over the governments or security services of Mediterranean partner countries. If oversight is to be improved, these bilateral agreements will need to be incorporated into a framework specifying acceptable policies and best practices. This kind of framework cannot simply be imposed by the EU, but would require the agreement and active cooperation of Mediterranean partner governments. The proposed Union for the Mediterranean may provide an appropriate institutional setting for this kind of framework.

IMPROVING OVERSIGHT OF ILLEGAL MIGRATION POLICY AND OPERATIONS: A UNION FOR THE MEDITERRANEAN PROJECT?

The "Barcelona Process: Existing EU Oversight Measures Union for the Mediterranean" first proposed by French President Nicholas Sarkozy during his election campaign and hotly debated by the French and German governments, launched to great fanfare in Paris on July 13, 2008. It may provide an appropriate institutional setting for an illegal migration oversight body. In theory, the Union for the Mediterranean (UPM) addresses two of what some analysts consider the EMP's greatest weakness: the lack of South Mediterranean 'ownership' of the EMP; and the tendency of political deadlocks to overshadow progress on issues where common interests exist. The UPM provides for greater non-EU influence over decision-making and a project-based focus on discrete issues of common interest. Like most European agreements, the UPM has the characteristics of a negotiated framework that can be expanded into more sensitive issues over time. Initially, the UPM would focus on relatively uncontroversial aspects, including motorway building and green projects.[22] However, President Sarkozy's original Mediterranean union proposal called for a multilateral council, similar to that of the EU itself, to deal with all of the major Euro-Mediterranean issues: energy, security, counter-terrorism, migration and trade. Although these ambitions were refined during intra-EU negotiations before the Paris Summit, there is no reason to believe that the UPM's mandate will not extend into more sensitive areas should the framework prove successful.

By introducing biennial Euro-Mediterranean summits, annual foreign affairs ministers meetings, a co-presidency, a joint permanent committee and a joint secretariat, the proposed UPM proposal provides non-EU countries with a greater say in decision-making regarding projects carried out under its mandate. Mediterranean partner governments may use this as an opportunity to negotiate a common position on any given project, thus combining their weights in negotiations with the EU. A common Mediterranean partner country position towards Europe also reduces the need for the EU and its members to deal with ten or more neighboring countries, each with different interests and demands. This promises to improve the efficiency of Euro-Mediterranean negotiations by enabling the EU to negotiate the terms of a project once instead of trying to satisfy a wide spectrum of third country interests. The requirement that the UPM secretariat arrange funding for projects also reduces the influence of the

European Commission in major strategic decisions as well as their day-to-day implementation. The UPM is—at least on paper—a less EU, and more Mediterranean, bargaining framework.

The UPM could be utilised to facilitate transparent oversight of migration policies and operations by incorporating them into a committee comprised of law enforcement, judicial, parliamentary and NGO representatives from both EU and Mediterranean partner countries. As an adjunct to the joint permanent committee or the Euro-Mediterranean Parliamentary Assembly, this body would be able to define the best practices for European and Mediterranean border control agencies and monitor adherence to these standards. Its day-to-day operations could be coordinated through the UPM secretariat. Such a body would not have any legal jurisdiction. Its role would be to provide independent, public oversight and to improve the transparency of unilateral and joint actions, with the possibility of case referral to the European Court of Human Rights. This institutional framework would enable co-ownership of oversight by having Mediterranean partner governments participate in the formulation and implementation of policies and practices in accordance with internationally recognized human rights principles. As an official body, a UPM illegal migration oversight committee would have the potential to improve the efficiency of oversight, which is currently conducted by NGOs.

The UPM is designed to be a Euro-Mediterranean rather than an EU organisation, resting on the principles of multilateral cooperation, regional integration and cohesion (European Commission 2008 c). Including illegal migration in its remit would be a clear acknowledgement by Europeans that the phenomenon is specifically a Mediterranean, rather than purely European, problem. While this change may seem merely rhetorical, it would take the wind out of claims that the EU protects its borders unilaterally, without regard for the interests of neighboring countries. This removes a potential reason for non-cooperation on the part of Mediterranean partner governments. Effective management of illegal migration depends heavily on the ability of Southern Mediterranean countries to adopt legal provisions and actions to counter regional irregular migration movements. Therefore, deeper integration of Mediterranean partner countries in the formulation, implementation and oversight phases of the policy and project development processes would increase the likelihood of cooperation, promote regional cohesion and foster the overall stability of the Euro-Mediterranean partnership.

CONCLUSION

Illegal migration is a long-term issue, with economic and social causes and consequences. These 'root causes' cannot be addressed in a time frame that is acceptable to most European voters. The push/pull factors that convince people to risk their lives to cross the Mediterranean and attempt to enter Europe illegally will still be prevalent for at least the next decade, if not beyond. It will be many years before the measures that the EU has put in place to encourage economic growth and to reduce incidences of socio-political persecution in sub-Saharan and Mediterranean partner countries start to make a difference to migration, assuming political elites in these countries implement the reforms the EU suggests. People will keep trying to enter the EU. Furthermore, as border security measures tighten and 'easier' routes are made more difficult, people will risk longer and more dangerous entry routes and will be more prepared to put their lives in the hands of people traffickers (Spijkerboer, 2007). The illegal migration problem will not go away because, in the foreseeable future, there will always be more people wanting to live in Europe than Europeans are prepared to allow. This means border security will remain an unpleasant necessity, and debates over how best to implement management strategies that uphold European and member state laws while protecting vulnerable migrants will continue for some time.

The EU's role in illegal migration management is based on three spheres of action. The first is providing an institutional framework for discussion, debate and declarations at the policy level; facilitating operations when multilateral coordination is necessary at the operational level; and, most importantly, supervising the member states' policies and operational standards with regard to illegal immigrants and undocumented residents at the oversight level. The EU's primary role is to act as a policy 'clearing house,' improving policy efficiency in the EU by providing member states with an institutional environment in which to coordinate their policy responses. At the next level, the EU aims to improve border management by facilitating operational cooperation among member states and third countries through agencies such as FRONTEX and EUROSUR. At the third level, the EU oversees member states' adherence to relevant European and international human rights conventions, especially with regard to their bilateral relations with third countries and their activities in enforcing border control policies. The EU does not wish to supersede the existing efforts of member states, but rather seeks to establish communal instruments to synergize and coordinate actions taken by national administrations through the addition of the European dimension (European Commission, 2001a). While member states maintain their responsibilities in border policing and bilateral cooperation partnerships, the EU provides coordinating assistance and oversees existing practices.

While the existing system has led to an increase in the apprehensions of illegal migrants attempting to cross the Mediterranean, it has also raised concerns regarding the transparency of practices and the legitimacy of oversight. Considering that effective management of the problem rests on deep, sustained cooperation between origin and destination countries, an institutional framework is required to facilitate such cooperation. This involves considering the expectations and interests of the neighboring countries in the policy formulation process as well as establishing a permanent oversight body to define the best practices and monitor adherence to them. The bilateral relationships established within the current system clearly lack a coherent institutional and legal framework. This increases the potential for unsavoury incidents, and the difficulty of dealing with them when they occur.

Establishing, implementing and overseeing a common framework for bilateral management of illegal migration represent an opportunity for the European Union and its Mediterranean partners. Facilitating partnerships may be best undertaken in the proposed Union for the Mediterranean, which offers a framework within which efficient and durable project-based cooperation could be incorporated. This framework, based on co-ownership between Northern and Southern members, has the potential to improve the consistency and structure of bilateral and multilateral partnerships. Establishing a permanent committee to supervise the implementation of existing agreements will greatly increase the coherence and transparency of migration management policies within a joint, legitimate framework.

Notes

1. This chapter resulted from research conducted under the 6th Framework Programme Project 'GO-EuroMed: The Political Economy of Euro-Mediterranean Governance,' generously supported by the European Commission DG Research. Naturally, all views expressed are those of the authors.

2. An August 2008 request to EuroPol for estimates of the annual flow of illegal migration to the EU, and the total number of undocumented persons residing in the EU declined.

3. August 2008 request to FRONTEX for estimates on the annual flow of illegal migration in the Mediterranean.

4. 'Italy and Libya: Undoing the damage,' *The Economist,* 2 August 2008.

5. See also Ministero dell'interno, *Lo stato della Sicurezza in Italia,* 2005, p. 41; Ministero dell'interno, *Note sulla sicurezza in Italia,* 2006, p. 16.

6. 'Turkish Organised Crime,' Worldpress, 12 November 2007, www.worldpress.org/europe, accessed 14/8/2008.

7. See, for example: Gunter Verheugen 'The European Neighbourhood Policy,' a speech to the Prime Ministerial Conference of the Vilnius and Visegrad Democracies, Bratislava, 19 March 2004.

8. See Zapatero and his Greek counterpart ask EU for support in migration issues, website of the Spanish government, 10 July 2008, www.la-moncloa.es.

9. See Memo/07/549, Brussels, 5 December 2007, available at www.euromed-migration.eu, accessed 15/8/2008.

10. For an excellent summary of the Hague Programme see www.euractiv.com.

11. See, for example, the Five Year Work Programme agreed at the EMP 10th Anniversary Summit, Barcelona, 2005.

12. Ilkka Laitinen, 'Frontex: Facts and Myths,' 11 June 2007, available at www.frontex.europa.eu, accessed 15 August 2008.

13. 'Keep Out: A special report on migration,' *The Economist*, 3 January 2008.

14 FRONTEX's annual budgets are published at www.frontex. europa.eu, accessed 15/8/2008.

15. See www.ec.europa.eu/justice_home, accessed 15/8/2008.

16. 'Incontro a Sirte (Libia) tra il Ministro dell'Interno Giuseppe Pisanu e il leader della Rivoluzione Muhammar Gheddafi,' Italian Ministry of the Interior press release, 17 January 2006.

17. 'Morocco: Investigate Migrant Deaths at Sea,' *Human Rights News*, Human Rights Watch, 9 May 2008, available at www.hrw.org.

18. See European Parliament 'Immigration: MEPs and the "return" directive in depth,' available at www.europarl.europa.eu, accessed 15/8/2008.

19. Regulation (EC) No 562/2006.

20. House of Lords European Union Committee, 9th Report of Session 2007-08, Frontex: the EU external borders agency, Report with Evidence, 5 March 2008.

21. See 'Joint Declaration of the Paris Summit for the Mediterranean,' Paris, 13 July 2008.

22. Speech by Mr. Nicolas Sarkozy, Tangiers, 23 October 2007, available at www.diplomatie.gouv.fr.

Bibliography

"Italian frigate takes migrants to Sicily after Malta refusal." *The Times* (Malta, 11 May 2009). Available at: www.timesofmalta.com.

"Malta insists it is not responsible for all migrants in its search area," *The Times* (Malta, 27 May 2009). Available at: www.timesofmalta.com.

Aardes, A (1980): *Algerian emigration in France: Provisional data.* Algiers.

Achoual, A (1983): *Le Salariat industriel au Maroc (1956–1980).* Mémoire de Diplôme d'Etudes Supérieures (DES) en Sciences Economiques. Rabat. Faculté de Droit-Agdal.

Achour, O (2003): *The temporary and spatial structure in the novel 'The Season of emigration to the north'.* University of Algiers.

Ait Hamou, M (1978): *Algerian emigration through the romantic works of Mouloud Feraoun and Mouloud Maamri.* University of Algiers.

Akacha, M (1973): *The legal status of Algerian workers in France.* University of Algiers.

Al Kut, B (2007): The Illegal migration in the African European Relations. *Dirasaat.* No: 28, Spring. pp. 51:62.

_____ (2008): *Libyan national security.* Unpublished study presented to Libyan National Planning Council.

Aleinikoff, T. A and Chetail, V (eds) (2003): *Migration and international legal norms.* The Hague, TMC Asser Press, 2003).

Aliboni, R, Ahmed, D, Schumacher, T and Tovias, A (2008): Putting the Mediterranean Union in Perspective. *EuroMeSCo* Paper N°68.

Alimazighi, K, Djabri, A, Labdelaoui, H and Sahraoui, B (1993): *The teaching of the Arabic language to the children of algerian emigrants who returned back to their country.* CNEPRU project, Report ronéoté, Sociology Institute, University of Algiers Amel Blidi.

Amnesty Internacional (2006): *Frontera Sur. El Estado da la espalda a los derechos humanos de los refugiados e inmigrantes.* Available at: http://www.amnesty.org/es/report/info/EUR41/008/2005.

Asociación Pro Derechos Humanos de Andalucía (2006): *Derechos humanos en la frontera sur. Informe sobre la inmigración clandestina durante el año 2005.* Available at: http://www.apdha.org/index.php?option=com_content&task=view&id=175&Itemid=32.

Assembly of Western European Union (2006): *Security and stability in the Mediterranean region.* Document A/1939.

Ayad Teisser, A (1994): *Jewish immigration in Palestine and its consequences on the economy of the occupied Palestinian territories since 1967.* Masters in Economics.

Azouz, N (1982): *Myths and space in an ideal topography for a characterized aggression of Rachid Boudjedra.* University of Algiers.

Bagtache, N (1995): *The return of young emigrant women at their country of origin and the difficulties of their socio-cultural adaptation.* University of Algiers.

Baldwin-Edwards, M (2002): Semi-reluctant hosts: Southern Europe's ambivalent response To immigration. *The Brown Journal of World Affairs*, Vol. 8, No. 2, pp. 211:229.

Baldwin-Edwards, M (2004): The changing mosaic of Mediterranean migrations. *Migration Policy Institute Migration Information Source*, June. Available at www.migrationinformation.org.

_____ (2006): Between a rock & a hard place: North Africa as a region of emigration, immigration and transit migration. *Review of African Political Economy*, Vol. 33, No.108, pp. 311:324.

_____ (2007): "Illegal migration in the Mediterranean" 5th International Seminar on Security and Defence in the Mediterranean (CIDOB, Barcelona: 2007), pp. 115:124.

Basch, L. Et al. (1994): *Nations unbound: Transnational projects, postcolonial predicaments and deterritorialized Nation-States.* Gordon and Breach. New York.

Basu, A.M (1992): The status of women and the quality of life among the poor. *Cambridge Journal of Economics*, No. 16, pp. 249:267.

Bauman, Z (2005): *Fear, security and the city. Living with strangers.* Polity Press.

_____ (2001): *Community. Seeking safety in an insecure world.* Polity Press.

Ben Attou, M (2003): Emigration internationale et production de la ville Agadir: une nouvelle génération d'acteurs économiques absentéistes. *Al-Misbahiya*, No. 6, pp. 87:111.

Benattig, R (1989): Assisted home comings: enquiry in Algeria. *European Journal on International Migrations*, No. 13, vol. 5.

Benchrifa, A (1993): "Migration internationale et développement agricole au Maroc. In Migration internationale et changements sociaux dans le Maghreb" *Actes du colloque international de Hammamet* "Tunisie. Tunis: Université de Tunis, pp. 243 :260.

_____ (1996) : "L'impact de la migration internationale sur le monde rural marocain" *Migration Internationale*. Actes du séminaire sur les migrations internationales, Rabat 6 et 7 juin, Rabat, C.E.R.E.D, pp. 403 :430.

Benyounes, A (1977): *Emigration and society: A village in Kabylie.* University of Algiers.

Berriane, M (1993): Impact de la migration internationale du travail sur la croissance du cadre bâti : le cas du centre de Zeghaneghan. *Revue de géographie du Maroc*, Vol. 15, No. 1-2, pp. 143 :163.

_____ (1997): "Emigration internationale du travail et micro - urbanisation dans le Rif oriental: cas du centre de Taouima, région de Nador, Maroc" *Migration internationale et changements sociaux dans le Maghreb*. Actes du colloque international de Hammamet, Tunisie, 21-25 juin 1993, Tunis : Université de Tunis I, pp. 75 :97.

Bockerman, G (1980): *Identity, motivation and attitudes of foreigners in Algeria: the case of the permanent members of the Christian church.* University of Algiers.

_____ (1983): *West Germans in the industry and cooperation with Algeria.* University of Algiers.

Boudou, M (1998): *Pour une sociologie de la science de l'émigration-immigration marocaine à l'étranger.* Institut universitaire de la recherche scientifique. Rabat.

Bougara, H (2006): *The consequences of emigration on Euro-Maghreb relations from 1985 to 1997*. University of Algiers.

Bourchachen, J (2000): "Rapport des transferts des résidents à l'étranger à la réduction de la pauvreté: Cas du Maroc" *Statistique, développement et droits de l'homme*, Montreux, 4-8-9, pp.4:6.

Boutaleb-Joutei, H (1996): "Réflexion sur l'enseignement supérieur et la recherche scientifique au Maroc" *Les enjeux du débat sur l'éducation nationale*: actes des journées d'études organisées les 8 et 9 avril 1995 par la Fondation Abderrahim Bouabid à Rabat, Casablanca. Editions maghrébines, pp. 77 :105.

Bouzahzah, M (2003): Libre-échange et migration marocaine: une approche par l'équilibre général calculable. *Critique économique* : No. 11, pp. 47:63.

Boyd, M (1989): Family and personal networks in migration. *International Migration Review*. Special Silver Anniversary Issue. 23.

Brock, D (1993): "Quality of life measures in health care and medical ethics" in Sen, A and Nussbaum, M.: *Quality of life*. Oxford University Press.

Brouwer, A and Kumin, J (2003): Interception and asylum: When migration control and human rights collide. 21 *Refuge* 4.

Bruckert, C and Parent, C (2002): *Trafficking in human beings and organized crime: A literature review*. Royal Canadian Mounted Police, June 2002, available www.rcmp-grc.gc.ca.

Calleya, S and Lutterbeck, D (2008): *Malta and the challenge of irregular immigration*. Report published by Today Public Policy Institute, Malta, November.

Carlier, O (1976): *Individuals, groups and propaganda, the process of politicization of Algerian emigration in France between the two World Wars, (The African north star of 1932 to 1936)*, University of Algiers.

_____ (1983): *For a quantitative history of the Algerian emigration history in France*. Oran, publications of the Centre of Information and of Documentation in Social and Human Sciences.

Carrera, S (2007): *The EU border management strategy. FRONTEX and the challenges of irregular immigration in the Canary Islands. CEPS Working Document*, No. 261 March, Brussels.

Cassar Torregiani, P (2008): *Migrant smuggling by sea: Combating a current threat to maritime security through the creation of a cooperative framework.* Martinus Nijhoff / Brill.

Castles, S and Miller, M. J. (2003): *The age of migration.* Third edition. Palgrave MacMillan. UK.

Chapkis, W (2003): Trafficking, migration and the law. *Gender and Society,* Vol 17. No. 6, pp. 923:937.

Charef, M (1995): Migrations internationales et mutations socio-économiques dans le Souss-Massa, Maroc. In *Les nouvelles formes de la mobilité spatiale dans le monde arabe,* Tours, Ed. l'URBAMA, pp. 167:175.

Chekroun, A (1992): *Literature of Crossroads; the nationality issue through the works of Leila Sebbar.* University of Algiers.

Churchill, R.R and Lowe, R.R (1999): *The Law of the Sea.* 3rd edition, Manchester University Press. Manchester.

CNES (1998): *Situation of the Algerian community settled abroad.* Report of the commission in charge of the Algerian community abroad. Algiers.

_____ (2003): *The Algerian community settled in France: what contribution to the economical and social development of Algeria?* Report of the commission in charge of the Algerian community abroad. Algiers.

Cogneau, D (1995): Libre-échange, répartition du revenu et migrations au Maroc. *Revue d'économie du développement,* pp. 27 :52.

Cohen, R (1987): *The new Helots: Migrants in the international division of Labour.* Aldershot, Avebury.

Collyer, M (2008): Towards Mediterranean migration management 2008? *Developing Discourse and Practices.* Real Insituto Elcano. Madrid.

Coluccello, S and Massey, S (2007): Out of Africa: The human trade between Libya and Lampedusa. *Trends in Organized Crime,* Vol. 10, pp. 77:90.

Commission (EC) (2001): A common policy on illegal immigration. (Communication) COM (2001) 672 final.

_____ (2002): Towards integrated management of the external borders of the member states of the European Union. (Communication) COM (2002) 233 final.

_____ (2006): Reinforcing the Management of the European Union's Southern Maritime Borders (Communication) COM (2006) 733 final.

Commission of the European Communities (2004): *Annual report on asylum and migration.* Available at www.ec.europa.eu/justice.

_____ (2005 a): *Proposal for a directive of the European parliament and of the council on common standards and procedures in member states for returning illegally staying third country nationals.* COM (2005) 391 final.

_____ (2005 b): *Communication from the Commission to the Council and the European Parliament, on improved effectiveness, enhanced interoperability and synergies among European databases.*

_____ (2006 a): *Communication from the Commission on policy priorities in the fight against illegal immigration of third country nationals.* COM (2006) 402 final.

_____ (2006 b): *Communication from the Commission to the Council, reinforcing the management of the European Union's southern maritime borders.* COM (2006) 733 final.

_____ (2008 a): *Communication from the Commission to the European Parliament, the Council, the European Economic and Social Committee and the Committee of the Regions, Report on the evaluation and future development of the FRONTEX agency.* COM(2008) 67 final. .

_____ (2008 b): *Communication from the Commission to the European Parliament, the Council, the European Economic and Social Committee and the Committee of the Regions, Examining the creation of a European border surveillance system* (EUROSUR), COM(2008) 68 final.

_____ (2008 c): *Communication from the Commission to the European Parliament and the Council, Barcelona Process: Union for the Mediterranean,* COM (2008) 319 final.

Commission Staff Working Document Commission (2008): Study on the international law instruments in relation to illegal immigration by sea. Staff Working.

Council Directive (EC) (2002): *Council Directive (EC) (2002): Defining the facilitation of unauthorised entry, transit and residence.*

_____ (2003): *Laying down minimum standards for the reception of asylum seekers.* OJ L 31/18.

_____ (2004): *On minimum standards for the qualification and status of third country nationals or stateless persons as refugees or as persons who otherwise need international protection and the content of the protection granted.* OJ L 304/12.

_____ (2005): *On minimum standards on procedures in Member States for granting and withdrawing refugee status.* OJ L 326/13.

Council Framework Decision (2002): On *the strengthening of the penal framework to prevent the facilitation of unauthorized entry, transit and residence.* OJ L 328/1.

Council of Europe (2005): Report by Mr. Alvaro Gil-Robles, Commissioner for Human Rights, on his visit to Italy, 10—17 June 2005, for the attention of the Committee of Ministers and the Parliamentary Assembly, available at www.wcd.coe.int.

Council of the European Union (2003): "Feasibility study on the control of the European Union's maritime borders: Final report" 11490/1/03 FRONT 102 COMIX 458. REV 1, 19 September.

_____ (2003): "Programme of measures to combat illegal immigration across the maritime borders of the Member States of the European Union" 15236/03 FRONT 170 COMIX 717, 28 November.

_____ (2003): *A secure Europe in a better world: European Security Strategy*, Brussels, European Council, 12 December 2003.

_____ (2007): Presidency conclusions, Brussels European.

Council Regulation (EC) (2003): *Establishing the criteria and mechanisms for determining the Member States responsible for examining an asylum application lodged in one of the Member States by a third-country national.* OJ L50/1.

_____ (2004): *Establishing a European Agency for the Management of Operational Cooperation at the External Borders of the Member States of the European Union.* OJ L 349/1.

De Lucia, A (2004): Human migratory flows. *International Journal of Anthropology. Springer.* Netherlands. Vol. 19. No.1-2. January, pp. 1:18.

de Vries, Gijs (2005): The European Union's role in the fight against terrorism. *Irish Studies in International Affairs*, Vol. 16, pp. 3:9.

Dejong, G. F. and Fawcett, J. T. FA (1981): "Motivation for migration: An assessment and a value-expectancy research model" in

G.F. DeJong and R.W. Gardner (eds): *Migration decision making: Multidisciplinary approaches to micro level studies in developed and developing Countries.* New York, NY: Pergamon Press, pp. 13:58.

Demleitner, N (2008): Linking organized crime and terrorism: The fight against undocumented migration in Europe and the US. Paper presented at annual meeting of The Law Society, Las Vegas, NV, 23 April 2008.

Djebaba, S (1980): *Capital strategy and emigration,* Masters in Economics. Algiers.

Doudah, A (2000): *The socio-cultural integration of the Jewish minority in Algeria, from the beginning of colonization to independence.* Masters in Sociology. University of Algiers.

Duteil, M (1972): *Emigration in France: the incidences of the Franco-Algerian crisis on Algerian emigration. Study of the Algerian press in french language from January to August 1971.* DES in Political Sciences, Institute of Political Studies, University of Algiers.

Eddeks, M (1971): *Social situations of Palestinians in Algeria. A theoretical and practical study.* DEA in Sociology. Institute of the Social Sciences. University of Algiers.

El Kenz, A, Benguerna, M and Khelfaoui, H (1993): *Report on Algerian scholarship holders of the Ministry for higher education and their integration abroad.* Investigation report, Algiers, C.R.E.A.D.

Elmadmad, K (1999): "Migration et Droits Humains" *La Migration clandestine: enjeux et perspectives.* Actes du colloque organisé à la Faculté de Droit-Agdal, Rabat, 29-30 April, pp. 65:76.

_____ (1999): Asylum in the Arab World: Some recent instruments. *Journal of Peace Studies.* Vol.6, Issue 1, Publication of The Centre for Peace Studies, New Delhi, pp. 24:34.

_____ (1999): The human rights of refugees with special reference to Muslim refugee women in Doreen. In *Engendering Forced Migration.* Berghahm Books, New York and Oxford.

_____ (2001): *Les réfugiés et les apatrides au Maroc: des étrangers pas comme les autres, in Regards Croisés sur le Maroc.* Publication de l'Université Moulay Ismail, Mekhnès. Morocco.

_____ (2005): *Les Migrants et leurs droits au Maghreb.* Editions La Croisée des Chemins, Casablanca.

_____ (1992): Asylum in past and present Morocco. *Journal of the Society of Moroccan Studies*, Vol. 2, SOAS, London, pp.29:34.

Ennaji, M (2006): "Social policy in Morocco: History, politics and social development" in Karhsenas, M and V. Moghadam, (eds): *Social policy in the Middle East*. London. Palgrave, pp. 109:134.

_____ (2007): "Migration, development and gender in Morocco. In Ennaji M (ed.): *Migration et diversité culturelle*. Publications of Revue LL, pp. 69:85.

_____ and Sadiqi, F. (2008): *Migration and gender in Morocco*. Trenton, New Jersey. Red Sea Press.

Erf, de R.V., and L.Heering (2002): *Moroccan migration dynamic: Prospects for the future*. No10, Geneva. IOM (International Organization of Migration) Publications.

European Commission (2005): "Technical mission to Libya on illegal immigration" 27 Nov—6 Dec 2004, Report 4.4.2005.

_____ (2006): *Communication to the council and the European Parliament on strengthening the European Neighbourhood Policy*. Brussels, 4 December 2006 COM (2006)726 final.

Fadloullah, A (1995): *Conditions de l'émigration et de la migration de retour au Maroc*. Cacucci editore.

Fargues, P (2005): *Mediterranean migration 2005 Report*. European University Institute, Robert Schuman Centre for Advanced Studies, available at http://cadmus.iue.it.

Fazouane, A (1998): Migration internationale et développement au Maroc. In *Population et Développement au Maroc*. Ministère chargé de la prévision économique et du plan Rabat. Centre d'études et de recherches démographiques, pp. 233 :242.

Fekete, L (2001): The emergence of xeno-racism. *Race and Class*, pp. 43:23. Sage.

Felipe, S (2005): "Conclusions on the working meeting regarding the Euro-Mediterranean Summit. Peace Research Center." Madrid.

Ferguène, A (2000): Infrastructures de recherche et volet scientifique et technologique du partenariat euro-méditerranéen: le cas du Maroc. *Critique économique*, No.3, pp. 21:36.

Frontex, (2009): "The impact of the global economy crisis on illegal migration to the European Union." Frontex.

Glick-Schiller, N (1999): "Citizens in transnacional nation-states: the Asian experience" In Olds, K. Et. Al (eds.): *Globalization and the Asia-Pacific: Contested territories*. Routledge, London.

Guild, E, Carrera, S and Geyer, F (2008): "The Commission's new border package: Does it take us one step closer to a 'cyber fortress Europe'?" *CEPS Policy Brief,* No. 154.

Hadib, M (2007): *Departure plans of young people in Kabylie*, CRASC, Algeria.

Hadj Naceur, M (1976): *Literature and emigration: Myths and realities.* Institute of foreign Languages. University of Algiers.

Haj Ali, O (2005): "Caractéristiques de l'émigration marocaine vers l'Espagne et son impact sur les transformations socio-spatiales: cas de la commune rurale de Sidi.

Halliday, F. (2005): Mare Nostrum after ten years. *InfoCip Bulletin.* No 8. Peace Research Center. Madrid.

Hamdouch, B, and M. Khachani (2005): Les déterminants de l'émigration internationale au Maghreb. *Critique Economique,* No 16, pp. 7 :22.

Hamimida, M (2001): L'investissement direct étranger au Maroc comme alternative à l'émigration. *Revue marocaine d'études internationales*, No.7. pp. 273.

Hammouche, A and Labdelaoui, H (2005): *Les migrations Algériennes à l'étranger.* Acts of the International Seminar organised in Alger on 11 and 12 June 2005.

Hamood, S (2006): *African transit migration through Libya to Europe: The human cost.* American University of Cairo.

Hanachi, K (1985): *The social adaptation of the reintegrated emigrants in national industry.* Institute of Social Sciences. University of Algiers.

Harbi, A (1982): *The training of executives abroad: Study and analyzes of the experience of the national enterprise Sonatrach.* Institute of Social Sciences. University of Algiers.

Hassan Sari, A (1992): *The Palestinian society in Jordan.* Institute of Social Sciences. University of Algiers.

Human Development Report (2009): *Overcoming barriers: Human mobility and development.* United Nations.

_____ (2006): *European Union: managing migration means potential EU complicity in neighboring States' Abuse of migrants and refugees*, available at www.hrw.org/backgrounder.

_____ (2008): *Libya: Summary deportations would endanger migrants and asylum seekers*. January 17, 2008, available at www.hrw.org.

_____ (2009): *Pushed back, pushed around. Italy's forced return of boat migrants and asylum seekers: Libya's mistreatment of migrants and asylum seekers*, 21 September 2009, available at: http://www.hrw.org/en/reports/2009/09/21/pushed-back-pushed-around-0.

Ibn Ameur, I (2002): *Emigration towards non-Muslim countries*. University of Algiers.

Içduygu, A (2007): The politics of irregular migratory flows in the Mediterranean basin: Economy, mobility and 'illegality. *Mediterranean Politics*, Vol 12. Issue 2. July, pp. 141:161.

Ihadiyan, A (2005): Emigration et développement économique: enjeux pour la région Maghrébine. *Critique économique*, No 16, pp. 37:56.

INEAP (1981): *Algerian emigration in France, socio-demographic and economic situation of emigrants*. Algiers.

International Centre for Migration Policy Development (2001): Migrant smuggling, trafficking in human beings and organized crime, available at www.icmpd.org.

International Centre for Migration Policy Development (2004): *Irregular transit migration in the Mediterranean*. available at www.icmpd.org.

Jeandesboz, J (2008): *An analysis of the Commission Communications on future development of FRONTEX and the creation of a European border surveillance system (EUROSUR)*, briefing paper for the European Parliament's Committee on Civil Liberties, Justice and Home Affairs.

Jennissen, R (2007): Causality chains in the International migration system approach. *Pop Res Policy Review*, No 26, pp.411:436.

Joffé, G(2008): The European Union, Democracy and Counter-Terrorism in the Maghreb. *Journal of Common Market Studies*, Vol. 46, No. 1, pp. 147:171.

Kacemi, O (2008): *The phenomenon of Algerian emigrants' marriage with foreigners, case study of Algerian emigrants in the United*

States of America. Master dissertation in sociology. Department of sociology of the University of Algiers.

Kaizen, J and Nonneman, W (2007): Irregular migration in Belgium and organized crime: An overview. *International Migration*, Vol. 45, No. 2, pp. 121:146.

Kebache, N (1980): *The legal status of foreign workers in Algeria*. University of Algiers.

Kharoufi, M (1994): Les effets de l'émigration sur les sociétés de départ au Maghreb : nouvelles données, nouvelles approches. *Correspondances*, No. 16, pp. 3:9.

Koudri, M (1989): *Demography, youth and emigration in the Maghreb*. Oran, URASC Publications.

Laadjel, M (1990): *Arabic brain-drain, the causes and the suggestions for its termination, the case of Algeria*. University of Algiers.

Labdelaoui, H (2005): *Migration and development in Algeria*. OIT, Geneva.

Labdelaoui, H, Amira, D and Akeb, N (2003): *International mobility of teachers of higher education in Algeria*. CNEPRU project, laboratory of social change of the University of Algiers.

_____, Hamadouche, R and Khelfaoui, H (2000): *The training of Algerian students abroad*, CNEPRU project, department of Sociology of the University of Algiers.

Lacomba, J (2004): *Migraciones y desarrollo en Marruecos*. Ed. La Catarata, Madrid.

Lacroix, T (2006): Les migrants et la démocratie dans les pays d'origine. *Homme et Migration*. No 1256, Juillet-août, pp. 93.

Larbi, M (1977): *Emigration and agricultural development*. University of Algiers.

Lavanex, S (2006): Shifting up and out: The foreign policy of European immigration control. *West European Politics*, Vol. 29, No. 2, pp. 329:350.

Lazaar, M (1997): Migration internationale et croissance des villes au Maroc: Tétouan, Tanger, Meknès et Fès. *Mobilités et investissements des émigrés: Maroc, Tunisie, Turquie, Sénégal*. Paris. L'Harmattan, pp. 114:119.

Le Masne, H (1974): *The Algerian emigrants and the perspective of return. The plans of 80 emigrants from the Rhône-Alpes region.* University of Algiers.

Lobkowicz, W (2002) : *L'Europe et la sécurité intérieure. Une élaboration par étapes.* Paris.

Lutterbeck, Derek (2001) : Der 'weiche Unterleib': Das Grenzkontrollregime an der Meerenge von Otranto. *Bürgerrechte & Polizei*, Vol. 70, No. 3, pp. 74:79.

_____ (2006): Policing migration in the Mediterranean. *Mediterranean Politics*, Vol. 11, No. 1, pp. 59:82.

_____ (2009): Small frontier island: Malta and the challenge of irregular immigration. *Mediterranean Quarterly*, Vol. 20, No. 1. 119:144.

Maarouf, N (1970): *A monographic study on the conditions of cult and life of North African immigrants at the mines in Freiberg.* University of Algiers.

Mabrouk, M (2007): *The attraction for emigration in post-graduate students Masters in Sociology.* University of Algiers.

Massey D. S, et. al. (1998): *Worlds in motion. Understanding international migration at the end of the millenium.* Oxford University Press.

_____ (1993): Theories of international migration: a review and appraisal. *Population and Development Review*, 19 (3), pp. 431:466.

_____ (1994): An evaluation of international migration theory: the north American case. *Population and Development Review* 20. No. ?, pp. 699:751.

Medken, K (2001): The meaning of space in the novel: *"The season of emigration to the North".* University of Algiers.

Menad, Z (2004): *The emigration issue in Euro-Maghreb relations, stakes and perspectives.* University of Algiers.

Menjel, I (1983): *The Spanish emigration in Algeria, 1936 to 1939.* University of Algiers.

MIGREUROP (2006): *Le livre noir de Ceuta et Melilla.* Paris, Editions Migreurop.

Miller, R and Mishrif, A (2005): The Barcelona Process and Euro-Arab economic relations: 1995-2005. *Middle East Review of International Affairs*. Vol. 9. Nº2. June.

Ministerio del Interior (2007): *Balance de la lucha contra la inmigración ilegal 2007*. Madrid.

Moch, L. P (1995): "Moving Europeans: historical migration practices in Western Europe" in Cohen (ed.): *The Cambridge survey of world migration*. Cambridge University Press.

Mokadem, Y (1977): *The image of Algerian emigration through literature*. University of Algiers.

Mold, A (2007): "To reciprocate or not to reciprocate? Is that the question? A CGE simulation of the Euro Mediterranean Agreements" in Mold, A. (ed.): *EU development policy in a changing world. Challenges for the 21ˢᵗ Century*. Amsterdam University Press.

Monar, J (2006): Cooperation in the justice and home affairs domain: Characteristics, constraints and progress. *European Integration*, No. 28, pp. 496:509.

Monzini, P, Ferruccio, P and Sciortino, G (2004): *L'Italia promessa: geopolitica e dinamiche organizzative del traffico di migranti verso l'Italia*. CeSPI Working Papers, No. 9.

Moulay Hadj M et. al. (2007): *International migrations in Algeria*. CRASC project.

Mter, A (1997) : "L'émigration internationale de travail comme facteur principal des mutations économiques et sociales des oasis du Dadess et du Draa, sud du Maroc" in *L'émigration maghrébine vers l'Europe: espace et investissement*. Centre d'Etudes sur les Mouvements Migratoires Maghrébins, Oujda: Université Mohammed, pp. 97 :110.

Musette, M.S (2006): *Rights of foreigners in Algeria*. Algiers. Working document, CREAD.

_____, Labdelaoui H, Belhouari-Musette D, Hammouda N.E (2006): *Statistics on the returned migrants* Algeria, MIREM-CREAD Report.

_____, Labdelaoui, H, Belhouari, A (2007): *Return migrants in Algeria: a new strategy in perspective*, MIREM-CREAD Report.

_____ (1984): *The Algerian emigrants in Europe: immigrated or aid workers*. Algiers, CREA Publications.

_____ (2006): *North Africans in international migration*, Algiers. CREAD Publications.

Nakache, D (2006): "La migration dans les programmes de coopération et de développement communautaire: un éclairage particulier sur la Roumanie, le Maroc et les pays ACP" In *Le sud de la Méditerranée face aux défi du libre-échange et Henri Regnault*, Paris, l'Harmattan, pp. 245-249.

Organization for Economic Cooperation and Development (2007): *International Migration Outlook: SOPEMI 2007*, Paris: OECD.

Ouali, B (2003): *The impact of arabic and foreign factors in the novel "Emigration to the North*. University of Algiers.

Pastore, F, Monzini, P and Sciortino, G (2006): Schengen's soft underbelly? Irregular migration and human smuggling across land and sea borders to Italy. *International Migration*, Vol. 44, No. 4, pp. 95:119.

Pei-Shan, L. (2001): Contextual análisis of rural migration intention: A comparison of Taiwanese and Pennsylvania data. *International Journal of Comparative Sociology* No. 42; 435:450.

Phuong, C (2007): Minimum standards for return procedures and international human rights law. *European Journal of Migration and Law*, Vol. 9, pp. 105:125.

Rea, A and Tripier, M. (2008): *Sociologie de l'immigration*. La Découverte. Collection Repéres.

REMADAE (2004): *La loi marocaine relative à l'entrée et au séjour des étrangers au Maroc à l'émigration et l'immigration irrégulières*. Série Textes législatifs et réglementaires, N°25, Publications de la REMADAE, Salé.

Residence. OJ L 328/17.

Riddel C. R (1999): The end of foreign aid to Africa? Concerns about Donor Policies. *African Affairs*. 319.

_____ (2007): *Does foreign aid really works?* Oxford University Press.

_____ (1987): *Foreign aid reconsidered*. James Currey. London.

Roque, M.A (1994): La migration: facteur de coopération et d'interculturalité entre les deux rives de la Méditerranée. *Quaderni mediterranei*, No.7, pp. 138:145.

Rotte, R-Vogler, M and Zimmermann, K.F (2002): South-North refugee migration: Lessons for development cooperation. *Review of Development Economics*, No. 1, pp. 99:115.

Sadek, A (2004): *The sources of the collective Israeli conscience and the effects on the pattern of representations of others*. University of Algiers.

Sahel, M (2002): *The phenomenon of the rise of the extreme right in Western Europe due to migration issues - from 1984 to 2002*. University of Algiers.

Salt, J (2000): *Trafficking and human smuggling: A European perspective*. *International Migration*, Vol. 38, No. 3, pp. 31: 56.

Santamaria, E. (2002): *Inmigración y barbarie. La construcción social y política del inmigrante como amenaza*. Universidad Autónoma de Barcelona.

Sarrica, F (2005): The Smuggling of Migrants. A Flourishing Activity of Transnational Organized Crime. *Crossroads*, Vol. 5, No. 3, pp. 7:23.

Sawani, Y (2008): *Migration and Migrants in Libya*. Tripoli. Libya.

Schloenhardt, A (2003): *Migrant smuggling: Human trafficking and organized crime in Australia and the Asia Pacific region*. Martinus Nijhoff, The Netherlands.

Sciortino, G (2004): Between phantoms and necessary evils: some critical points in the study of irregular migration. *IMIS Beitrage*, Vol. 24, pp. 17:44.

Sefrioui, F (1995): *Marocains de l'extérieur et développement*. Fondation Hassan II.

Seglow, J. (2005): The ethics of immigration. *Political Studies Review*, Vol. 3, pp. 317:334.

Sen, A. (1977): Rational fools: A critique of the behavioural foundations of economic theory. *Philosophy and Public Affairs*, Vol. 6, N° 4, Summer, pp. 317:344.

Sfreiff-feinart, J (Ed.) (1992): *Comparative research on student migrations of southern Mediterranean countries to European Universities*, University Sofia Antipolis, groupe SOLLIS.

Simon, J(2006): "Irregular transit migration in the Mediterranean : Some facts, figure and insights" in Sørensen, N (Ed.): *Mediterra-*

nean transit migration. Copenhagen: Danish Institute for International Studies.

Skeldon, R. (2003): Migration and poverty. Paper presented at the conference on "African migration and urbanization in comparative perspective" Johannesburg, South Africa.

Spijkerboer, T (2007): The human cost of border control. *European Journal of Migration and Law,* Vol. 9, pp. 127:139.

Taftaf, M (1993): *The situation of the families of Algerian emigrants in the Country of Origin.* University of Constantine.

_____ (2004): *The familiarization of Algerian families in France and the socio-cultural changes of emigration.* University of Algiers.

Tamim, M (1993): Effets de l'émigration internationale sur la vallée de l'Ouneine, Haut Atlas occidental. *Revue de géographie du Maroc,* Vol. 15, No.1-2, 1993, pp. 93 :104.

Tezanos, S (2008): *The Spanish pattern of aid giving.* WP. 04/2008. Universidad Complutense de Madrid.

Thieux, L (2005): *The democratic deficit: A pending objective for the Barcelona Process.* Peace Research Center. Madrid.

Trucco, L (2005): *Lampedusa : A test case for the subcontracting of EU border controls,* European Civil Liberties Network, ECLN Essay No. 13.

_____ (1992): *Handbook on procedures and criteria for determining refugee status under the 1951 Convention and 1967 Protocol relating to the Status of Refugees* HCR/IP/4/Eng/REV.1 (UNHCR 1979; re-edited, Geneva, January 1992).

_____ (2000): *Interception of asylum-seekers and refugees: The international framework and recommendations for a comprehensive approach.* EC/50/SC/CRP/17.

_____ (2001): *Refugee protection and migration control: Perspectives from UNHCR and IOM. Global consultations on international protection.* EC/GC/01/11.

_____ (2002): *Background note on the protection of asylum seekers and refugees rescued at sea* (18 March 2002) (final version as discussed at the expert roundtable *Rescue-at-Sea: Specific aspects relating to the protection of asylum-seekers and refugees.* Held in Lisbon, Portugal on 25-26 March 2002).

Ureta, I (2009): The blurry line: Economic performance, migration policies and public opinion in the Euro-Mediterranean area. Working paper. BRISMES Annual Meeting. University of Manchester. UK.

Varady, D.P (1983): Determinants of residential mobility decisions. *Journal of the American Planning Association,* 49, No. 1, pp. 184:199.

Weinzierl, R and Urszula, L (2007): *Border management and human rights. A study of EU law and the law of the sea.* German Institute for Human Rights. Berlin.

Widgren, J, Jandl, M and Hoffman, M (2005): Migration and security in Europe after the Madrid bombings. *Migraciones,* No. 17, pp. 1:8.

Contributors

Naima Baba is a Ph.D. candidate in public law at the University of Casablanca, Morocco.

Abderrazak Bel Hadj Zekri is Director of Studies, office of Tunisians Abroad, Institute of Labor and Social Studies.

Fethi Boulares is a lecturer in politics and international relations at the Université M'Hamed Bouguerra, Algeria, and a Research Fellow of security and governance issues at the University of Toulousse, France.

Khadija Elmadmad is an attorney with Rabat Bar Association of Law and English and an international consultant. She holds the UNESCO Chair, "Migration and Human Rights," based at University Hassan II Casablanca Ain Chock, Morocco.

Moha Ennaji is a full professor who has been affiliated with Sidi Mohamed Ben Abdellah University since 1982. Ennaji is President of the South North Center for Intercultural Dialogue and Migration Studies, Morocco.

Mark Furness is a Research Fellow at the German Development Institute (DIE) in Bonn, Germany.

Alina Khasabova is currently studying for a double master's degree at the University College London and Charles University, Prague. She works in the EC public diplomacy department in London.

Bashir el Kot is a professor at the Political Science Department at Al Fateh University, Tripoli and director of Research and Development at Gaddafi Foundation.

Hocine Labdelaui is a professor of sociology at the University of Algier, Algeria and runs the Migration Studies Programme. He is associate consultant at the Center for Research in Applied Economics, Population and Development.

Derek Lutterbeck is a lecturer in international history, Deputy Director of International Affairs and Holder of the Swiss Chair at the Mediterranean Academy for Diplomatic Studies, University of Malta.

Patricia Mallia is a lecturer in public international law and heads the Department of International Law at the University of Malta.

Ivan Ureta is a senior researcher and oversees Migration Studies at the Institute for Mediterranean Studies, University of Lugano. He is also Visiting Research Fellow at the Department of Middle Eastern and Mediterranean Studies (King's College London) and at the Department of Arabic and Middle Eastern Studies (University of Leeds).

Index